CONFESSIONS {OF A} PRAIRIE BITCH

CONFESSIONS {OF A} PRAIRIE BITCH

HOW I SURVIVED NELLIE OLESON AND LEARNED TO LOVE BEING HATED

Alison Arngrim

AN IMPRINT OF HARPERCOLLINS*PUBLISHERS*

HarperCollins books may be purchased for educational, business, or sales promotional use. For information please write: Special Markets Department, HarperCollins Publishers, 10 East 53rd Street, New York, NY 10022.

Designed by Jaime Putorti

Library of Congress Cataloging-in-Publication Data has been applied for.

ISBN 978-0-06-196214-1

10 11 12 13 14 OV/RRD 10 9 8 7 6 5 4

For Jess:

The Pig Woman speaks at last.

{ A N D }

For Lucy:

I think I understand you a little bit more every day.

CONTENTS

INTRODUCTION

The Los Angeles County Fair is probably not the first place you'd go if you were seeking to be forgiven of your sins, but I have a tendency to find strange things in strange places. Or, more accurately, they find me.

A few years ago, the fair decided to host a celebrity autograph show as a novelty attraction. Plunked down in a tent, right there with the Ferris wheels, prize-winning cows, and endless fried food, fairgoers could also find their favorite TV celebrities happily chatting away and signing our names to stacks of eight-by-ten glossies. My husband, Bob, and I thought this would be a fun way to spend the day (besides, they gave us free tickets, so we could go on all the rides afterward). So, as we were sitting there in the intermittently air-conditioned tent, passing the time with some of the more amusing celebs—Pugsley from *The Addams Family* is always a delight!—a woman strolled in and stopped dead in her tracks.

She stood, frozen in front of my table, not moving, not speaking, just staring down at the sign with my name on it. Then she slowly looked up at me. She was perhaps in her early forties, with long hair, casually dressed in jeans and some sort of vaguely western shirt, like 90 percent of the people I'd seen at the fair that day.

She looked like someone who'd spent a lot of time in the sun. But I couldn't tell if she was really sunburned or not, because she was so incredibly angry that her face was turning several different colors, one after the other. She quickly went from what seemed to be abject shock and horror to boiling rage. She was even shaking. She shut her eyes and took several long, deep breaths through her nose, in an obvious effort to compose herself. She then swallowed hard and opened her eyes. I thought she was going to burst into tears, but she held her head up proudly, looked at me, and announced in all seriousness, "I forgive you!"

Then she turned on her heels and marched out of the tent. No autograph, no "Hi, how are you?" No "*Loved* your show!" Nothing.

Bob, who, after more than fifteen years of being married to me, had come to accept these scenes with a Zen-like sense of bemusement, said matter-of-factly, "You know, we *really* have to start bringing the video camera to these things."

I was still openmouthed in amazement. "What the hell was THAT?!"

Bob looked on the bright side. "Well, she forgave you. Of course, she didn't really say for what. Maybe for everything you've ever done? That's great! My God, you've just been absolved at the L.A. County Fair! How many people can say that?"

"You have a point," I replied. "Maybe they should advertise: 'The L.A. County Fair—where you can receive complete absolution and eat a deep-fried Snickers bar at the same time!' "

We laughed, but we both knew what she meant. This woman

didn't know me. She had never seen me before in her life. She had no knowledge of what transgressions I may or may not have actually committed. But she knew what *She* had done. Bob and I knew she was talking about *Her.*

Nellie Oleson.

A grown woman had been driven to a state of rage and was forgiving me for what I'd done on television . . . while pretending to be someone else . . . nearly thirty years ago.

Welcome to my world.

I live every day with the knowledge that what was supposed to have been simply a really good gig, a major role on a long-running TV series, with lots of good times and fun memories, has instead morphed into a bizarre alternate version of reality, where I am repeatedly held to account for the actions of a fictitious character as if they were my own. And not just any character. A bitch. A horrible, wretched, scheming, evil, lying, manipulative, selfish brat, whose narcissism and hostility toward others knew no bounds. A girl who millions of people all over the world had grown to hate. But she was a girl I grew to love.

And why wouldn't I? She's given me everything I've ever wanted and more. She put food on my table, clothes on my back, and a roof over my head for most of my life. She got me out of my house when I thought there was no escape. She aided and protected me like no other creature, real or imagined. She transformed me from a shy, abused little girl afraid of her own shadow to the in-your-face, outspoken, world-traveling, politically active, big-mouthed bitch I am today. She taught me to fight back, to be bold, daring, and determined, and, yes, to be down-right sneaky when I needed to be.

Despite the occasional outburst and stray can of soda thrown at my head, I meet people from all over the world who grew up watching *Little House on the Prairie* (and still watch it) and tell me the most amazing things about what the show means to them. There was the chef of a four-star restaurant who grew up watching it in Bangladesh and the bookstore manager from Borneo who told me his grandmother still watches the show in their village. Then there's the man who grew up on an island near Singapore, where his family, who had electricity for only a few hours a day, used it to watch *Little House*. They had one of the few TVs in the town, and the neighbors would gather in front of their house and stare through the living room window to watch the show. I was in a bar in New York where the bartender was from Israel, the waitress was from Argentina, and the manager was from Iran. They compared notes on their favorite episodes. I receive fan mail regularly from Poland, Germany, Japan, Argentina, Sweden, Denmark, Finland, and dozens of other countries. The show is popular in both Iran and Iraq. I am told that even Saddam Hussein was an avid fan and never missed an episode. (I have not heard from Osama bin Laden, but I read that he used to like *Bonanza* when he was young, so what are the odds? Did even he follow Michael Landon's Little Joe all the way to the prairie?)

I know several totally unrelated people who have never met each other, who each told me a heart-wrenching story of terrible illness or incapacitation—horrible tragedies involving car accidents, full body casts, cancer, severe depression, blood diseases. But all their tales had one thing in common: each of them, while lying in bed, unable to move and on the verge of giving up all hope, had turned on *Little House on the Prairie*.

They watched episode after episode, forgetting about their pain and gradually recovering their strength and sometimes even their will to live.

I cannot count the number of people who have told me that *Little House on the Prairie* saved their lives or the number of ways people have incorporated it into their lives, going so far as to name their children Laura and Mary and, of course, Michael. But no Nellies. I have heard from people who name their cats and even their cows Nellie, but they don't dare name their daughters after her.

Well, I, for one, am happy I was "the Nellie." No, not just happy, proud. And eternally grateful. All I can say is, thank you. It's like I tell people at my stand-up shows: by making me a bitch, you have given me my freedom, the freedom to say and do things I couldn't do if I was "a nice girl" with some sort of stupid, goody-two-shoes image to keep up. Things that require courage. Things that require balls. Things that need to be done. By making me a bitch, you have freed me from the trite, sexist, bourgeois prison of "likeability." Any idiot can be liked. It takes talent to scare the crap out of people.

And if enjoying that as much as I do makes me a bitch, well, *goody.* Playing Nellie and being marked a bitch for life is the best thing that ever happened to me. I constantly hear actors complain about being strongly identified with a character they played ages ago. They reject the character, refuse to talk about "that old show," and dismiss their fans as silly and "uncool." Not me, buddy. It took me a long time to figure out which side my bread was buttered on, but once I did, I never turned back. I will happily, wholeheartedly embrace Nellie Oleson, *Little House on the Prairie,* and all the fans worldwide until the last bitchy breath leaves my body.

Perhaps now, in writing this book, I can finally explain how much it all meant to me. Sometimes people tell me that the reason they loved the show so much was because, sadly, their childhood just wasn't like that.

Neither was mine.

And I've had people tell me they really needed Nellie Oleson in their lives. *Nowhere as much as I did . . .*

CONFESSIONS {OF A} PRAIRIE BITCH

CHAPTER ONE

MOM, DAD, AND LIBERACE

> **LAURA: My pa works hard.**
>
> **NELLIE: So does a mule.**

I always envy people whose detailed memories extend back to the womb. What I remember mostly are places. When I was growing up, my parents, my older brother, Stefan, and I usually moved at least once a year, so I can always tell how old I was at a particular time by where we were living.

The Chateau Marmont? Ages three through five. Famous stage and screen comedienne Beatrice Lillie attended my fifth birthday party. Waring Avenue off La Cienega? Ages five through seven. Carlton Way in the Hollywood Hills? I was eight. That would be the party with the plastic Day-Glo Indian headdresses.

The earliest memory I can come up with is from when I was about three. We had only recently moved to L.A. from New York and were living at the Chateau Marmont in Bungalow B. (No, that's not the one where John Belushi died. That was Bungalow D.) I was watching *Peter Pan,* not the Disney cartoon version, but the truly weird, almost creepy, televised play version with Mary

Martin and Cyril Ritchard. (I still like those old 1960s "teleplays," Hallmark Hall of Fame, and that sort of thing. The video used at the time gives them a surreal, almost dreamlike quality.) I was totally fascinated with Captain Hook. He had all the best songs, like "Hook's Waltz" ("Who's the swiniest swine in the world?"). Every one was either a rollicking sea shanty or a tango. My favorite number in the whole show, however, was the bizarre sequence where Captain Hook and Peter Pan chase each other around a large papier-mâché tree, singing "Oh, My Mysterious Lady." A grown-up, somewhat older woman, pretending to be a young boy, pretending to be a grown-up, younger glamorous woman by doing not much more than prancing around with a green scarf over her head and singing in a very high register, yet the guy in the pirate suit *believes her.* Wow. To me it was proof that grown-ups really are insane. And so began the launch of two major themes in my life: my love for and fascination with villains of all kinds and my total lack of respect for traditional definitions of gender.

By the time I was four, it was all over. My parents made a last-gasp effort to put those dainty ballerina candleholders on my birthday cake, but by that fall, the dreaded signs were there. Dainty was not my thing. I wanted to be a villain. Halloween was my favorite holiday. In previous years, they'd managed to stuff me into those cute Halloween baby-pajama costumes, so that I was dressed as a clown or some such cuddly character. But the minute I was old enough to pick out a costume, I wanted to be a witch with a big, pointy black hat. By the next year, I would insist on dressing as the devil himself.

I *looked* like a nice little girl. People were always getting me gifts like Mary Poppins dolls or tea sets. But I loved action movies and would have much preferred something like the *Krakatoa: East of Java* Exploding Volcano Set, complete with Maximilian Schell and Sal Mineo action figures. (Sadly, there was no such set—I just always wished there was.)

One of the advantages to growing up in Hollywood in the 1960s was that one was allowed a great deal of latitude as far as weirdness was concerned. And at my house, weirdness was the order of the day. I know everyone thinks their parents are weird, but I may have an unfair advantage in this department. To start with, both of my parents were actors. And Canadian. (New game show: *Weird or Just Canadian? You Be the Judge!*) They married each other essentially on the grounds that they would never have to "behave themselves." I can honestly say, when it came to this promise, they both succeeded admirably.

My parents got married in 1954 at the height of an era of total repression. The rules and expectations for married people, especially women, were staggering. I think if I had been around then, I would have simply never gotten married at all. My mother, Norma Macmillan, as the daughter of a prominent Vancouver obstetrician-gynecologist, was expected to marry someone reasonably rich, educated, and preferably from the same type of neighborhood and private school background she had been brought up in. As a wife, she would be expected to severely limit, if not give up entirely, her career aspirations, such as acting and writing. She would also be expected to give up the usual things like drinking, partying, and sleeping around. And there was the dreaded "cooking and cleaning" clause.

My mother could not cook. *At all.* I remember as a child having to show her how to fold the foil back from the dessert on the Hungry-Man TV dinner. She told me that when she was growing up, her mother had forbidden her or her sister, my Auntie Marion, from participating in any cooking or cleaning around the house. They had staff for that sort of thing, don't you know! Her mother told them, "Men will marry a woman to get free household help. I did not raise you to be maids. If a man wants to marry you, he can hire you a cook and a maid as befitting your station." No, Grandma wasn't kidding.

If my mother was considered all wrong as marriage material, my father would be a worst-case scenario. First of all, he was gay. Unlike most wives of gay men at the time, my mother was completely in on the game from the get-go. She had decided that gay, bi, or whatever, my father could offer her a better life than the stodgy Canadian straight boys available at the time. This doesn't mean he was what you could actually call "out." My father's sexuality seems to have been something that was revealed to people on a case-by-case, need-to-know basis. (It was apparently decided that my brother and I didn't need to know—although we figured it out pretty quickly.)

My father's sexuality was hard to miss; he was a very, shall we say, "flamboyant" personality. He was always immaculately, fashionably dressed. As a child, when I first saw the TV show *The Odd Couple,* I thought the character of Felix Unger was based on my father. He had a lot of friends—male friends—most of whom seemed to be other handsome, well-dressed, flamboyant gentlemen in the artistic professions. Yet, if I or my brother commented about this, or even asked our parents outright if "perhaps there was something you would like to tell us," we were given the brush-off. My father wasn't gay. Oh yes, all of his friends were, of course. But no, not him. He was just . . . *theatrical.*

My dad had been born out of wedlock at the height of the Great Depression to a young Irish-Canadian woman who named him Wilfred James Bannin and put him in the Salvation Army orphanage. We later found out she did not simply abandon him; she worked in a restaurant and sent money to the orphanage every month for his upkeep. Sadly, it seems the orphanage totally ripped her off, and by the time my dad was adopted, he was suffering from rickets and malnutrition. (Yes, my father's childhood *is* the plot of *Les Miserables*. This explains a great deal!)

He got adopted by an Icelandic-Canadian family with ten children, some their own, some adopted, and was quickly nursed back to health and put to work milking cows, feeding livestock, and tending the crops. His new family renamed him Thor—not for the comic book hero, but for the original god of thunder. When you're Icelandic, being named Thor is like being named Joe. His full name was now Thorhaüler (pronounced "Tor-Huddler") Marvin Arngrimson. When it came to names, my father could not catch a break. Arngrim (he eventually changed it legally) was a little shorter and snappier—and fit better on the theater marquees.

He went to classes in a one-room schoolhouse, where he was related to half the other students by adoption, and even the teacher was a cousin. He learned to chop wood and churn butter and survived not only the Great Depression, but blizzards, locusts, and tornadoes.

Dad left home at fifteen to pursue his dream of working in the theater, much to his family's relief, no doubt. Between milking cows and plowing fields, he had insisted on putting on lavish spectacles in the barn, complete with stage lights made from milk cans. This sort of behavior was confusing to people in a small town like Mozart, Saskatchewan, and it frightened the animals.

He moved to Vancouver and became an actor and a producer and an entrepreneur and an "impresario"—basically, all of those things that don't require a high school education. He did very well, because he was willing to do absolutely anything to keep the theater open. One summer, he decided to "invent" air-conditioning. Well, not really, but close enough. It was a hot, humid summer, and none of the other theaters on the same street had air-conditioning, so he saw a golden opportunity. He purchased a large block of ice and a really big fan. He positioned them in the attic of the theater, creating a primitive but effective cooling system, and proudly put out a sign: WE HAVE AIR-CONDITIONING! It was a smash. The other theater owners were terribly jealous.

But not for long. The ice was heavy and unstable, and the theater was very old. One afternoon, during a musical rehearsal, the block of ice came crashing through the ceiling and into the expensive rented piano. It just barely missed the actor and his accompanist who were rehearsing. They were not amused.

His "invention" of the drive-in theater went much better. The company was doing "Theater under the Stars," major theatrical productions with well-known actors performed in the park. The audience would sit on blankets and picnic. It was very successful. In fact, it was sold out. Then during one performance, it rained, and people started demanding their money back.

"Not on your life!" said my father. He convinced everyone to simply pull their cars up onto the grass, close to the stage. Unlike a drive-in, however, there were no speakers. People rolled down their windows and leaned out of them, straining to hear. The actors simply projected louder over the storm. Everyone thought it was a great novelty, and not a single ticket was refunded, which was a good thing, because my father, I'm sure, had already spent every penny.

My father eventually founded his own theater, the Totem Theatre of Vancouver, with his friend Stuart Baker, when one day in walked my mother. Dad and Stuart had become popular young producers in Vancouver, to the point that they were being referred to in the press as "The Gold Dust Twins." The two of them were straight out of Mel Brooks's *The Producers.* My mother showed up at the theater and announced that the two of them had no idea how to actually run a business, and that she, having just graduated from the local business college, was capable of keeping their books correctly and thus keeping them both "out of jail." She told them she would happily keep the finances in order and run the office in exchange for the lead female role in *every* production. As my father said, "She made me an offer I couldn't refuse." So my mother became well known in Canada for her brilliant performance as Laura in Tennessee Williams's *Glass Menagerie* and in any other role she felt like having. (She sometimes let the other girls have a turn.)

The theater eventually ceased to be as profitable as they wanted, and my parents, having worked their way romantically through the entire theater company and most of Vancouver, realized it was time to get out of town. My father proposed to my mother on a used car lot. He must have had a hell of a sales pitch, because she agreed. They were married right away, with Stuart as best man. Then the three of them moved to Toronto to get fabulous new careers in radio. Back then, a career in radio was the happening thing to have. Saying you wanted to be on TV in the '50s would be like saying today that you wanted a show on the Internet. Interesting . . . but not yet profitable. My dad and Stuart were the ones with the contact; a friend had gotten them a meeting with a major producer. They only had a couple of radio credits between them, and my mother had none, but they decided to take her along to the meeting anyway, just in case. There might be a small part for her if they were lucky.

At the meeting, my father and Stuart gave their best pitch about why they should be big stars, and the producer seemed to be buying it. Then he asked my mother, "And what do you do?"

"I do children's voices," she replied without missing a beat. Stuart and my dad nearly had a seizure. They didn't know what the hell she was talking about. Children's voices? She'd never done any voices. The producer chatted with her politely, then told them he'd call.

When they left, my dad really let her have it. "Children's voices? Where in the hell did you come up with that bullshit?" He and Stuart thought she was nuts and hoped she hadn't ruined their chances.

The script soon arrived. They had all been hired to be in a new radio soap opera. They celebrated madly and began leafing through the script, seeing how many lines they had. My father shouted, "Look! I'm on page ten!" Stuart found his part: "I'm on page twenty and twenty-one!"

My mother sat silently, slowly turning the pages of her script. My father asked her, "Which page are you on?"

"All of them," she replied calmly.

It turned out the entire plot of the soap opera revolved around a disturbed little girl and her family's attempt to deal with the medical and psychological crisis. She was the little girl.

My father and Stuart soon learned to bow before her prowess in voice-over. Because she worked so much, she often had to run back and forth across the street from studio to studio in Toronto, recording several programs and commercials at the same time. My brother, Stefan, was born in Toronto in 1955, so she was doing all this while carting around a newborn.

In the early 1960s, my mother became the voice of Gumby, the walking, talking "little green ball of clay." At this point, they had moved to New York and had been living there for a few years. She was also a ghost, Casper the Friendly Ghost, to be exact. Known by her maiden name, Norma Macmillan, she was one of the most prominent voice-over artists of the late '50s through the '60s. She played everybody. She was Sweet Polly Purebred, intrepid reporter and girlfriend of Underdog. She was Davey of *Davey and Goliath,* absolutely the world's most religious Claymation program ever made. (My mother used to joke, "C'mon, Goliath, let's go outside and *pray*!") With her high, childlike voice, she was also, by default, Davey's mom, his sister, and all his friends. She was Gumby's mom, sister, and his blue friend Goo. She was nearly everyone in Casper's town with a voice over middle C—Nightmare, Wendy, and even Spooky. In fact, she was so many voices, that sometimes I could sit in front of the TV on Saturday mornings and hear her in every third cartoon. She was even in commercials. Before the hyperannoying Cocoa Puffs bird, there was a choo-choo train that shouted, "Cocoa Puffs, Cocoa Puffs!" She was the little girl in that.

In 1962, while we were living in New York and shortly after I was born, she was cast in the first comedy album ever to mock a seated president, "The First Family," about JFK and Jackie and the whole gang starring stand-up comedian Vaughn Meader. She was the voice of Caroline Kennedy and baby John-John. It sold so many copies so fast (seven and a half million, to be exact), it made the *Guinness Book of World Records* for fastest-selling album in history. It was played over loudspeakers in department stores and won the Grammy for Album of the Year. Even President Kennedy was said to have loved it.

A second *First Family* album was recorded and set to be released Christmas 1963, but, since JFK was killed on November 22, that was the end of that. The album disappeared from the airwaves, and poor Vaughn Meader's career never really recovered. It's still a major collector's item, and yes, that's my forty-year-old mom on the cover wearing knee socks and holding a balloon.

By the time I was in first grade, my mother was so well known in cartoons, that on the occasions she would walk me to school, the other kids would beg her to perform: "Do Gumby!" "Do Casper!" And there, in the school yard, at eight in the morning, in her coat and scarf, even on days she was fighting a hangover, she would smile bravely and say, "Hi! I'm Casper the Friendly Ghost, and I want to be your friend!" On some mornings she could even be persuaded to sing: "Where oh where has my Underdog gone? Oh where oh where can he be?" Not only were her early-morning performances impressive in quality, but I was amazed just by the fact she did them at all. I have to hand it to her; I don't know if I could have done that before my first cup of coffee.

I, of course, loved this. At that age, kids think you're nuts when you tell them your mother is Gumby. Having her come down to the school yard in person and *prove it* was more than I could ever dream of. It gave me a smattering of what would pass for "street cred" in the first grade.

My mother was very beautiful, and she had that whole '60s style going. She had very, very dyed red hair, although I believe it was called strawberry-something. It was teased into a bouffant not unlike the hairdo of her cartoon character Sweet Polly Purebred. Because she liked to wear smart suits with three-quarter-length sleeves and black pumps, the resemblance was positively disturbing; the only difference at all was she was missing the big cartoon doggie nose. Sometimes I went with her to the hairdresser's, where her stylist would smoke endless Benson & Hedges while spraying her and the whole room with Aqua Net. I don't know how either of them was able to breathe. I nearly passed out.

My mother didn't do the usual "mommy" things. She wasn't into all the arts and crafts activities that other mothers so enjoyed. I can just imagine the look I would have gotten had I suggested she make me a Halloween costume. Mine all came from the store, until I got older and started making them myself. It wasn't really a problem, except for the Girl Scouts. All my school friends were in the Brownies, the lead-in to being in the Girl Scouts, and I wanted to join, too. My mother and I went to a meeting where the program directors explained the whole process, as well as their very pressing need for more den mothers.

This is where things went south. When we got home, my mother sat me down and told me very solemnly that we needed to talk. She explained that at the meeting, they had suggested that she become a den mother. She explained that if I joined my local troop, she would be expected to join as well and fulfill the duties of a scout den mother: driving girls around, going camping, making treats for meetings, helping with arts and crafts, etc.

She said, "I'm very sorry. I know you want to be a Brownie. But seriously, ask yourself, do you honestly see me as den mother material?" I was six, but I knew she was right. The images were horrifying: I tried to visualize her in a schoolroom, handing out little Dixie cups of Elmer's glue and glitter with her shaky hands, and I could just see the ensuing disaster. I saw her standing around in a supermarket parking lot helping me sell cookies, with the far away, sad, deadened look of someone who's been waiting in line at the DMV for several hours. Did I really think *she* was going to make lunches for a troop of twenty little girls? This was a woman who had trouble cutting the crusts off my peanut butter sandwiches, for God's sake.

I told her I understood. And I did. I did not join the Brownies, and I never became a Girl Scout. In retrospect, I sincerely doubt I was what they were looking for either.

After we moved to Hollywood in 1965, Dad became a personal manager. This is like an agent, only weirder. Being an agent is simple: you have clients; you get them jobs; they pay you 10 percent. The end. The personal manager's job is to "counsel and advise." But personal managers are not lawyers. They are different from business managers, who handle bank accounts and investments. They do not specifically procure employment. But they get paid 15 percent instead of 10. So what the hell does a personal manager actually do? If they're a bad one, not much at all. And if they're a good one? *Everything.*

The agent may get you the three-picture deal and negotiate for the raise and the bigger trailer. The publicist may get you the cover of *People,* but the manager is the one who will come in the middle of the night to bail you out of jail. The publicist might spin the story of your arrest to the press and try to make you sound innocent. But the manager will come before the cops arrive, flush the dope down the toilet, give the girl cab fare home, and wipe the prints off the gun. My father was a manager.

Before he started his own firm and became my manager, he worked for Seymour Heller and Associates. This was how he wound up working for Liberace.

It was 1969, so Liberace was famous by this time. Back in the '50s, he had his own TV show (called *The Liberace Show*; what else?) and was now touring to packed houses. As strange as it may seem to young people now, at the time, Liberace was in fact the highest-paid entertainer in the world. I had the hilarious privilege of going to see his show when I was just eight years old.

My parents prepared me for this by admonishing, "Now, whatever you do, don't say anything, because no one must know that Liberace is gay."

"Excuse me?" I said. "I'm eight. I know he's gay." I thought they had to be kidding. No grown-up person really thought this guy was straight, did they?

"No, no!" they said. "His fans are in love with him. You mustn't say a word!"

I agreed to behave myself, under protest. If I thought hiding Liberace's gayness was a ludicrous proposition before I saw the show, I was absolutely in hysterics afterward. He came onstage in hot pants—spangled, gleaming, red, white, and blue hot pants covered in sequins and rhinestones. He tap-danced in this outfit and did a baton-twirling routine. He also had a floor-length cape that lit up. Really, it was wired with thousands of little bulbs. The house lights would go down, and he would blaze away like a Christmas tree. He wore elaborate makeup and gallons of hair spray. He sat at the piano and played (quite beautifully, by the way) and sang, simpering and winking and giggling the entire show. And in case anyone still didn't get it, he raised his arms over his head, soared into the air, and flew across the stage.

Yet there they were, his legions of female fans, mostly older women dressed in fur coats and jewels, with that well-sprayed, perfectly coifed, slightly blue hair that was considered cool at the time. I watched them in amazement at intermission as they scooped up all the merchandise. Liberace was crazy about merchandise. He was ahead of his time. People didn't sell things at concerts as much as they do today. But old Liberace did. He had records and coffee mugs—he even had soap, for the love of God, with his picture on it. I tried to imagine who in their right mind would actually get off on bathing with Liberace. It was too icky to contemplate. Yet as the cash registers rang furiously, I began to understand why Liberace's most famous quote was, "I cried—all the way to the bank!"

I overheard some of the fur-coated ladies talking. They paid no attention to the eight-year-old in the frilly yellow dress and white tights hovering near them. They assumed, of course, that my mother must be nearby purchasing scads of Liberace merchandise, so I could eavesdrop with impunity. They whispered and giggled like teenagers, and I heard bits and pieces: "Oh, he IS!!" (Shriek!) "Just darling!" and finally, "You'd be safe with him!" followed by gales of laughter. THEY KNEW!

They didn't call it "gay," but they knew perfectly well what it was when they saw it. If you had walked up to any one of these women and asked flat out: "Is Liberace a homosexual?" she would have slapped you soundly across the face and screamed, "How DARE you!" But if you asked something along the lines of "So, why do you think he's not married?" she would have winked at you and said, "Oh, *really,* dear!" That's how they liked it, and that's how he gave it to them. Just as he floated over the stage, Liberace eternally hovered over the concepts of gayness and straightness, never really touching down on either side. It was genius.

CHAPTER TWO

THE CASTLE

NELLIE: My mother says we're not like the rest of the children.

The Chateau Marmont is probably not most parents' first choice as a place to raise their family, but like most actors, it was where we landed when we came from New York in 1965. It wasn't yet the infamous location of Belushi's death, but it was already notorious. For those who haven't been on the tour of Hollywood and seen it yet, the Chateau is a big, gorgeous pretend–French castle, sitting right smack in the middle of Hollywood on the Sunset Strip, surrounded by liquor stores, banks, and nightclubs. It really stands out. Built in the late '20s, it was meant to be a fashionable, high-end apartment building for very respectable people, but it became both semipermanent and totally transient lodging for people in show business and those who *think* they are in show business. It now has a fancy bar and restaurant and is frequented by many notorious, drunken, pants-dropping celebrities. This observation is not meant in a negative way or considered a sign of the Chateau's falling from grace. It was always the home of notorious, drunken, pants-dropping celebrities.

I, of course, loved it from the minute I set eyes on it. All little girls of four and five think they are princesses, but I was the only one I knew who could tell people she really did live in a castle. We moved in just as the 1960s were breaking right there on the Sunset Strip. We had come to California because my older brother, Stefan, was supposed to star in the movie *The Singing Nun* with Debbie Reynolds. I say "supposed to" because between the time he was cast and the time shooting began, he grew and was deemed much too big—and therefore replaced. He then had to settle for playing Kirk Douglas's son in *The Way West.* Stefan, who's six years older than I, had started acting when he was barely five, playing sad-eyed orphans on soap operas. This led to an article in a New York paper about "the theatrical Arngrim family: Dad's a monk, Mom's a ghost, and their son's an orphan!"

No one seemed to question the parts he got. I remember my mother proudly telling the story of how when he was very little, she had begged him to smile at an audition, to "try to look happy." He didn't, but when he came out of the reading, he was thrilled. "They didn't want a happy little boy! I got the part!" He worked like crazy, playing everything from the French war orphan on the series *Combat!* and the embarrassing illegitimate spawn on a soap opera to the moody "disturbed child." There was no shortage of parts for the cute boy with big, sad brown eyes, who looked like he had the whole world on his shoulders. But no one seemed to want to know *why* he looked that way.

By the time he was twelve, he was officially a "teen idol." He played Barry Lockridge in the Irwin Allen sci-fi cult classic *Land of the Giants,* released in 1968. Yet another in a series of unhappy orphans, Barry was on his way to a new family, when the suborbital plane he's on, the *Spindrift,* crashes on another planet, inhabited by, well, giants. He's then left to be raised by the crew and passengers of the ship, including Mr. Fitzhugh, the constantly sweating and panting "embezzler on the lam." Luckily, Barry had his faithful dog, Chipper, with him, resulting in endless scenes of him shouting, "No! Chipper! Chipper, come back!" It was sort of like a warped, sci-fi version of *Gilligan's Island,* but without the laughs. Stefan should have been happy then; he was making tons of money and was now world-famous. Yet he still managed to remain in a seemingly permanent state of gloom.

Living with an official teen idol was very bizarre. Every month he was in one of the magazines or all of them—*16, Tiger Beat, Teen Beat*—they all seemed to blur into one big mass of teenage girl squeal speak: "Who's your Fav?" and pages and pages of "Luv," "Fax," and "Pix," all "cos they're the grooviest!" I did not think my brother or anything he did was remotely "groovy."

This didn't stop the media from dragging me into his "fab" world. I hadn't worked a day in my life, yet articles began to appear with titles like "Meet Stefan's Cool Kid Sister!" with pictures of me modeling the latest in cool children's wear. I even technically have a song-writing credit. My brother and I wrote a song called "Otis the Sheep." It was sort of an homage to the Lewis Carroll nonsense poem "Jabberwocky" with lots of "cool"-sounding, made-up words. It was perfectly stupid, but by God, they printed it, "lyrics by Stefan and Alison Arngrim." I was famous, and I hadn't done a damn thing.

One day, a fanzine came over to interview the family ("Meet Stefan's Groovy Family!" "See Stefan's Groovy Dog!"). The woman who interviewed us was very nice; she even stayed for lunch. Back then, we had the great status symbol of a maid. She was primarily for symbolic effect, since with my neat-freak father around, there just wasn't that much left to clean. My brother and I must have been unusually well behaved that day, because the maid had baked us a lemon meringue pie. It was fantastic, and of course we served it to the lady from the magazine.

When the article came out, I was stunned. Not one single word anyone actually said all day was in there. There were lots of other words, all very nice, but all completely made up. I was only six, but I had *been* at the lunch table. These people in the article didn't even talk like anyone in my house! They were total strangers! And to top it all off, it included the ridiculous claim that my mother had made the lemon meringue pie. Bewildered, I asked my father, "Why? I don't understand—we were all there—why not write down what we said? And Mom *bake a pie*? Everyone knows Mom can't cook!"

And that's when I learned one of the most important lessons of my life—at age five. "That's what they do in magazines," explained my father patiently, "they make things up. No one cares if it's true. So they write whatever they think will make a better story." This blew my mind at the time, but I'm so glad I learned this warped lesson then, long before I was ever on TV and had to deal with the *National Enquirer* and *TV Guide*. It's good to have your expectations lowered as much as possible before you go into show business.

We Arngrims arrived in Hollywood just in time for the riots. In the summer of 1966, there was a teeny little rock club on Sunset called Pandora's Box. Well, not really on Sunset, but on what was actually a traffic island in the middle of the street. It was that teeny. And apparently it was ground zero for the entire L.A. hippie population. As a kid, I was fascinated with it, since it was painted purple and looked like some kind of kid's playhouse, just sitting there in the middle of the street. I couldn't understand why I wasn't allowed to go in. Turns out a lot of people didn't want their kids going in, and the police shut it down one night, resulting in a series of demonstrations and riots, so huge, that they became the basis of the Buffalo Springfield song "For What It's Worth." You know, "It's time we stop, hey, what's that sound? / Everybody look what's going down." Yeah, that one. There really were "a thousand people in the street." Probably quite a bit more than that, actually. At one point, the rioters even turned over a bus.

We were living up on the fifth floor of the Chateau, giving us the best view of the scene. My parents and their friends gathered on the balconies to drink wine and watch the spectacle. I wasn't allowed out on the balconies, so I felt quite put out. My mother explained to me that it wasn't safe because there might be something called "tear gas." I remember hearing the adults talk and asking my mother, "What's a riot?" The explanation I was given about people fighting in groups, etc., didn't make a lot of sense, and I became convinced it was some kind of sporting event. I had visions of organized teams in something like karate robes with wooden poles taking turns hitting one another. It's not surprising I thought it was all a game from the reaction of the grown-ups on the balcony. They were yelling and laughing: "The peasants are revolting!" "Let them eat cake!"

But riots weren't the only thing I could see from our perch in the castle. From my bathroom window, I had a perfect view of a revolving billboard. No, not just any revolving billboard, but a giant Bullwinkle. For also on Sunset were the offices of Jay Ward, the creator of Rocky and Bullwinkle. At the corner of Sunset and Marmont Lane, he had erected a perfect replica of Bullwinkle J. Moose, in a glittering, cut-away showgirl costume, with Rocket J. Squirrel perched on his outstretched hand. Every time I went to the bathroom, I watched Bullwinkle go round and round and round. I thought he had been put there just for me.

Back then, children were permitted to play in the halls at the Chateau. But they weren't the only ones roaming aimlessly. Some of the more stoned or spaced out adults could also be found wandering about. One day, I found an old woman in my hallway. She was very well dressed and had an accent. She sounded British, like the people in that annoying *Mary Poppins* movie. She had a wonderful smile and seemed sort of funny and dotty. As if I had found a stray kitten, I brought her home to my mother and asked if I could keep her.

She turned out to be the famous music-hall star and actress Beatrice Lillie. No, I couldn't keep her, as she really did have her own apartment down the hall, but she did officially become my new best friend. I made it clear that she was specifically *my* friend, and my parents were allowed to play with her only when I was busy.

We all went to see her in her movie when it opened: *Thoroughly Modern Millie,* with Julie Andrews, Carol Channing, and Mary Tyler Moore. Bea played Mrs. Meers, the scary old lady with the chopsticks in her hair who kidnaps the girls in the movie by chloroforming them and dumping them into a large wicker basket. I absolutely loved her. She was the villain.

Bea was delighted to come to my big event as well—my fifth birthday party, held in our apartment in the Castle. She brought me a present. It was in a big box with lots of tissue paper. When I got it open, I pulled out a ceramic sculpture—of what appeared to be a disembodied head. The grown-ups all stared at Bea in horror. She said simply, "Oh, I just never know what to get for children."

I thought it was the most beautiful thing I had ever seen. It was a sculpture of what looked like a beautiful dark-eyed East Indian boy. I eventually named it Mowgli, after *The Jungle Book* character, and kept it on my dresser and stored hats on it. I still consider it one of the top-ten best gifts I've ever received.

I liked surprises, and my childhood was full of them. I never knew who in the way of friends my parents were going to spring on me next. Some of my parents' pals were more fun than others, some I just barely tolerated, but I couldn't say any of them were boring. One of my favorite grown-ups was named Christine, whom I befriended when I was about seven. She was an older lady, but I liked her because she didn't talk to me like I was stupid. Because I was so small for my age, a lot of adults treated me as if I were younger than I was. But Christine wasn't one of those. She would look me in the eye and listen to what I was saying. She would ask me sensible questions and pay attention to the answers. If I asked her a question, she didn't laugh and say, "Oh, how cute!" She just answered it like a regular person. In other words, she was capable of holding a normal, intelligent conversation.

She met my mother through their shared publicist. My mother was at the height of her *Casper* and *Gumby* fame, and

Christine had a book that she discussed on the lecture circuit and in a nightclub act. She, like my mother, had become quite famous in the late '50s and early '60s. Her name was Christine Jorgensen—the recipient of the world's first "publicly acknowledged" sex-change operation.

She had at one time been a soldier named George Jorgensen, who one day realized that certain *things* were just not what they should be. So he went on a quest for medical assistance with what at that time was thought to be a rare condition. He found his way to the doctors in Denmark who were pioneering this new treatment, and several very experimental surgeries later, *she* returned to America to live out her new life as a woman, in peace and total anonymity.

Except it didn't quite work out that way. The press found out, and the 1950s equivalent of today's rabid paparazzi met her at the airport, where all hell broke loose. The headlines read: "Ex-GI Becomes Blonde Beauty!" and "Operations Transform Bronx Youth!"

I didn't have a clue about Christine's past, but then one day, my parents came to me and said, "We need to talk to you about Auntie Christine." I was worried and thought maybe she'd been in an accident or something.

"It's just that Auntie Christine is famous, and, well, you might hear about this on the news," my mother said delicately. (I was surprisingly up on current events for the average second grader. A major news junkie, I never missed Walter Cronkite.)

My parents seemed to be hemming and hawing, which was unusual. Finally, they said, "Auntie Christine used to be a man."

"What?" I said and stared at them. I knew they were nuts, but

I thought maybe this time they had finally gone the rest of the way around the bend.

"She used to be a man," they replied nervously. "She's a woman now, of course. Uh . . . you see, she was born a man, and, well, she had an operation . . ." The whole explanation tumbled out quickly.

"Oh." I mean really, what can you say to a story like that? But then my curiosity was piqued. "So wait, you mean people can change? Men can become women, and women can become men?"

They looked even more nervous. "Uh . . . well, yes. But it's very complicated."

"So then, if I wanted to, *I could become a guy*?"

The furious backpedaling began: "Oh, well, technically, yes. Of course, you'd have to be an adult, and, of course, it's a major medical procedure; several operations, you know, very expensive."

I was ecstatic. "Wow! That is so cool!"

I hardly think that was the response they expected, but it was cool. This strange thing they were describing with such discomfort was nothing short of a miracle. I knew I was living in what was quickly becoming an age of scientific wonder; I had just recently seen men walk on the surface of the moon, right there on TV in my own living room. And now they were telling me of yet another astounding scientific triumph. This was cause for celebration!

Of course, I didn't really grasp the implications of Christine's sex change. I also wasn't clear about whether or not one could have multiple operations and just go back and forth, from gender to gender, as one needed. I thought that a person could then, by logical extension, have surgery to become *anything*: a monkey, a giraffe . . . a fire engine. But what I did get was the underlying principle: a person was no longer permanently defined by the circumstances of his or her birth. Biology was no longer destiny. I had no real desire to become male at that time, and so far, the female thing has really worked out for me. But all my life, I have known, deep in my heart, that if it didn't, I knew my options. Because of this realization, I feel that I am, and have always been, a woman by choice.

As fabulous as this news was, I had no idea what I was supposed to do the next time I saw Christine. It seemed rude to ask. I knew she'd written a book; I figured I'd eventually just go get a copy and read it. But now I couldn't help staring at her. I'm not sure what I was looking for. A seam running up the back? Bolts in the neck? A zipper? In my cartoon-addled mind, I thought perhaps it would be something like when Bugs Bunny just unzips his head and becomes something else. There were no signs. Whatever the medical technology at the time the procedure was performed in Denmark, they must have really been on to something, or the doctor was having a *very* good day. I've seen pictures of her over the years, and she really did look fabulous.

This is why I find it odd now, that with all the medical advances in the last forty years, there are still transsexuals who settle for less than top-drawer results. I swear, there's no pride in workmanship anymore. When asked by a transsexual friend what I think of her new look, I am all too often forced to admit: "I knew Christine Jorgensen, and you, sir, are no Christine Jorgensen."

CHAPTER THREE

KEEPING SECRETS

> **OLGA: My grandma says you can tell what's inside a person by the face they wear.**
>
> **MARY: I guess. I never thought of Nellie that way, I mean, being poor and all. It kind of makes me feel sorry for her . . . almost.**

I'm all for a change of scenery now and then; out with the old, in with the new. But when I was growing up, my parents barely let me unpack my stuffed animals before we were on to the next locale. I'm not really sure why we moved so much, but I think it had something to do with money. Being actors, our family income varied wildly from year to year. And being actors, we were cursed with a constant sense of misplaced optimism. If we came into a little extra money, my father would say, "Oh no, we can't live *here*!" and we'd move somewhere much nicer and more expensive. And then, a year to two later, when the money ran out, and no jobs came in, we'd pack up and move to "something more practical." We sometimes stayed as long as three years, sometimes less than one.

When I was born, my family lived in Queens, New York, in a two-bedroom in Kew Gardens. We moved when I was a year old to Eighty-third Street and East End Avenue in Manhattan. My dad got a job on Broadway in the show *Luther* with Albert Finney, so this apartment building was ritzier; it had a doorman. Two years later, we were at the Chateau in Los Angeles.

Obviously, all our apartments were rentals. My parents did not own a home until Auntie Marion left them hers when she died in 1985. They didn't own a car until I was a teenager. When we first moved to L.A., their credit rating was so nonexistent they couldn't even get a charge account at a department store. They had a friend use his card to buy us a TV and paid him back in cash installments.

Once we moved to L.A., the places we found to live were all deluxe, mind you. After the Chateau, we bounced around the Hollywood Hills and West Hollywood, but my father would not venture so much as "east of Fairfax" (let alone "east of La Brea"—*quelle horreur*!). We were the snobbiest bunch of broke people you ever met.

Still, my parents always wanted to be able to say their children lived in a real house, and they finally got their chance. At one point, when our income was particularly high, we moved out of the Chateau to a house literally across the street. Even though it was huge and had a yard full of trees, all my brother and I did was complain that it wasn't the Chateau. He even got up every morning and walked across the street to use their pool (again, this was the '60s, and he was an actor, so nobody stopped him). I pressed my nose against the window and sighed, "I used to live in a castle!" My parents missed the laundry service. After a few months of this nonsense, my father asked why in hell we were paying more rent just to carry on like this all day, and we packed up and happily moved back to the Chateau.

Sadly, we couldn't stay there forever. We moved into the heart of West Hollywood, to Waring Avenue just off La Cienega Boulevard. It was another attempt at a "real house." It was adorable, with a yard, hardwood floors, a big kitchen, and a breakfast nook. Unfortunately, it only had two bedrooms. My parents put me in one, my brother in the other, and they slept on the pull-out sofa in the living room. It's possible they could have afforded a house with more bedrooms, but it would have meant moving to a slightly cheaper neighborhood. And that was *never* going to happen. My father would have slept in the bathtub first. For him, it was "location, location, location." He would rather have an eight-by-eight room in a luxury building than a five-room ranch house in the type of neighborhood he always referred to as a (sharp intake of breath) "bad address."

I liked Waring Avenue. I had a good-sized room, and I loved that breakfast nook. There were lots of children in the neighborhood and things to do within walking distance, and I was given pretty much free rein to go where I wished. And back then we had Beverly Park. At La Cienega and Beverly, where the Beverly Center shopping mall sits now, was an amusement park, with roller coasters, a haunted house, the whole bit. Oh, and a fully functioning, active oil well. Well, the whole area was rich in oil, and you couldn't very well expect them to cap it off because there was an amusement park full of children on the premises, could you? Environmental hazards were not as well understood by the general public then as they are now, so we all thought it was just great to ride the Ferris wheel and watch the pump go up and down, up and down, happily churning up oil and carcinogens all day.

So Dad's hanging out with Liberace and trying to "pass," Mom's managed to successfully escape from traditional women's work by becoming a cartoon, my brother is a successful (if somewhat miserable) brooding teen idol, and I'm a cute blond six-year-old. What could possibly go wrong?

Just about everything.

My parents went out quite a lot, so I was often left home with a baby-sitter. That should have been fine, except that my parents had some strange ideas about who was considered a reasonable choice as a baby-sitter. I encountered a long parade of actors, friends, acquaintances, and friends of friends. Some of them were amusingly eccentric, some had severe drug and alcohol issues, and some were actually certifiably insane. (I once took a count and realized that three out of four people who baby-sat me later wound up committed to a mental hospital. I think the ones who weren't simply went undiagnosed.)

But all of them were preferable to my parents' favorite (translation: cheapest and most available) baby-sitter, my brother. Why would any parent think that a teenage boy, who no longer attended regular school, had already been to a psychiatrist, and had been caught smoking, drinking, and trying drugs, would be a suitable baby-sitter for a six-year-old girl? I think they thought it would teach him responsibility.

The best explanation I can give for what happened next is this: he was really angry, and I was home. A lot of it's a blur. I wish a whole lot more of it was. I know a lot of kids beat up their younger siblings (and, no, that's not good for anybody either), but most of the time, they don't break out the kitchen carving knives and demonstrate how they're going to cut your throat if you tell anyone what they're doing.

It wasn't like I didn't try to tell my parents my brother was abusing me. It was just hard to explain how low things had really sunk, and they didn't want to believe anything like that was even possible. Stefan was famous, after all, and could therefore do no wrong in my parents' eyes. I'd beg them not to leave me alone with him, and they'd say, "Don't roughhouse with your sister!" and split. And the next thing I'd hear was: "Now you're really going to get it . . ."

I soon learned to shut up. Besides, Stefan clearly had some kind of magical powers; grown-ups seemed to believe absolutely anything he told them, no matter how ludicrous, and everyone talked about how he was a genius. So when he spoke, I listened. Sometimes he didn't make a whole lot of sense. Sometimes I'd question him; this was not a good idea. If I asked a question that he didn't know the answer to, or was perhaps a bit too logical for his taste, he'd beat me up. I was amazed at how the adults didn't seem to want to question him either. Did he beat them all up, too? In this environment, what happened next wasn't really much of a surprise.

I was six years old, and I didn't know what sex was or where babies came from. And frankly, I hadn't asked. But the guy who insisted he knew everything wasn't going to let that stop him. I had seen our two dogs, Rex and my brother's ill-treated mutt, Pork Chop, romping in the yard and as dogs will do, occasionally attempting to mate. I had asked what they were doing, and why everyone was giggling so much about it. My brother took it upon himself to enlighten me . . . in the garage, with the door closed.

I was innocent, but not a moron. I demanded to know why his explanation would require me to disrobe and lie down. But his answer was the same he gave to most questions: "JUST DO IT!" Having no clue as to what would come next, I did. As weak as some of the "sexual abuse prevention" literature may be, if I had been told even as little as "Don't let anyone touch you there," things could have gone quite differently. But no one had ever said anything about my body belonging to me. And my brother always made it quite clear who he thought it belonged to.

I don't remember pain. Or fear. I remember utter confusion. And a coldness, both physical and emotional. I was naked and flat on my back on a cold, filthy steamer trunk, in a dark, cold, dirty garage. Stefan explained what he was doing, but not why. And then, it was as if I wasn't there. There was no pretense of affection, no emotion, no talking. I was an object he'd found to serve this odd purpose. He was on top of me, and it was as if he was all alone in the world.

Afterward, I tried as usual to question him as to exactly what the point of this activity had been. His explanation was vague, to say the least. I wasn't sure if this now meant I was going to have a baby, give birth to a litter of puppies, or grow a second head. The only part I understood clearly was the very last thing he said: "Whatever you do, don't tell anyone. *Or else.*"

The abuse became a regular occurrence; it was happening at least three times a week, sometimes every day. After several months of this, not surprisingly, I wanted to get out of the house. I asked my parents if I could move out and get my own place.

They explained that six-year-olds did not have their own apartments. Besides, these things cost money. "How much?" was all I asked.

It was oddly my brother who explained that I needed a job and that the only job for kids that paid well enough to get an apartment was acting. Perfect! I already had a press clipping file and an audition tape from the supermarket. Well, sort of. The Arrow Market in West Hollywood was the first market to put in video security cameras. It was such an innovation, they didn't try to hide it. You could watch the video monitor at the checkout line. So every time we went shopping, I marched into the cheese aisle and practiced my tap routine. I wasn't very good, but the people at the checkout counter were very entertained nonetheless. I had turned theft prevention into art.

I soon joined the Arngrim family ritual—the audition process. Everyone in my family—in fact, everyone I knew—went on these things they called "auditions." I liked them at first, because I enjoyed dressing up and making sure my hair was absolutely perfect—no small feat in my case, with my nearly waist-length, super-fine, fly-away Barbie doll hair. (I think they invented the No More Tears and No More Tangle hair products just for me.) But I didn't care for the long car rides. I was then and still am prone to motion sickness and became famous for starting off auditions by brightly chirping, "I frew up in the car!"

At that age, auditions didn't demand any acting, seldom even dialogue. I was just asked to smile, then turn, and smile. It was sort of like posing for a cheerful mug shot. I finally landed a national television commercial, a major gig in anyone's book. It was for Hunt's ketchup. It was a series of commercials featuring a whole bunch of kids. The premise was children trying to figure out "how they get those tomatoes into the bottle." We were all given a sealed bottle of ketchup and a large tomato and told to do our worst. Some pushed, some tried to jam the tomato down the neck of the bottle. It was pretty funny.

So there I was on my first set, in an adorable white tennis outfit. No, I did not play tennis, but it was the '60s, and those cute little tennis skirt and top sets were very popular. And against my pale skin and white-blond hair, it made for a striking look. I fiddled with that bottle and tomato in every way possible, squinting and biting my lip, finally pressing down on the tomato with the bottle. Small problem: my tomato was apparently just a little bit riper than the others. Finally, during one take—squish!—the tomato exploded. Juice, seeds, and tomato flesh flew everywhere, splattering all over my fabulous, brand-new white tennis outfit, all over my face, landing in my hair, in my eyes, everywhere. I froze with my juice-covered arms extended away from my body.

The director and all the adults stood frozen, too, stifling hysterical laughter. Finally, the director, a very nice woman, came up to me and said, "Can I get you anything, honey?" (By which I suppose she meant, did I want a towel?) To which I replied, in a very deep, un-six-year-old girl voice: "Yes. GET . . . THIS . . . GODDAMN TOMATO JUICE OFF OF ME!"

At that point, any attempt on anyone's part to stifle laughter went right out the window. I think some of those crew members are still laughing. I wasn't really mad. I was just appalled. Not to mention cold and wet. Later, I did thank the nice lady for wiping me off. But my reputation in Hollywood was off to a hell of a start.

For the next several years I led a double life. I did my best to behave normally at school and in public, while at home nothing was normal. My brother had decided that his experiment in the garage was a success and now insisted on repeating this activity as often as possible. New activities were introduced, usually with the aid of whatever pornographic magazine he was reading that week, and insurrection was punished swiftly and mercilessly. I still have some of those awful visual memories, like the time I almost made it to the front door, my hand slipping off the doorknob as I fell to the floor, and watching my fingernails scrape the hardwood floor, as I was dragged back by my feet.

I understand how people in these situations can develop multiple personalities. I sometimes wish I had. I learned a whole bunch of stuff nobody, particularly not a child, should learn. I learned how to pretend that hours, days, entire weeks had simply never taken place. I learned how not to cry, how not to show pain, and what to do to guarantee myself a few hours of peace and quiet. I learned how to pretend to be happy when I wasn't. I learned to play dead. I learned how to lie. I've always been fascinated by what people are willing to do to survive, physically and mentally; how the human mind will warp, bend, twist, and adapt itself to even the most unbelievable situations if it thinks there's a chance of survival. When I was a bit older, my friends used to ask me why I had so many weird books about people in horrible situations—stuff about wars, plagues, the Holocaust. It was because I was fascinated by how these people lived through such horrors and survived, not just physically, but mentally and emotionally. I was looking for help in that department.

I also learned how to do drugs and get high. I understand that some people get through childhoods like this without using any substances at all. They must be a lot tougher than I am. I grabbed a break anywhere I could get it. Of course, the drugs weren't for my benefit. Stefan was taking every substance known to man and didn't want to "drink alone," as it were. I learned to roll joints. I learned to smoke pot, but I would cough too much to hold it in. So he taught me to drink it in tea. That worked.

By this time, I was eight, and my brother was home all day. He was no longer working. After his show, *Land of the Giants,* was canceled in 1970, his voice changed, and he grew to over six feet tall. All fourteen- and fifteen-year-olds want to look older, but for a kid actor, that's death. This freed up his time for other activities. School wasn't one of them.

He'd long ago managed to convince everyone that he didn't need to go to school like "regular people." The whole business of dealing with teachers and other children, let alone doing homework, seemed impossible for him. It was a great relief to everyone when he got a series where he could be tutored on the set. The trouble arose when they weren't filming, and he was expected to enroll in a school—somewhere, anywhere.

For a while my parents tried putting him in what was then the premier school for rich hippie parents in Los Angeles, Summerhill. The only decent thing he got out of that school was a cat. Really. The school cat was named Malcolm X because no one figured out, until it was too late, that Malcolm was really a female (basic biology being one of the many subjects outside of its core curriculum). Malcolm gave birth to seven kittens in our garage. I promptly picked out the cutest one and named it Bonnie after the movie *Bonnie and Clyde.* It died before its eyes even opened, and we buried it in the front yard as my brother played taps on his kazoo. So I got to pick another kitten, which I called Maude, and she lived for fourteen years.

Summerhill was a great school for Stefan, as they didn't ask him to do anything, and he didn't have to go if he didn't feel like it. I found this fascinating and begged my parents repeatedly to take me out of public school and send me to this magical place.

All they said was, "Finish your breakfast, or you'll miss the bus."

So from the time I came home from school, until the time my parents came home, which some days might not be until the early evening, or all day during summer vacation, I was alone in this huge, rambling house on a hill with Stefan. And his friends. He had the room on the side of the house with its own entrance, so he and his friends simply came and went at all hours of the day and night as they pleased. They liked to have parties.

One day, when I was about eight, I walked into the kitchen and saw that someone had baked a cake. Now, this was unusual, as I was the only one who did any baking in that house. My mother certainly didn't, my father only did stuff like that at the holidays, and besides, they weren't home. My father taught me how to make scrambled eggs when I was five, and cooking became my great passion. By the time I was nine or ten, I could make anything: cakes, pies, Cornish game hens in orange sauce, whatever. And here was a great big chocolate cake and an enormous bowl of purple frosting. What with the lurid purple color, I quickly deduced this to mean my brother and his friends must be having another party. I decided to inspect their handiwork. The frosting tasted pretty good, sweet with a slight hint of peppermint extract. Just as I was having my second or third spoonful, my brother and one of his buddies walked into the kitchen.

I heard a gasp. I looked up, spoon still in my mouth, to see them both staring at me wide-eyed. The boy next to my brother was getting very pale and looked as if he might start crying. My brother remained calm. "Put down the spoon and step away from the frosting," he ordered.

"What?" I said, my mouth full of frosting.

"Don't . . . eat . . . any . . . more . . . *frosting*!"

I put down the spoon.

"Okay, how much frosting have you eaten?" he asked.

"I dunno, a couple of spoonfuls. I licked the beaters."

At this point, his friend began to hyperventilate. He started whispering hysterically, "Oh, shit! Oh, shit! We're going to go to jail, man! We're going to go to jail!"

My brother turned to him. "Shut up" was all he said. The friend complied.

Then Stefan explained the situation to me: "We're having a party. We made a cake and put LSD in the frosting. Since we calculated the correct dose to be about one slice per person, and you've just eaten several large spoonfuls—and licked the beaters, where most of the acid we poured may still be concentrated—you've just taken enough LSD to pretty much fuck up all of West Hollywood."

His friend made a painful, gurgling noise and almost fainted.

"So what exactly does this *mean*?" I asked.

He smiled in a way I never liked to see. "It means you're coming to the party." I shrugged and followed him downstairs.

As they like to say in the drug books, "LSD's psychological effects vary greatly from person to person." Now, there's an understatement. I was nowhere near as stoned as the other guests, who each had way more than one piece of cake, along with champagne, pot, and anything else they could get their hands on. At one point I asked for a glass of champagne, and someone protested that I was too young. My brother laughed and said, "She's dropped more acid than all of you put together; what possible difference could it make now? Give her whatever the hell she wants!"

So I sat back, sipped my champagne, and watched the other guests. Some seemed to be enjoying themselves, chatting and laughing. Others were acting like people on acid in an antidrug film—sitting in the corner all freaked out, staring at their fingers. Someone even kindly gave me a balloon. I soon figured out that all of these people had been instructed that I was to be kept amused and happy at all costs, because if the kid freaked out, everybody was going to jail.

As soon as I realized the power I had, I began to mess with their heads as much as possible. "Let's play Monopoly!" I shouted. If they didn't look interested, I put on a face that indicated I might be about to lose it. "I really, *really* want to play Monopoly!" Then I sat back, smiling behind my champagne glass, while I watched a bunch of hapless stoners panic and scramble to find a Monopoly board. Why, there was fun to be had here after all!

The best was when I lost my balloon. It went over the side of the balcony. One big-eyed look from me, and three terrified, hallucinating young men were dispatched on a quest to find a balloon in the dark, in our huge, unlit, overgrown backyard. Mean? Sure. But these crazy bastards were giving drugs to small children. I figured they had it coming.

And where were my parents during this particular bout of insanity? Upstairs in another part of the house, paying absolutely no attention whatsoever. At one point, their dinner guest, a friend of my dad's, actually came downstairs to see "what the young people were up to." He didn't notice anything out of the ordinary. So my brother, grinning, gave him a piece of cake. And he ate it. He went back upstairs to watch TV with my father.

I heard later that he began to hallucinate, and he turned to my father and said, "Holy shit! There was LSD in the cake!" My father blithely denied the whole thing. "Oh, don't be silly. They wouldn't really be doing acid! You probably just ate a pot brownie." Well, if he didn't believe another grown-up, his own buddy, why ever should I think he would have believed me?

And people actually still ask me why I didn't tell anybody anything. *Sheesh.*

CHAPTER FOUR

SOMETHING'S GOTTA GIVE

> **LAURA: Hard-working folks only smell bad to people who have nothing better to do than stick their noses in the air! Well, whenever you stick your nose in the air with me, Nellie Oleson, it's going to get punched!**

It was 1971. Somehow, I'd managed to survive the '60s. I was nine years old and still being abused by Stefan; his sexual demands had only increased over the past three years. But now I was old enough to actually understand what it was he was asking me to do, and what it meant. If I didn't like the situation before, I liked it even less now. I hadn't the slightest idea what to do about it, though. There were no public service announcements on the TV advising "what to do if someone hurts you." There were no brochures. There was no *Something About Amelia.* Nothing. I was on my own dealing with this.

As far as the general public was concerned, the entire concept of incest and child molestation simply did not exist. You couldn't learn about it on an *ABC Afterschool Special,* because no one was talking about it. Hell, the *ABC Afterschool Special* series itself wouldn't be invented for another year. When I was a little girl, teachers were told they were forbidden to call the police about child abuse. "Mandated reporting" didn't exist until after 1974, when Congress passed something called CAPTA—the Child Abuse Prevention and Treatment Act. Until then, it was just understood by nice people everywhere that "these sorts of things" only happened very rarely, in poor, backward, rural, or slum families. And if, God forbid, you did manage to accidentally hear about it, your job was to "not interfere."

And what if someone did get caught back then? Did he go to jail? Not terribly likely. Jail for child molesters is actually a new concept. Until 1950, the penalty for child rape in California—not "fondling," not "molestation," but flat out, unquestioned, forcible rape of a child by an adult—was (drum roll, please) thirty days in the county jail. After all, child rape was only a misdemeanor. The victim was only a child; it wasn't like raping a real person. But then, in November 1949, Linda Joyce Glucoft, a six-year-old girl in Los Angeles, was raped and murdered by a man named Fred Stroble. The story was front-page news in the *L.A. Times* for a week as police and the FBI searched for Stroble. Turns out he had just finished his thirty days for raping another child. The public went berserk, and the law was changed, so that the rape of a child could at least be considered a felony.

I found out that I might have some recourse entirely by accident. I was at day camp and heard some older campers joking about someone having "gotten raped." I asked my father what rape was, and he gave me an explanation about someone making someone else have sex "when they didn't want to," and that this was actually illegal. I was floored—not by the illegal part, but by the "didn't want to" part. My brother had gotten so good at making everyone cater to his slightest whim, that the very idea of my "wanting" or "not wanting" anything had become an alien concept. I didn't know that sex was something people did because they wanted to. I thought it was something you had to do when you were told. And I could hardly imagine anyone wanting to do *that* on a voluntary basis.

So I refused Stefan's next "request." When he started the usual ranting and raving and threats, I took a deep breath and informed him that I had just found out that making me do this was against the law, and that if he didn't get out of my room, I would call the police. Bluffing? You bet. Even then I figured the cops probably weren't going to do much about a "familial" molestation case. I would have been right. Stefan laughed and taunted me, but then decided not to take the risk, and walked out of my room, zipping up his pants on the way out. How long would this reprieve last? I didn't know, but I knew I had to do something to make sure he never touched me again.

What I really needed was to get out of town. As luck would have it, I got a movie part in a real honest-to-God feature film. I was the lead. Well, the lead kid anyway. It was called *Throw Out the Anchor,* and the stars were Richard Egan and Dina Merrill. It was a poor imitation of a typical Disney flick: handsome, widowed dad and his two adorable kids—the precocious, blond tomboy (yours truly) and her teen idol–type brother—go to Florida to "get away from it all" and rent a houseboat. Dad meets gorgeous heiress type, and romance and adorable high jinks ensue.

Oh wait, this sounds familiar. That would be because somebody already made this movie, in 1958. It was called *Houseboat* and starred Cary Grant and Sophia Loren. But I was too young to know that (and thankfully too young to compare Richard Egan to Cary Grant—yikes!), so I thought it was great. The best part was the whole movie was going to be filmed in Florida for three months. Hooray!

My mother and I moved to Orlando for the summer of 1972. We stayed in a nice hotel called the Park Plaza. I was thrilled because the room had a kitchen, so I could stock the fridge with Dr Pepper and pickles and all the other ghastly things I liked that nobody else could stand. On the set, I had not just my own dressing room, but an entire Winnebago. The set was in the middle of nowhere on the St. Johns River; not quite the Everglades, but close enough. The whole area was crawling with thousands of frogs, fish, armadillos, raccoons, possums, snakes, and, yes, alligators—real-live alligators that could actually maim and kill. And unlike California, whose only poisonous breed of snake is the rattler, Florida is home to every kind of poisonous snake you can name: rattlesnakes, water moccasins, coral snakes, and copperheads. As a huge fan of nature's villains—not to mention all things weird and scaly—I was in heaven.

My character, Stevie Porterfield, also liked wild animals, even snakes, and one of the movie's subplots was her quest to save their habitat from being destroyed by developers. Like me, Stevie was a tomboy, who preferred jeans and sneakers to dresses and romping through the underbrush to playing with dolls. For the next three months, I got to play a character who could be my real-life best friend, and I didn't have to see, hear, speak to, or so much as smell my brother.

This was probably the healthiest I'd been in years, because

I was sleeping eight hours a night and, during the day, getting more exercise and fresh air than I ever had. And I was certainly eating. The impossibly thin Dina Merrill and I drove everyone crazy by making a show of how many hot dogs, hamburgers, and Twinkies we could eat without gaining weight. (We both apparently had the metabolism of hamsters.) We just burned them off as fast as we could scarf them down.

I gained a little weight, which was a good thing. Until then, I was always in trouble at school whenever the school nurse decided to check everyone's height and weight. I was always at least twenty pounds under whatever the number was supposed to be. Notes were sometimes sent home. I ate constantly, but I suppose it was stress. During *Throw Out the Anchor,* I had a growth spurt, and I proudly went all the way up to fifty-eight pounds.

To top everything off, I even got a pet, just the kind of inappropriate pet every kid wants: a possum. On the way to the set, Dina Merrill found a dead mother possum and her babies. Some were still alive, so she rescued one and presented me with an adorable baby possum in a laundry basket full of Spanish moss. It sat there hissing, spitting, and snarling as all baby wild animals do. I was thrilled; my mother wasn't. She admonished me not to get too attached, as this probably was *not* going to be a big hit at the hotel. Several older cast members said that possums were very dangerous—they bit, had rabies. They encouraged me to return this creature to the wild immediately.

Before a decision could be made, a boat pulled up on the river. Sometimes visitors arrived on the set this way, as it was actually easier to get in by boat than by car, and this stretch of the river was a vacation spot for rich tourists with houseboats. An older couple disembarked. The lady had white hair and tons of jewelry and even carried a small poodle. The man wore a neck scarf and captain's hat. They looked like Mr. and Mrs. Howell from *Gilligan's Island.* They wanted to drop by and see "the movie stars," they said.

The woman suddenly looked down at my basket. "And what do you have there?"

"A possum," I replied.

"Oh, *how adorable*!" she squealed.

My mother interrupted. "Yes, well, it may be cute, but I think they're not going to feel the same way at the hotel!"

The lady brightened. "Oh? What hotel are you staying at?"

"The Park Plaza," replied my mother.

"Ahhh!" The rich lady said and laughed. "What a coincidence! We own it."

They thought the possum was darling and absolutely insisted that we bring it back to the hotel as an honored guest. My mother looked at me and asked, "How do you always manage to do these things?"

So what did I name my new pet? I named him after a bizarre subplot in the film. In *Throw Out the Anchor,* there's a scene in which an old man tells me a convoluted story about "second chances in life" and how this all has something to do with an egg cream soda. Since my furry little friend had been facing certain death when I got him, I figured this would be a good name for him. So he became Eggbert Crème II, or Eggy for short. When we finished filming, I knew I couldn't bring Eggy back to Los Angeles, so I left my pet with the director's daughter, who was about my age and also an avid animal lover. She had a rat named Sweetheart that she had taught to run up her sleeve. She happily took Eggy into her menagerie. Later she wrote to me that, when Eggy got too big to keep in the house, they took him out to the location where they first found him and let him go. Somewhere in the forests along the St. Johns River in Florida, there is a possum sitting on a stump trying to tell the other possums and squirrels and raccoons, "No! I am *not* making it up!! I really *did* live at the Park Plaza Hotel!"

By the time my mom and I returned to L.A. from the movie, it was, of course, time to move again. My brother was also sort of out of the house. I say sort of, because he couldn't seem to make it stick. He would find an apartment, move out of my parents' house, usually trading up for an apartment with a girl, a couple of guys, and a big pile of drugs. He'd pay the first and last month's rent and then stop. This became a joke around our house: "With Stefan, the first and last month's rent really are the first and last month's rent." He and his friends would stay until the landlord threw them out or until someone got arrested for drugs. It was a toss-up as to which happened more often. But it was decreed that Stefan "lived on his own now," even though my parents wound up paying for everything, and he spent more time moving back home than he did out. His time at home with us was considered "just visiting."

My family moved to an apartment, a fabulous place in West Hollywood called Hayworth Towers. It was built in the early 1930s, and each apartment had high ceilings, white art deco moldings, a fake fireplace, and floor-to-ceiling mirrors. My room even came with its own bathroom. I particularly loved that it was in the heart of West Hollywood, where there were 7-Elevens, Thrifty Drug Stores, and Baskin-Robbins as far as the eye could see. There was so much sidewalk, I even got a skateboard.

Sadly, though, I was unemployed. I continued to go to auditions. After the movie, I was considered a marketable commodity, and my parents and I thought my career would be off and running. No dice. Auditions, even callbacks, came and went with no bookings. Was I doing something wrong? Was the market glutted with blond eleven-year-old girls? Hmmm . . . and there was always that damn Jodie Foster. My God, she got everything! She was fantastic, an unstoppable force. I loved her movies, but every little child actress in Hollywood knew that if they saw her at an audition, it was time to go home.

My father, having now started his own management business, Arngrim and Associates, soon to become Arngrim and Petersen, sat me down for a managerial talk. "It's not going well," he began. "It happens. Sometimes people do a movie and work like crazy afterwards, and sometimes they never work again. You may need to accept the idea that you might not work until after you're eighteen."

He was right, of course. Show biz is inherently an unpredictable business, but for child actors, it's downright impossible. You grow, you age. You might have a "look" that sells, then wake up one morning looking like someone else entirely. Children are often hired as "accessories" to the grown-up members of the cast. A child might get a role because he or she bears a physical resemblance to the star playing one of the parents in the film or TV show. If that star stops working for some reason . . . well, so much for the kid. Was this me? Was I "done"? It was possible: I could be washed up, over the hill, past my prime. At eleven.

It was less than a week after my dad's speech that I auditioned for the part of Nellie Oleson on *Little House on the Prairie.*

Now, it was not my first trip down to this particular office. I had been called in when the concept of the show was first being discussed. I remember wearing my frilly, girly yellow dress, the one I deemed nauseating and only to be worn for special occasions or at gunpoint. I was not asked to read any lines. It was a bizarre meeting where producer Ed Friendly showed me a set of *Little House* books and asked ominously, "Do you know what these are?"

"Um, books?"

I figured I didn't get the job, as I had not read the *Little House* books and had actually never heard of Laura Ingalls Wilder until that day. But this, apparently, didn't destroy my chances. Weeks later, I returned to read for the part of Laura. Obviously, no sale there. I was called back yet again, a week later, to read for the part of Mary. The only thing I found surprising about any of this was that I kept getting called back. As I said to my father at the time, "What could they possibly be thinking? I am *so* not the farm girl type." So when I got the call that my presence was requested yet again, I thought, *How the hell many people are in this thing? It must have a cast of thousands!*

When I auditioned the fourth time, on Friday, May 17, 1974, I had dispensed with all manner of pretense, yellow dresses, etc. I was wearing cutoff shorts and a T-shirt—my usual wardrobe. I remember sitting on the stairs outside Paramount Studios with my father, going over the script. As I began to skim the pages, I noticed something odd—a tone I had never seen in any other role I had read for. This was not some ordinary, insipid child character, blandly responding to her parents and pretending the usual sickening cheer about incredibly boring things no actual child could possibly get excited about in real life. "Gosh, Mom, help you with the church bake sale? You bet!" "Wash the car? Gee, Dad, you're the keenest!" This was a girl who wouldn't be caught dead doing any of that crap, and would tell you so to your face.

I looked up at my father. "Uh, Dad?"

"Yes?"

"This girl's, like, *a total bitch.*"

"Read it," he told me. So I read the lines. My father laughed so hard, tears ran down his cheeks. He gasped, "God, whatever you do, don't touch it! Just read it EXACTLY LIKE THAT!"

I went into the room for what was now my fourth tryout. Michael Landon was there, along with Kent McCray, the show's producer, and a third man I can't recall. The three of them asked me if I would be so kind as to please read for them. I sat down and proceeded to read the script. I remember the main part of it was the "My Home" speech, where Nellie, under the cover of writing an essay for school, gloats over every expensive item in her house and how much her family paid for it. I began to recite, "It's the nicest home in all of Walnut Grove. We have carpets in every room . . . and three sets of dishes . . . one for every day, one for Sunday and one for when somebody special and important comes to visit—which we've never used. . . ."

As I read, these men became hysterical, as my father had been minutes earlier. They actually threw themselves around on the couch and elbowed each other in the ribs. "Would you please read the last part again, dear?" one of them asked.

"Yes," I replied politely, awaiting direction. "What would you like me to change?"

"Nothing," said the trio, "just read the part about the house again. *Please!*"

And so I did, exactly the same way—with exactly the same shriek-inducing results. They hired me on the spot.

By the time my father and I made the ten-minute drive home and got in the door, my agent had already set a price, accepted the producers' offer, and scheduled my wardrobe fitting for the following Monday. I can honestly say, this was the easiest role I ever landed before or since. I asked my father if I should be concerned that I was turned down for the parts of both Laura and Mary, but for the great bitch role of Nellie, I was hired instantly. Did this say something about me as a person?

"Hey, if the shoe fits, wear it," was all he said.

Well, technically, he did say a few other things, like "This thing won't last one season!" "Who on earth would actually watch this drivel?" "Why the hell are they spending so much money on sets? My God, if this is still on TV a year from now, it'll be a miracle!" Needless to say, we didn't take my dad to the track much. Unless we wanted to know what horse *not* to bet on.

To be fair, he was not alone in his disbelief at the success of *Little House.* Nobody, I mean *nobody,* except for maybe one person, thought for an instant that it would be the phenomenon it turned out to be. Obviously, crazy old Michael Landon was way ahead of us all on this one, but I don't think even he anticipated this level of worldwide "cultdom."

The first episode of *Little House on the Prairie,* titled "A Harvest of Friends," aired September 11, 1974 (not counting the pilot, which aired March 30, 1974), and the last episode, "Hello and Good-bye," aired March 21, 1983—plus they threw in some spin-offs and a few more TV movies for fans in withdrawal. Nine years in all on the air; 203 episodes. Insane! And *Little House* lingers; it's syndicated daily in over 140 countries, including Borneo, Argentina, Iraq, and Sri Lanka. There's even a sixty-DVD boxed set shaped like a covered wagon you can buy for two hundred bucks. The French set comes in a little house; it's much prettier.

Back then (and even today) *Little House* was a bit of a rarity: a TV show that actually advocated morals, faith, and community. There was no T&A, no police chases, no bionic body parts, not even a musical number (unless you count the Walnut Grove gang singing "Bringing in the Sheaves" in church). What it was, was wholesome: churning butter, milking cows, helping your fellow man, that kind of wholesome stuff. And it was old; the actual children's book series was written way back in 1935. As if that wasn't bizarre enough, all the action took place in late-nineteenth-century Minnesota.

But there was something about this show that struck a nerve; at its core, even with all the crazy plotlines that Michael and company cooked up (Blindness! Rabies! Anthrax!), *Little House* was simply about a family trying to achieve the American dream. Maybe it's what the world needed after the crazy, druggy debauchery of the late 1960s and early '70s. In the '50s and'60s, country shows like *The Beverly Hillbillies, The Andy Griffith Show, Hee Haw, Gunsmoke,* and *Bonanza* abounded; then they disappeared despite the fact that people loved them. The networks wanted to appeal to a younger demographic, so they "deruralized" TV. Only Michael Landon wanted to buck this trend. He realized that *Little House* was exactly what audiences were missing. Every episode was filled with family values, love, and friendship. The show made you feel good; it made you appreciate what you had and stop bitching about what you didn't. You don't have enough money to pay your rent? Buddy, those Ingalls girls didn't have a penny between them to buy a slate pencil. Now, that's poor.

Still, I was puzzled back then, and I remain in shock now. *Little House* was *big*. It was number one in the ratings in the 1974–1975 season and always held a spot in the top thirty; even up against shows like *Rhoda, Phyllis,* and *The Captain and Tennille*. It was a force to be reckoned with. An estimated forty million viewers watched us every week at our peak. There were dolls, lunch boxes, Colorforms, even a tea set.

I loved my first script, "Country Girls," because I had the punchline: I got to read that haughty essay about how wonderful my home was. But the books were another story. For the life of me, I could never figure out how Ed Friendly or Michael Landon had read them and envisioned a hit TV show. We had to start shooting so quickly after my audition that I had no time to cram, no time to read the *Little House* books for more perspective on what I was doing. It was actually weeks before I went out and bought a copy of *On the Banks of Plum Creek*. When I read it, I was shocked; it was pretty slow and boring. But the Garth Williams illustrations were dead on. When I saw the picture of Nellie clutching her doll away from Laura, it looked exactly like me. She had my nose. It's just spooky.

Because the books lacked soap operaesque drama, Michael took great creative liberty; poetic license ran rampant on *Little House*. Michael added adventure, excitement, and tears (even the men cried!) in nearly every episode. Someone once asked him, "So, why don't you stick closer to the books?" He replied, "Have you read them? There's an entire chapter on how to make an apple fritter. I can't film that."

Instead, he brought out the true nature of all the characters; he said things about them that Laura Ingalls herself only implied. And that is why the show was so brilliant and so well received: it spoke universal truths about human nature. Everybody's problems were the Ingallses' problems.

All I knew at age twelve was that I was just cast as one of the biggest brats on TV. I had no idea what I was getting myself into.

CHAPTER FIVE

WELCOME TO WALNUT GROVE

> **NELLIE: You know, the Oleson family goes all the way back to royalty. We come from heads of state, and there were titles for most of my relatives.**
>
> **LAURA: Like Nero and Ivan the Terrible?**

No one could have prepared me for the *Prairie*. There had never been a set—and there will never be a set—quite like it. It was so enormous that we needed two stages—Stage 31 and 32 at Paramount Studios. In 1978, when we moved to MGM Studios, we actually needed the biggest set they had, Stage 15, where they filmed *The Wizard of Oz*.

Paramount housed the indoor sets—places like the Mercantile, the store owned and operated by my parents on the show, Nels and Harriet Oleson, and the ornate Oleson living quarters, the church/school, Doc Baker's office, and the Little House interior itself. The Little House and the barn existed in their entirety inside the building: there were dirt floors, haystacks, and Mary and Laura's loft. When we had to shoot exteriors—in and around the school, anything at the mill, all the ring-around-the-rosies in the yard, and the endless running over the hills—we filmed at

Big Sky Ranch in Simi Valley, forty miles from Paramount. All the facades of the buildings in the town, Walnut Grove, had four sides, but they were hollow. That's why the scenes were always shot out of sequence; we had to shoot the exteriors and interiors days apart. On Monday, for example, I'd walk into the school and say hi to Miss Beadle. Then on Thursday, I'd take my seat in class.

After my victorious audition, I had just the weekend before I was to report to wardrobe for fittings. It was Monday, May 21, 1974, and Auntie Marion and I walked into a set of dark, musty rooms in the costume department, deep in the bowels of Paramount Studios. They kept bringing out dress after dress and pinning them on me, checking to see what was too big or too small. I started to feel a little giddy and light-headed—just how many costumes would I have? Were we making *Gone With the Wind* here? The few parts I'd had were all modern-day kids, and I'd worn my own clothes half the time. I'd never seen a petticoat up close and in person in my entire life. By the time I left, I'd tried on so many things, I had no idea what I would finally end up wearing.

Marion was my guardian on the set. She was my mom's older, somewhat more socially conventional sister. Being retired, she was deemed to have more time on her hands. As far as my parents were concerned, that and owning a car were qualifications enough to be my set guardian. And it so happened, Auntie Marion loved me. She called me her "favorite niece," even though she didn't have any other nieces. She had been a classical singer and claimed to have always suffered from terrible stage fright. But she was the bravest shy person I ever met. Just ask the burglar. One night, in the early '70s, a burglar attempted to break into Marion's house in the Hollywood Hills. He was halfway through the bedroom window when she awoke and spotted him. She was completely alone in the house, my uncle Beach having died some years before. What did she do? She spoke: "And just what do you think you're doing?"

The burglar was stunned. Instead of screaming for help or hiding under the bed, this woman was chastising him like his third-grade teacher. He pulled himself back out the window and fled. This was possibly also due to the fact that she was holding the samurai sword that Uncle Beach had brought home from World War II. The burglar likely didn't feel up to confronting a woman who could stand there in a fuzzy pink housecoat, clutching a three-foot steel blade, and exhibit no fear whatsoever. So there was no doubt, as I braved my first day on the set, that I was in the best possible hands.

A few days after the wardrobe fitting, it was time to film my first episode, "Country Girls." This was actually the third episode of *Little House*—Nellie didn't make an appearance until then because the Ingalls are busy braving storms, fires, hostile Native Americans, etc., all en route to settling in Minnesota. In my episode they're finally living in the Little House, and Mary and Laura are off to school, where they have to battle an even more terrible force: that would be me.

The first person we met on arrival at the set was Reed Rummage. Yes, that was his name, poor man. He was wearing polyester pants with a short-sleeved shirt, bearing some sort of stain (mustard?), tucked in. He had the utterly thankless job of second AD, or assistant director. This position has very little to do with "directing" as most people think of it, and everything to do with desperately trying to keep things on schedule, figuring out where the hell the actors and crew disappeared to after lunch, and generally yelling at people. It's more of a factory floor foreman–type job. He was quickly nicknamed Reed Rubbish.

I was, thank heavens, not only on time, but early. Number one item on this man's job description was "screaming at people who are late." A good set boasts a well-defined chain of command. If several of the actors go missing or something is wrong with the shooting schedule, a director or producer doesn't want to yell at a bunch of different people, so he just yells at the second AD. Hence, Reed Rubbish's constantly pained expression and flawless timekeeping. He actually carried a stopwatch and a clipboard like some kind of demented gym teacher. ("You are three and one-half minutes late!")

Reed greeted us not with "Good morning" or "Welcome to our set" or any such pleasantry one might fantasize about hearing if one were to arrive for one's first day starring on a TV show. The moment my aunt explained who we were, he looked me up and down, glanced at her, and barked, "This child's hair is supposed to be in curlers! Why isn't she in curlers?" We hadn't the slightest idea what he was talking about. They had never mentioned this when I was in wardrobe, and I had endured no hair or makeup tests like in the old studio days. I wasn't even aware of Nellie's whole "ringlet" issue, not having read the books. Reed then began snarling into a walkie-talkie to someone about my not being in curlers. My aunt desperately tried to explain that we really had not been told this, and, of course, had we been informed, we would have gladly complied.

He finally let out a long-suffering sigh and said, "Okay, never mind. Go get dressed!" We scurried away to my dressing room. With all of the gigantic *Little House* sets, the soundstage was not big enough to accommodate the dressing rooms. So we had to go out the back door, often into the rain, onto what appeared to be a loading dock of some kind, and walk down a wooden plank until we reached a series of small wooden structures. Each dressing room was maybe ten feet deep at most and about five feet wide. Mine contained a beat-up old motel couch, two end tables with a truly ugly lamp on one of them, a makeup table (more like a very small desk, really), and an old, rickety wooden chair. There was an old-fashioned wooden cupboard in the corner that held my costumes. I couldn't decide whether it more resembled a small suite in a skid row hotel or a big bedroom in a mobile home. But, hey, it was clean and dry, and within a few weeks, I would find the sight of this room at the end of a long, hard day to be the most wonderful in the world.

Safely ensconced, Auntie Marion and I began the process of getting me into wardrobe. I had seen the clothes in their half-finished state at the wardrobe fitting, but they were even more lavish and beautiful now. Every outfit had lace and flowers on it (unless it was taffeta with stripes): lace at the collar, lace at the cuffs, lace on the hem. Gorgeous, really. Okay, incredibly scratchy and uncomfortable, but beautiful, just the same. On the first day, I already had four dresses: a blue one with short, puffed sleeves; a long-sleeved yellow floral number; an adorable pink one with a starched white pinafore, and my favorite, the dark purple-striped taffeta party dress.

My wardrobe offered a stark contrast to Laura's two dresses, both of which seemed to be made out of sackcloth. One of the major plot points of this first episode was Laura and Mary getting their first remotely attractive outfits, the pretty blue calico dresses that Ma makes for them rather than sewing a dress for herself. They then proceeded to wear these dresses daily for the next several years. All our costumes were one-of-a-kind and dry-cleaned at the end of the week. We were given just one duplicate that was "the stunt dress." Mine was the blue puffy-sleeved outfit—which is why anytime Nellie is in a fight, she's wearing it.

All of those dresses had what seemed like hundreds of those little hook-and-eye catches. I also had these weird thigh-high stockings with elastic garters, which I'd certainly never worn before. I actually don't think anyone had really worn anything like this in some fifty or sixty years. And I had pantaloons, of all things, plus the world's largest, heaviest petticoat. I swear, if the dresses didn't kill me, the underwear would.

Thankfully, Richalene Kelsay, a very kind, intelligent, down-to-earth woman who was in charge of the show's wardrobe, suddenly materialized to save us. She strolled into my dressing room and showed my aunt and me how to operate all these elaborate trappings, then told us we were the lucky ones: "You just have black Mary Janes for shoes. Those other poor girls have high-button boots to put on. We actually had to go out and buy buttonhooks for everyone, so they could get dressed."

My aunt was positively aghast. She was old enough to have put her shoes on with buttonhooks when she was a little girl in the 1910s. She had been relieved to see that and all the other complicated fashions go, and had applauded the advent of zippers and Velcro. She really thought she'd manage to make it through the rest of her life without having to deal with nonsense like buttonhooks ever again. And here she was, late in the twentieth century, at seven in the morning, helping me into pantaloons and garters and doing up hook-and-eye closures.

We had just gotten me into my straitjacket of 1800s finery, when there was yet another knock on the door. This time, I was greeted by a tiny girl with long braids, freckles, and the biggest set of front teeth you ever saw in your life. It was Melissa Gilbert. She was about nine years old. I was barely twelve and small for my age, but she looked as if she might fit in my purse—and could chew her way out if she had to.

She marched right in and introduced herself and began explaining things to us, all kinds of things: who was who, who did what, how everything worked. She was filling us in, in no uncertain terms, mind you, as to the way things were around here. We stood there openmouthed, paying rapt attention to her lecture. It was terribly surreal, yet informative. Then came her stern warning, delivered with the intensity of Edward G. Robinson, in the vocal range of Shirley Temple: "And whatever you do, you watch out for that Melissa Sue Anderson. She's very dangerous. She's evil, and I hate her."

Now, my aunt could not sit still for this. Melissa Sue Anderson? The girl cast to play Laura's big sister, Mary? She was a little girl, for heaven's sake! My aunt chided, "Oh, honey, you don't mean that! You don't really *hate* her now, do you?"

"Yes, I do!" Melissa squeaked. "I hate her, and she hates me. She tried to kill me, you know. And she'll kill you, too, if she gets the chance!" And then she ran off.

It was as if we were suddenly in the middle of a really bad prison movie with an all-midget cast. We had just been told to "watch our backs" by someone who looked like a talking Holly Hobby doll. And this "terror of the cell block" we were to fear? What was she, *ten*? Melissa Gilbert had to be putting us on. Obviously, this was not true. She didn't mean "kill" for God's sake—the kid was a major drama queen already. But there was something very unsettling and insistent about her warning. My aunt and I slowly turned and stared at each other. Just what sort of place was this?

After imprisoning myself in my fabulous costume, we proceeded to makeup. On some shows, depending on the studio, there might be a whole makeup room or department, but in most cases, it was more what you would call a "makeup and hair area." That's what *Little House* had, and entering it was like falling into a time warp. The makeup tables were the old white-painted wooden kind, with the huge mirrors lit up with dozens of bulbs like you'd see in the movies. There were wigs on old-fashioned cloth wig heads and manual curling irons—not those cute little thermostatically controlled things you plug in, but clattering, scissorlike iron rods (no Teflon coating here!) you put in the oven to heat.

The hairdressers put the irons in the oven until they were so hot, you could run a cloth ribbon through them to take out the wrinkles. And you always knew when you accidentally picked up a synthetic ribbon because it melted and smoked. This is what they announced they were going to run through my hair every morning.

All of the equipment was the same stuff they had been using for decades. Also apparently in continuous use for decades were the hair stylists, Larry Germain and Gladys Witten-Coy. They, along with the equally ancient makeup crew, Allan "Whitey" Snyder and Hank Edds, had worked with every major star since the beginning of time: Marilyn Monroe, Bette Davis, Joan Crawford. Many child and teen stars fancy themselves divas and cop quite the attitude in hair and makeup. I would have paid money to have seen any of them try that on *Little House*. Really, go on, try it. Strike a pose with people who kept Bette Davis in line and told Joan Crawford where she could bloody well get off.

Makeup and hair quickly became known as a demilitarized zone. Absolutely no arguing, no yelling, no pushing, no shoving. Just "Yes, ma'am," "No, ma'am, "Yes, sir," "No, sir." If you had somehow, God forbid, gotten into any sort of an argument with anyone elsewhere, you weren't going to finish it here. Not only would the tribal elders of hair and makeup not put up with it, but absolutely anything you said and did while in the chair would be immediately reported to those in charge. You were cordially invited to leave your bullshit at the door. In a way, it was the safest place on the set.

It was probably for the best that this is where I had my initial encounter with Melissa Sue Anderson, the girl who had been selected to play the sweet, beautiful Mary Ingalls, the girl who, I had just been warned, might be dangerous. She didn't look like a "killer." She looked like, well, a little girl. But not just any little girl. She had a large, round face (what Auntie Marion would eventually take to calling "that great moon face of hers"), with her hair pulled back to show an enormous smooth, high forehead. She had the most gorgeous, huge blue eyes, small, perfect lips, and the same adorable, TV-ready pug nose that I saw on Linda Blair and all those girls at auditions who got the part of the cheerleader instead of me. Her hair was not mixed dishwater blond like mine; it was perfect, shining, yellow-white blond, like a Breck commercial. She was spectacular.

She was the prom queen, the head cheerleader, the girl with the perfect hair and teeth. *Oh crap,* I thought. Girls like this *always* hated me. As if on cue, Melissa Sue Anderson turned to look at me, her huge, round blue eyes narrowing to slits. Her cheeks puffed slightly, and her perfect nose wrinkled. As she was in the "makeup/hair safe zone," she smiled in a disturbing, artificial way, like a well-trained beauty pageant contestant with smooth, perfectly polished teeth. "Hello, I'm Missy," she said.

I was momentarily confused. I had never met anyone who used her nickname or anything other than her real name. Because of the two Melissas, the producers had been forced to create a system of identification: Melissa Sue Anderson was to be Missy, and Melissa Gilbert would be Melissa (until they started calling her "Half-Pint").

"Um, good morning. I'm Alison."

That appeared to be the end of the conversation. I was now even more confused by Melissa Gilbert's warning. Where was this big, bad, menacing creature she had described? Not only was this girl about my age, she was actually a bit younger, closer to Melissa's age. But she did have that eerie quality some girls have that makes them appear older than they are. Something in her eyes did make her look older. Much older. Like, about forty-two. I retreated to the safety of the makeup chair. I decided to suspend judgment but proceed with caution.

It was time to get my hair done. This was going to be a hellacious process, as I had not arrived "in curlers" and sported some of the straightest, most curl-resistant hair on earth. But it was no match for Gladys. Gladys Witten-Coy was a tale unto herself. With another long-term survivor of Hollywood stationed above my head, I learned to follow her advice, and over the next seven years, she was my protector, confessor, adviser—essentially the closest thing I had to a guru. She never steered me wrong.

Gladys Witten-Coy had grown up in terrible poverty, living in two rooms with something like fourteen brothers and sisters in Appalachia. Hers was pretty much the same as Dolly Parton's childhood. The two women were not dissimilar in personality or blond glamour, although by this time Gladys's hair was a blazing white, perfectly styled wig.

She had started in the business way back in the 1940s and worked with absolutely everyone. She told me, as soon as she got any money, she had bought a tiny shack. She soon sold that and found a slightly larger place, and so on and so on. This led to her not only owning her fabulous home in Laguna, but her getting—and keeping current—a real estate license. She explained to me that this gave her an enormous sense of independence and allowed her to tell any out-of-control diva actresses, "I don't have to take any of this! I own my own home and have a real estate license!"

Gladys commanded my undivided attention and worship as soon as I found out that she had been the hairdresser on *Bonnie and Clyde*. The famous blond flippy bob of Faye Dunaway's that I had imitated since childhood? That was her creation. Of course, it was also the source of one of Gladys's greatest frustrations. She said it wasn't authentic to the period at all; that none of the actors, especially Faye Dunaway, wanted to alter their looks to conform to the 1930s period in which the film took place and kept insisting on more attractive "modern" hairdos. Over the years, she regaled me with wild tales of the on-set antics of Faye Dunaway and others—and her zero tolerance for such behavior.

Gladys was single. Well, divorced. And widowed. And divorced. Her relationship history was sort of confusing. She had been married several times—"Not my fault!" she explained. But she still wore the various rings and wedding sets given to her by the various husbands. She would point to each in turn and explain to me, "Well, you see, this one died. This other one, well, he was an alcoholic. . . ." She went down this list and matter-of-factly showed me how she had really tried, in good faith, to be married just once for life, but fate (and what sounded to me like the hopeless stupidity and daredevil lifestyles of the men involved) just made it impossible for her to achieve her goal. But the moral was, she never gave up. Gladys always kept trying.

My hair was going to need all her best efforts. Gladys put the curling irons in the oven until they were so hot that a drop of water on them sizzled and boiled away. If the irons were so hot they smoked, she cooled them by spinning them around by the handles, creating a metallic clanking sound, and looking and sounding just like a gunslinger twirling a couple of Colt pistols. Gladys was the Wyatt Earp of hairdressing. My hair gave up in terror and curled.

Having my makeup applied seemed merciful after this. With my one film experience, *Throw Out the Anchor,* I'd had makeup put on before and was familiar with the feel of the wet sponge and the smell of the typical film makeup, usually served up in a flat blue container labeled Max Factor Natural Tan. I always thought it was hilarious that they called this stuff natural. It was without a doubt the most unnatural color you could possibly paint a person. But the set lighting back then was so bright and harsh, if you didn't paint people several shades darker than normal, we'd have all looked pale and deathly ill on your TV screen.

The run-of-the-mill makeup artist tended to just slap on a coat, indiscriminately covering your facial features, so that you went around all day looking weirdly brown and featureless and had to spend hours scrubbing this stuff off when you got home. The makeup was much better on *Little House* and improved year by year as both the actors and the makeup artists got more comfortable with each other, we girls got older, and our individual features got more attention. It was also hard not to feel more beautiful when we found out that the man doing our makeup had been the makeup man for Marilyn Monroe. Allan "Whitey" Snyder—we never called him anything other than Whitey—was a stout, white-haired, middle-aged man who looked as if he had spent the last twenty years crossing a desert. He was a cautionary tale of the dangers of excessive sun exposure. Not only had he done Marilyn Monroe's makeup, though, he had been her makeup man from her very first screen test all the way to the day she died . . . and beyond.

Whitey always carried a gold money clip. One day when Gladys was telling me about how fabulous Marilyn had been to work with and how much they all loved her (this really kind of blew the lid off the whole "diva" mythology—those who worked with her described her as a sweet, vulnerable, almost delicate creature), she showed me the gold pendant necklace Marilyn gave her and told Whitey to show me what Marilyn had given him. He took a wad of bills out of his pocket; he didn't just keep the money clip, he actually used it for its intended purpose on a daily basis. It was engraved with the words "While I'm Still Warm—Marilyn."

I thought the inscription was very weird and started to open my mouth to ask what on earth that meant, when he put it away hurriedly, and Gladys gave me a "don't you dare" look and shook her head. After Whitey left the room, she explained that he was very sensitive about the whole thing. What the engraving referred to was this: Marilyn used to laugh and tell Whitey, "Oh, Whitey, your makeup is so wonderful; when I die, I want you to make me up while I'm still warm!" One day, she gave him the engraved clip. The gift would have remained a cute, funny story, except that when she died, tragically and horribly at thirty-six, he in fact went to the funeral home and applied makeup to the face of his now dead friend.

According to Gladys, this task was extremely traumatic for him and required large amounts of alcohol to complete. She said he never fully recovered emotionally and told me that I should always be careful when discussing Marilyn in his presence and, if I had any sense, to never say anything else about the money clip again. I heard and obeyed.

The rest of the day flew by. I couldn't keep track of all the people I met, although I could tell I was going to love our new teacher. Oh, not the real on-set teacher, Helen Minniear, who had the thankless job of making us child actors spend at least three hours a day in a room doing our homework when we all wanted to be elsewhere. I liked her, too. In fact, I admired her patience and fortitude. The kids of *Little House* were of all different ages and educational levels, and she was responsible not only for assisting all of us with our homework, but riding herd on the producers to make sure we all got in our required hours. Our "classroom" was basically any makeshift room that could hold a bunch of chairs and desks. When we were on location at Simi, they set up a long table behind the actual schoolhouse facade. Mrs. Minniear was the two Melissas' full-time teacher since they were in thirteen out of thirteen episodes a year and could only attend a regular school during spring hiatus. I, on the other hand, was contracted for only seven out of thirteen episodes. I often had several weeks off at a time, so I could go to my local public school and just bring my assignments with me to the set on the days I was working.

Sure, I liked Mrs. Minniear, but like everyone else, I was utterly enthralled with Miss Beadle. The character of Laura Ingalls Wilder's favorite teacher was played by Charlotte Stewart. She had blond hair, blue eyes, and the most radiant smile you ever saw. She was every little girl's dream of a teacher. As soon as I saw her, I wanted to run out and buy her an apple. Later, we would all nearly *plotz* when we found out that this smiling vision of innocence had just come from the set of David Lynch's *Eraserhead.* Our Miss Beadle was secretly Mary X.

All in all, it took virtually no time to get into the groove of filming. We started in mid-May, worked all summer, had a brief Christmas break, then resumed shooting until we broke for the standard hiatus in late February. It took just seven working days to film a one-hour episode, maybe ten days if we had to go out of town on location. Things happened so fast, before I knew it, several episodes were in the can. Michael Landon liked to work at a breakneck pace. He was incredibly efficient; we were routinely ahead of schedule and under budget.

Thankfully, I had little trouble stepping into Nellie's patent leather shoes. I look back now on one of my very first scenes in the schoolroom, when I snarl at Laura and Mary: "Country girls . . . don't even know what a blackboard is." I sound a little strange, like I just got off the plane from Brooklyn. It took me a few more days to nail Nellie's prissy voice and evil inflection (a perfect imitation, if I do say so myself, of my mother's upper-crust Canadian accent). To this day, when I call to reserve a flight on an airline or even check my credit balance, my voice is recognized over the phone: "Are you Nellie Oleson?" So I guess I truly became her.

WILL THE REAL NELLIE PLEASE STAND UP?

Laura Ingalls Wilder actually based the Nellie character on three tormenters in her life:

1. Nellie Owens of Walnut Grove, the closest to the Nellie we know. She had a brother called Willie, a father named Nels, and her parents did indeed run the Mercantile. But her mother's real name was not Harriet, but Margaret (which is coincidentally my middle name). It seems that, after leaving Walnut Grove, the Owens settled in Tillamook, Oregon, where they became very big in cheese. Nellie married a Mr. Henry Kirry (sorry, no Percival), and she had three children, named Zola, Lloyd, and Leslie. Nellie later divorced Henry.

2. Genevieve Masters. It seems Genevieve was a real-live, card-carrying bitch, and much of Nellie's nastiest deeds in the books were based on her. So why didn't Laura simply name her character Genny as payback? Rumor has it that Genevieve's family was in publishing, and since Laura wanted her books published, she decided to cover up Miss Masters's misdeeds and blame them all on Nellie Owens.

3. Stella Gilbert (no relation to Melissa). She wasn't as evil as the other girls, but she did try to make time with Laura's boyfriend, Almanzo, so Laura captured some of her sneaky, underhanded antics when she was writing about Nellie.

CHAPTER SIX

TAKING SOME HEAT

> **NELLIE: A chicken can squawk, and a bird can flutter, but Anna can't talk, all she can do is st-st-st-st-stutter!**

Most kids look forward to summer as a time to kick back, relax, veg out. For me—and for all of the child actors on *Little House*—summer vacation meant work. Intense work. The creative team took full advantage of the fact that we didn't have to go to school during the day, and summer was our busiest time filming.

The heat only made things harder. In August and September, one hundred-plus degrees was a normal daytime temperature for Simi Valley. And I was wearing a wig . . . and a full-length dress with a five-layer petticoat . . . and tights and boots. I discovered that sometimes, just as you can be in so much pain that eventually you become numb, and the pain no longer bothers you, you can actually be so hot that everything stops, and you just feel this weird, neutral sense of having no temperature at all. It doesn't really feel good, but at least you don't feel hot anymore. Of course, a few minutes after that happens, you usually pass out.

That's what happened my first day in Simi Valley. We arrived horribly early, so early that the crew was still hammering away on some of the sets. They had already shot the pilot, and we were now ready to film the first episode set in the town and the first one featuring Nellie. The episode was "Country Girls." Not only was this the title, but it was in fact my very first line of dialogue on the show. I had to sit there for an hour and a half while Gladys curled and singed my hair into ringlets, and I got lacquered with Aqua Net. I was wearing the lovely yellow dress with the pointy lace.

Many other scenes were being shot that day, and they took longer than they should have, so there was a lot of waiting around. I didn't get to do my scene until after lunch. *Little House* had fabulous catering for the most part, but I thought tri-tip steak was an odd selection for lunch, what with the suffocating heat. Maybe something lighter would have been a better choice. No doubt I should have just had a salad. But I hadn't eaten breakfast—a terrible habit I would eventually come to change—and was hungry. The meat was heavy and greasy, and by the time lunch was over and I was back down the hill to work, all I wanted was a nap.

We were being directed in this episode by William Claxton. He had worked with Michael years back as a director on *Bonanza,* so Michael trusted him to direct nearly as often as himself. Claxton had had a very impressive career before that, directing some of the most prestigious TV shows, including *The Twilight Zone,* but Michael never let up teasing him about his great film "triumph": *Night of the Lepus,* a ghastly horror film about a town overrun by a horde of giant, man-eating rabbits.

A strange, quiet, shy man, Claxton sometimes reminded me of a large white rabbit. He seemed ancient to me at the time, even though he was just around sixty. He was very pale with white hair. I wondered how he didn't burn to a crisp instantly out there in Simi. He seemed almost albino, to the point I tried to see if he had pink eyes. They were blue, but he squinted so much in the sun that they were almost always half closed. When he spoke to me, or any of the other actors, he came up close, then looked down at the ground and spoke in a near whisper. He always seemed to be involved in a deeply personal and important conversation with his shoes.

Ironically, this was the man who taught me to stop looking at the ground and actually look people in the eye. At first, when he complained about my gazing down when he spoke to me, or the fact that I didn't raise my chin and look grown-ups right in the eye, I thought this was positively bizarre coming from him. A man who never spoke over a whisper was telling me to speak up. A man who talked to his loafers all day was admonishing me to "look at me when I'm talking to you!" and complaining about my being shy.

But then I thought about it. If he didn't know the drawbacks of living like this, who would? Maybe he knew what a drag it was to be shy and was trying to snap me out of it for my own good. In any case, he was right. Going through life with my chin up and staring down my adversaries is much more fun than all that skulking about I did with my head down and my eyes half shut.

Around one that afternoon, it was time for my big moment. This was it, Nellie's historic entrance. This was the first time the audience would see her and the first time they'd hear me speak. And all I had to do was walk up to Melissa Gilbert and Melissa Sue Anderson, give them the look of death, and scoff, "Country girls!" Piece of cake.

I don't know how hot it was under the lights; I'd approximate about 120 degrees. As we were standing there setting up the scene, I started to feel woozy, but I didn't dare say anything. I didn't want anyone to think I wasn't up to the job or that I was some kind of wuss. I remember thinking, *Well, at least it can't get any hotter.* But then it did. The sun was beating down on us. Not only was I suffocating in that long-sleeved frilly dress, it was so bright, my eyes were watering. The sun and lights reflected off the white schoolhouse and the Mercantile and the sandy dirt road so brightly, I felt as if I were going to go snow-blind. Finally, it was time for my scene. Claxton called action, and I staggered toward the girls. I suddenly realized I could barely see them. I continued anyway. I took a breath and said, "Country girls." I was so weak I sounded like I was speaking from a hospital bed.

Understandably, Claxton was not satisfied with this performance (if you could even call it that). He approached me and began talking to his shoes once more. He quietly explained that he understood that I was nervous, but this was, after all, my entrance scene and that I really had to try to pull myself together. He was going on in this fashion, and I was nodding, but after a while all I heard was this thrumming noise. We tried to shoot it again, but then I saw the most amazing thing. The sky turned green like the grass and the ground blue like the sky. They just switched. Bing! Just like that. I was fascinated with this reversal, but then I realized it was not a good sign. In fact, this probably meant something really bad was about to happen, but I couldn't think what.

So I staggered up to the assistant director, Maury Dexter, the closest person handy, and said politely, "Excuse me, I think I'm going to faint." Then I blacked out completely and fell to the ground. For a few moments, everything was very dark and quiet. Suddenly, there was ammonia. And salt. I gagged. When I came to, I was flat on my back. Several people were leaning over me, including the set medic, who had just broken an ammonia capsule under my nose and shoved a salt tablet under my tongue. If you've never tried salt tablets, believe me, you're not missing anything. They taste really, really terrible. And as much as I like the smell of a little ammonia in my cleanser when I'm mopping my kitchen floor, this is not something you want shoved up your nose—especially by surprise when you're unconscious. But it is a surefire way to get someone un-unconscious in a hurry. And when you keel over from heat prostration, salt is one of the things your system needs. After the medic made sure that I could talk and knew where I was and that my pulse was within nonfatal range, Auntie Marion took me up the hill to my dressing room to recover. Oh no, I was not going home. There were several more scenes to film, not to mention the one I blacked out in before finishing.

I took a short nap and ate a peach. The air-conditioning kicked in, and I began to feel human again. There was some discussion of blood sugar, lack of breakfast, combined with excessive heat and high stress. When I finally emerged somewhere between a half hour and forty-five minutes later, I was greeted by Melissa Gilbert. She had waited outside my dressing room the entire time, pacing back and forth like an expectant father at a maternity ward. She had told Auntie Marion, in that little munchkin voice, "Please say she's okay. She has to get better! She just has to!" Auntie Marion tried to comfort her. Melissa continued breathlessly, "We still have to film our fight scene!"

And that was the day I knew Melissa loved me and I her. We went back down the hill to beat each other senseless. It was the beginning of a great friendship. The rest of the day was fainting-free, but to this day, the *Little House* cast and crew have never let me live it down—I truly made an entrance.

So I had done it. I had gotten a series, arrived on set, made it through the first episode without getting fired, and lived to tell the tale. And now it was actually going to be on TV. I remember when I saw the first promos, I became hysterical. I was having my dinner in front of the TV, as usual, watching *Columbo,* when a promo for *Little House* came on. Suddenly, THERE I WAS! Nothing major, it was just me in those curls and that yellow dress, running. You almost couldn't tell it was me with the bonnet. But I could tell. I screamed. I flipped over my TV tray, knocking my Swanson Hungry Man turkey TV dinner and my bottle of Dr Pepper to the floor. I was on television!

As my mother reminded me while she helped me salvage my dinner and got me another Dr Pepper, it wasn't as if I hadn't been on TV before. But those were just commercials and small parts. This was a series, and now it was on, and I knew in my bones that this was different, and there would be no turning back. Everything was going to be different.

"Country Girls" aired on September 18, 1974. It was fantastic. Everyone in my house howled with laughter at my every haughty line, and they even thought I looked good in the dress and curls. It was a hit.

The next day, I had to go to school. I was in the eighth grade at Bancroft Junior High. *Would any of my classmates have seen it?* I wondered. I walked onto the school grounds at about eight in the morning. I was a little late as usual, so there weren't hordes of people around. The bell had just rung, and the students had already started heading into the building. I figured I wouldn't hear anyone's reactions, if they had any, until recess. I was wrong. As I walked alone across the playground, a girl way up on the second-story landing saw me. It was a girl I knew, but not someone I could call a friend. It was one of the popular girls. She spotted me. And then she opened her mouth. Her voice rang out, echoing off the buildings: *"You biiiitchhhh!!!!"*

I froze. Surely this was directed at someone else. I looked around. There was nobody else there. Just me. Oh.

I tried to think what to do. People had called me names before—skinny, shorty, shrimp. Being small, I was always fodder for bullies. But I don't think anyone had ever yelled at me from the top of a building before. It occurred to me that this was technically my first review. And if this was the response I was getting at eight in the morning, what could I expect for the rest of the day? The rest of the year? The rest of . . . my life?

I realized that if there was even the slightest possibility that people screaming obscenities at me from balconies was going to become a regular occurrence, I had to decide *right now* how I was going to handle this. There was no room for error. I had to take charge of the situation. I knew that whatever I did at this very second was going to set the tone for all future interactions. If I caved now, if I allowed myself to be intimidated or to show an ounce of fear, I was done for.

There was only one thing to do. I stopped, stood up straight, turned toward the sound of her voice, stuck out my chin, and said as loudly and bravely as I could manage: "*THANK YOU!*"

And then, as if I were onstage, I bowed, deeply. For the first time in my life, I marched into school with my head held high.

I realized I would have to become much more durable if this show was going to continue—and so was my hair. After a few miserable weeks of sleeping in the dreaded curlers (which my nonhairdressing mother fumblingly crammed into my hair before bed after slathering my hair with Pantene setting lotion) and arriving at the studio at 4:30 in the morning to be tortured with curling irons for hours, someone on the set finally came to their senses and decreed that the only solution was to design and create a wig.

This task was assigned to the lead hair stylist, Larry Germain. Another overly tan and weathered veteran of the golden age of Hollywood, Larry had worked with everyone, too, but his show-stopper credit was Bette Davis. He told me how one of his very first jobs at the studio was washing Bette Davis's hair. What a thought! At the time, he was young and inexperienced, and had been told only that Miss Davis would be coming in for a shampoo and that he'd better see to it that her needs were met.

Her reputation was already legendary, and he had no idea what she would want. He said he gathered up every brand of shampoo and hair product he could find in the entire studio makeup department, hoping that he had her favorite brand, gathered towels, cleaned up the place, and waited in fear. As she swept into the room, he tried not to stammer when he showed her the array of shampoos.

She ignored the entire lot, grabbed a towel, and headed for the sink. "That's okay, honey," she said. "I'll just rinse it out in the sink with some Dreft!" And the great Miss Bette Davis proceeded to wash her hair, right in front of him, with a box of Dreft laundry detergent. He said that they became great friends after that, that she was utterly down to earth and straightforward and never gave him a minute's trouble.

So it was only fitting that Larry would be the one most instrumental in designing the infamous Nellie wig. Larry called in a wigmaker, not just any wigmaker, but the famous "Ziggy," aka Siegfried Geike, "Wigmaker to the Stars." It was the first time I'd ever seen anyone in real life with a Salvador Dalí mustache. He was, after all, an artist. He arrived with an enormous black case filled with mysterious gear and numerous samples of hair. His aura was all very mad scientist.

Ziggy and Larry sat me down in the makeup chair and began to design the wig, right there on my head. They placed a plastic bag on my head, wrapped it around my skull, taped it in place, and cut off the excess, making a plastic wig cap. They then began to draw on it with a black marker.

They talked about how there would need to be a comb in the front and drew a large black symbol on the front of my head. They selected the site for each ringlet, making mysterious black markings accordingly. They continued with great solemnity conferring with each other, disagreeing occasionally on the location of a curl, negotiating each detail of this elaborate project. They um-hmmed and tsk-tsked and nodded as they went, Larry with his ever-present cigarette clenched in his teeth, drawing away on my head as if I weren't even there.

When they were done, my head was covered with what looked like the symbols a coach would draw on a blackboard to illustrate a football play. They carefully pulled off the cap, and Ziggy put it in his case to take back to his "laboratory" or wherever he made these things. Then Ziggy pulled out the hair samples, not small samples, but huge, thick blond locks of real human hair. Larry told me that this was "Swedish virgin hair." I snorted, and Larry, seeing that I was already going there, made a crack about not knowing there were that many virgins in Sweden. He then explained that this, of course, really meant the hair was "untouched"—it had never been dyed or processed in any way.

They held up all these different curls against my hair. They were matching it, not all at once, but strand by strand, shade by shade. Everybody has more than one color of hair, and mine ranged from very light Malibu Barbie blond to much darker "dishwater." He and Ziggy found a hunk of hair for every single color on my head. They explained that these would be mixed together, then tiny strands would be individually hand tied to the base, which would be constructed using the custom design they had just drawn on my head.

I have no idea what this thing actually cost, but I was told that at that time, it was considered one of the most expensive wigs ever designed for a TV show. And they were going to *strap this thing to my head every day.* Gee, no pressure at all!

When it finally arrived, I had to admit, it was fantastic. It shone and shimmered, as if it were alive. It was thick and heavy. It fit my head perfectly, having been custom fitted to the last millimeter. But I wasn't prepared for the metal comb. They'd mentioned the comb, of course, in the fitting, but I had no understanding of what that meant. The metal comb is what kept the whole thing in place. It was a hunk of steel with teeth, like the ominous metal contraption in a parking lot entrance where the sign reads DO NOT BACK

UP. It had precisely the same effect. As Gladys or Larry would place the wig on my head, I would hold the front, and they would pull the whole thing down in the back tightly onto my head. The metal comb would then be jammed into the base of the hair, at the very front of my hairline, right smack in the middle of the top of my forehead. Even after this, dozens of hairpins were strategically placed to hold it on.

The number of pins was impressive. First, my real hair was coiled and wrapped around my head and pinned in place. Then a nylon stocking cap went on over that, and more pins were added, both little bobby pins and those old-fashioned long, straight metal hairpins. Lots and lots of them. There was a minimum number of hairpins that had to be inserted to hold the wig steady, and if they weren't jammed in tightly and in contact with my scalp, it wouldn't stay on.

Two small pieces of hair were pulled out, one on each side to be combed into the wig. These were curled with the hot iron, making me look like an Orthodox rabbinical student with side curls and a yarmulke. My head would have easily set off a metal detector. The metal comb in front was the only way to hold it in place during all the mud fights and running around. And yes, it hurt all day. Not excruciatingly so; that was just in the morning when it first went on. But there was no point at which it felt comfortable, or when I didn't turn my head a certain way and feel the pins dig in.

The worst was lying down. If I had to lie down and put my head on a pillow in a scene, or if I tried to lie down for real and get in a nap at lunchtime, it took great effort to position my head just so as to not crush the bobby pins against my scalp, or to pull it on one side, causing the comb to rip into my flesh and pull my hair out.

We found ways to have fun with the wig. When Gladys was having a hard time putting it on, she would sing and encourage me to sing along. I had to hold the front with the comb very tightly while she pulled it on, so she'd sing one of the old Andrews Sisters' songs: "Hold tight, hold tight! . . . Fododo-de-yacka saki, want some seafood, Mama!" At twelve years old, I wasn't familiar with the Andrews Sisters, but I became a fan, as the song seemed to fulfill its purpose. And then we'd do it again the next day.

Some days, if I was in the wig for a very long time or had to do a lot of activity that caused my hair to get pulled in any way, the comb and the pins would dig in and cut my scalp in places. On those days, if I ran my hand through my hair and rubbed my scalp, when I pulled my hand out, there would be little flecks of blood on it. Gladys always made sure there was lots of Sea Breeze around for antiseptic. It stung and burned in the cuts at first, but it made my scalp feel better later. And it was better than getting an infection.

The only thing worse than the constant pain was when it stopped hurting. Sometimes, at the end of the day, my scalp would be almost numb. The circulation had been cut off, which meant that when Gladys pulled the whole thing off, the blood would come rushing back into my skin along with sensation. Sometimes I screamed. But then Gladys would sing to me and gently massage my scalp, bending my hair back into place until my head stopped throbbing. And I would learn the words to yet another obscure Andrews Sisters' tune.

Forever connected to the endurance of pain, I still sometimes hum the songs when I'm at the dentist's office.

THE PRAIRIE PLAYERS

There were so many characters on *Little House* over its nine years on the air, it's hard to keep them all straight. (Lars who?) So here is my cheat sheet:

CHARLES INGALLS (MICHAEL LANDON): **The poor but proud farmer, carpenter, and patriarch of the Ingalls family. In the original books by Laura Ingalls Wilder, he is the all-perfect Pa, hero to nine-year-old girls everywhere. But as played by Michael Landon, he is transformed into "The Big Hunk on the Prairie," stripped to the waist, glistening with sweat, and grabbing his wife around the waist with a lust not normally publicly displayed in the 1800s. But don't buy the macho man act completely; Charles also cries real tears in every other episode.**

CAROLINE INGALLS (KAREN GRASSLE): **The epitome of the ideal American mother, Caroline is an endless font of unconditional love for her children—but she also won't take crap from anyone (especially Harriet Oleson). My kind of woman! She can cook, sew, harvest crops . . . heck, she's even prepared to cut off her own leg with a hot kitchen knife in an emergency.**

LAURA INGALLS WILDER (MELISSA GILBERT): **The real star of this extravaganza, as the whole story is told through her eyes (she wrote the books, after all). She is a freckled, buck-toothed, "everychild" girl or boy, since she acts as her pa's surrogate son for most of her childhood: fishing, hunting, fighting, and spitting long distances. Despite her parents' attempts at a proper Christian upbringing, Laura refuses to stifle her feelings of rage, joy, jealousy, or passion, or her** right to act on them at any time. She is a fighter for truth, justice, and the American way. If Nellie Oleson wants to start something, Laura will finish it.

MARY INGALLS KENDALL (MELISSA SUE ANDERSON): The beautiful, blonde, blue-eyed, and later blind as a bat older sister of Laura. An eternal goody-goody who does her chores and gets straight A's, Mary can always be counted on to tell Laura that she's wrong, then run off to rat her out to their folks. Eventually, she manages to bag the most ridiculously hot blind guy ever born, Adam Kendall. They start their own school for the blind, which later burns to the ground, killing their baby. Mary temporarily loses her marbles, then regains her sanity, only to have her husband miraculously get his sight back, threatening their marriage.

CARRIE INGALLS (LINDSAY AND SIDNEY GREENBUSH): An adorable but extremely accident-prone dumpling of a child, with no visible neck and a serious communication problem. Baby Carrie regularly falls into wells, mine shafts, outhouses, etc., and even manages to accidentally take off in a runaway hot air balloon. She smiles and gurgles, seemingly up to the age of ten or so, speaking an unintelligible dialect that only her family understands. In real life, Carrie Ingalls went on to become a successful real estate agent in South Dakota.

GRACE INGALLS (BRENDA AND WENDI TURNBAUGH): Charles's and Caroline's fifth and final child (thank God!). Another cute blonde, she is so young, we do not have as much insight into her personality. But on first glance, she's a genius compared to Carrie.

JACK: The brave yet floppy family dog who was replaced by Bandit when he died in Season 4. Amazingly, he continued to appear in the closing credits long after his death, watching after the Ingalls girls as a ghostly presence.

ALBERT QUINN INGALLS (MATTHEW LABORTEAUX): Orphaned Albert is a street waif, a stealing, gambling, Artful Dodger type that Charles brings into the Ingalls family. Sad eyed with pouty lips, he is a magnet for tragedy. If someone is going to accidentally burn down a building, befriend a teenage rape victim, get addicted to morphine, or come down with a bizarre fatal disease, it's this kid. He's such a hit, it starts a ghastly irreversible trend on the show: dozens of orphans and lost children being taken in by the Ingallses, the Edwardses, and eventually even the Olesons.

JAMES COOPER INGALLS AND CASSANDRA COOPER INGALLS (JASON BATEMAN AND MISSY FRANCIS): Part of the tribe of orphans who populated the show in its last years. Their parents die in a horrible buggy crash. The episode is even called "The Lost Ones" in case any of us missed the point.

NELS OLESON (RICHARD BULL): Proprietor of the Mercantile, the only store in town. Sure, there's a feed and seed, but if you're buying anything for humans, not horses, this is *the* place. A kind, sensible, slightly sad-looking man, Nels tries to run a fair business, make a profit, and still help the less fortunate, while enduring the total insanity of his crazy wife, bitchy daughter, and spaced-out son.

HARRIET OLESON (KATHERINE MACGREGOR): The imperious co-proprietor of the Mercantile, Mrs. Oleson attempts to control everyone and everything in Walnut Grove, with positively grand operatic gestures and terrifying emotional outbursts. As seen through nine-year-old Laura's eyes, she is every child's nightmare, the archetype of the school head mistress, the evil stepmother, the wicked witch. Her greatest pleasure is spoiling her daughter, Nellie, whom she has made into her own personal Barbie doll on the prairie.

NELLIE OLESON (*MOI!*): Nellie decides to take out her misery on everyone in her path. Okay, maybe I'm a little prejudiced here, but can you blame her for being cranky? She's stuck in a small town in the middle of nowhere in the 1800s with a bossy mother, an insipid brother, and a Shirley Temple do that she's forced to wear way past puberty. She's bored, frustrated, and ridiculously overdressed for the climate and the occasion. Feisty new girl Laura Ingalls pisses her off from day one, starting a seven-year spiral of cruelty, backstabbing, blackmail, and terror.

WILLIE OLESON (JONATHAN GILBERT): Nellie's small, weakling, not quite all there baby brother. Clearly the runt of the litter, he makes the perfect henchman, happily doing her bidding, if only to have something to do.

PERCIVAL DALTON (STEVE TRACY): Five feet, four inches and all man. Don't let the glasses and the conservative suits fool you; Percival doesn't run from a fight. In his first episode, he achieves national hero status by telling Mrs. Oleson to zip her lip. Brought in to teach Nellie how to run her hotel, he wins her heart, not just because he loves her, but because he is the first to expect anything of her. She falls madly in love and becomes *nice*. He proposes to her in the middle of the street and informs Mrs. Oleson there will be no church wedding, because "I'm Jewish!" causing her to nearly fall out of a window. He and Nellie opt to raise their twins, Benjamin and Jennifer, in a mixed-faith household.

ADAM KENDALL (LINWOOD BOOMER): Blind Mary's way hot hubby, who at first is a blind teacher, then becomes a blind lawyer, then a sighted lawyer. All their children die.

ALMANZO WILDER (DEAN BUTLER): The blond, earnest, plain-talkin' guy known as "Manly," who marries Laura. He's the Wilder in the famous Laura Ingalls Wilder name, but despite his best efforts, he's overshadowed by Laura, both on the show and in history. It's all too clear who's driving the covered wagon in their relationship. Manly will also never be as manly as Pa.

MISS EVA BEADLE (CHARLOTTE STEWART): The teacher we all wish we had. Everyone wants to bring her an apple, and she's the type who will always graciously thank them, even if she's got a bushel out back. Always patient and kind, she never berates her students (unless they truly deserve it). She is the woman who taught one of America's most famous authors to read and write.

DR. HIRAM BAKER (KEVIN HAGEN): Poor Doc Baker. He tries so hard, but it's the 1870s. There are no antibiotics, no X-ray machines, no ultrasound—they hadn't even discovered antidepressants yet, for heaven's sake. He's smart and makes some very impressive educated guesses, occasionally keeping a few of his patients alive. But generally, the poor guy's got nothing. You get sick, you die. Being a doctor in the 1800s totally sucked.

REVEREND ROBERT ALDEN (DABBS GREER): It's never been clear what denomination the church in Walnut Grove was. Lutheran? Methodist? They're the most likely for that time and location, but with Reverend Alden, it could be anything. He manages to work in an awful lot of 1970s liberated church–type talk for a Protestant minister in the 1800s. And he somehow keeps the congregation from getting bored, even though they seem to sing the same four hymns over and over again for nine years.

ISAIAH EDWARDS (VICTOR FRENCH): He's the bearded, dagnab-it, consarned, baccy-chawin', jug-swillin' best friend of the Ingalls family. He even has his own theme song, "Ol' Dan Tucker," which he can be counted on to sing in most episodes. Famous for teaching Laura to spit, amazingly he later gets married to a very attractive woman (Grace Snider) and adopts three kids.

GRACE SNIDER EDWARDS (BONNIE BARTLET): The widowed postmistress who somehow decides that Mr. Edwards is a "good catch." (Maybe she's just turned on by guys with beards?) She's proper, but with a sense of humor. Between Mr. Edwards and the tribe of orphans, she'll need it.

JOHN SANDERSON EDWARDS (RADAMES PERA): The oldest adopted son of Isaiah and Grace, he is a handsome, high-cheek-boned, sensitive-artist type. A real tree hugger, he flunks hunting and all that pioneer stuff but teaches his dad to read. He goes on to become a writer and has an ill-fated romance with that uptight Mary Ingalls.

CARL SANDERSON EDWARDS AND ALICIA SANDERSON EDWARDS (BRIAN PART AND KYLE RICHARDS): Orphans come in sets on this show, so the Edwardses also get a cute, mischievous blond boy and a doll-like little girl.

LARS HANSON (KARL SWENSON): Why does anyone live in Walnut Grove, anyway? Because of this guy, the founder of Walnut Grove and proprietor of the Hanson Lumber Mill. A classic "yumpin yimminy" Swedish character, he returns to Walnut Grove in later episodes to die with dignity in a dramatic two-parter. Right before the episode aired, Karl Swenson died in real life.

JOHN CARTER, SARAH CARTER, AND THEIR ADORABLE KIDS, JEB AND JASON (STAN IVAR, PAMELA ROYLANCE, LINDSAY KENNEDY, AND DAVID FRIEDMAN): With Michael Landon wanting to spend less time on the show in the last year, the Ingallses move out of the infamous Little House and go to Iowa. Laura and Almanzo have long ago established their own homestead, so what are they supposed to do with the house? Tear it down? Instead, a handsome blacksmith and his family arrive from New York, just in time to move in and have all the same warm, laughing moments by the creek we're all accustomed to.

JENNY WILDER (SHANNEN DOHERTY): Because Laura and Almanzo had to adopt someone, too, didn't they? Jenny is played by a pre-*90210* Shannen Doherty, who tries her damnedest to do an impersonation of Melissa Gilbert in the early years. She is part of the "cloning process" that took place in the last years of the show, where new little girls with braids fought new little girls with ringlets.

NANCY OLESON (ALLISON BALSON): Speaking of clones . . . The Olesons are not left out of the orphan follies. After Nellie leaves, Mrs. Oleson, not surprisingly, has a breakdown and can only be consoled by finding another blond child to permanently screw up. She meets her match in little Nancy, who's psycho-bitchery is more closely modeled on the movie *The Bad Seed*.

CHAPTER SEVEN

PALACE ON THE PRAIRIE

> MR. OLESON: Sounds like Doc Baker.
>
> NELLIE: I wonder what he's doing here.
>
> MR. OLESON: He probably heard your singing and thought someone was dying!

I don't like getting up early in the morning now if I can avoid it, but as a teenager, I considered it a fate worse than death. The days we were shooting at Simi, I had to set my alarm for two a.m. so I could shower. I was on the road by three and on set at four. It was brutal; there were days I begged for death. But other times, I did see the good side of getting an early start. At that hour, there's virtually no traffic, which is a rarity in Los Angeles. It's quiet, and you can actually hear the birds. There was something exciting about arriving at the set in the dark, as if we were doing something dangerous and secretive, like sneaking up on the enemy for a surprise raid at dawn.

The makeup trailer was like a cabin in the forest, the only source of heat and light for seemingly miles around, and it felt cozy at that hour. And you haven't seen a sunrise until you've seen the sun come up over the set of *Little House on the Prairie.* Suddenly, for a moment, Laura Ingalls's hometown is real. The light hits the church, and you expect the bell to ring, and you start wondering if there aren't some crops you should be bringing in or some cows you need to milk. Then the sun ascends in the sky, and it's just a big wooden set again. But for a minute . . .

Another saving grace was the coffee. God, I love coffee. Yes, I started drinking coffee much, much too young, at twelve. By fourteen, I was a full-blown caffeine addict. I think this is a common problem for many child actors. It's just so hard to stay awake, and everyone is drinking the stuff constantly. The addiction potential is increased by the fact that the coffee on sets is not normal strength. It is made by and for the crew, the key grips and best boys—the electricians, horse wranglers, and truck drivers. It's similar in blackness and thickness to the coffee served at Alcoholics Anonymous meetings, the kind of stuff that could perk up even a stone junkie. I believe there are three strengths of coffee in this world: normal strength, AA strength, and grip strength. To this day, I take my coffee grip strength. This probably explains why I like France.

The big decision in the morning was "costume first, then makeup, or makeup first, then dress?" Multiple factors were considered: How busy were they in makeup, how cold was it, and how flimsy was the costume that day? Or conversely, how ridiculously hot was it, and how swelteringly suffocating was the costume? The weather never seemed to cooperate. If it was cold, we would be shooting some happy springtime episode, perhaps involving falling into some nice freezing water, and when it was hot, I would be wearing the dark scratchy wool dress with layers of petticoats.

Though it was a demilitarized zone, the hair and makeup trailer was always abuzz with conversation. Michael could be counted on to come barging in with a smart-ass remark or joke. He once told a guest star who was complaining about her age that his secret to youth was birdseed: he ate a cup of it every day. It was totally untrue; he wanted to see if she'd be gullible enough to do it. Of course she did, and when he spied her snacking on seeds a few days later, Michael shrieked with laughter. Mission accomplished.

But mostly I liked the smell of the makeup trailer. The makeup on sets smells a little different than the stuff in the stores. It's a very distinctive, clean sort of smell, almost slightly medicinal, but sweet. And the sponges were real latex, not that weird non-latex stuff that everybody insists on now. I know they came out with nonlatex sponges because so many people are allergic, but I absolutely love the smell of latex in the morning. I had smelled it before on the set of my brother's show, *Land of the Giants,* and I swear it was one of my top ten reasons for becoming an actress. I would eat latex sponges soaked in pancake makeup if I could.

When I wore short sleeves, I had to have makeup put on my arms. This was a diluted solution made by dunking the sponge in water until it was sopping wet, not just lightly dampened as usual, and dragging it across the pancake, so that the stuff dripped off my arms as they applied it. Sort of like whitewash, but in tan. On cold mornings this was a very unpleasant procedure, so in an act of mercy, Whitey would dip the sponge in hot coffee instead. Then I was covered in warm, wet makeup, and I smelled like latex and coffee. I was in heaven.

So, painted, petticoated, fully caffeinated, bewigged, and in pain, I would march down the hill, or across the meadow, or to the other end of the soundstage and go to work. In the first couple of seasons of *Little House,* I was in only a few scenes in each episode; occasionally, I was absent from an episode's plotline altogether. Then, my part got larger. Michael loved using me for comic relief. By Season 3, the battle between Laura and Nellie had become a focal point of the show, and there were several episodes where Nellie's schemes or hissy fits were the main story. At that point, I had to put in about eight hours a day on the set—the maximum number of hours a minor was allowed to work by law.

The dinner scenes were my favorite. For one, they were indoors at Paramount, and I didn't have to deal with Simi Valley; also, I got to sit down. A great deal of time on the show was devoted to me—and Melissa, Missy, and the other children—*running.* Endlessly running. Running up the hill, down the hill, running to school, running away from school. Taking turns running away from each other. Every single episode had at least two scenes involving running. It was even worse for Melissa Gilbert, since every time Laura got upset, she responded by running out the door and across the hills, sobbing, her braids flying. And to think people actually still ask us why we were such skinny little girls.

Any chance to spend the whole morning sitting on my ass was a welcome relief, even the church and school scenes that required sitting for hours on those wooden benches. They weren't really the beautiful, fully grained dark wood they appeared to be on screen. Just like all the doors, molding, and hardwood floors on the show, they were just plain old lumber from the studio carpentry shop, painted brown with a swirly design to look more like real finished wood. But they were very authentic in their own way. I believe they were exactly as uncomfortable as the benches the Olesons and Ingalls would have sat on in the 1800s.

The chairs at the Olesons' dinner table were the height of comfort by comparison. The Olesons' digs were impressive, even by 1970s standards. The dominant decorating theme was red velvet: red velvet cushions on the mahogany chairs, red velvet curtains in the parlor, even a red velvet swag with enormous tassels hanging at the entrance to the dining room. Is it me, or did the Olesons' abode look a lot like a brothel?

Everything on the Olesons' set was luxurious, including the food. The first time I sat down to dinner in a scene, I knew I had really lucked out. My brother openly confessed his jealousy at the time. He explained that I had enormous good fortune to play a rich person on television, while he was always the poor boy, forced to eat Dinty Moore beef stew or that god-awful Van de Kamp's pork and beans—*off tin plates*! "But you," he said, "you bitch, you're getting fucking leg of lamb with mint jelly on bone china!"

He had a point. We did have better food, not just better food than the Ingallses; I was getting better food than I got at home. Leg of lamb, roast beef, roast turkey with dressing, boiled new potatoes with butter and parsley, fresh green beans, peas, all kinds of gravy—and the biscuits: the greatest, fluffiest biscuits ever. One day, I finally asked the prop men where the hell they were getting this stuff. Some was brought in, ordered from restaurants, but most of the food was actually cooked by the prop men right there on the set. And the biscuits? They were just good old Pillsbury Poppin' Fresh. With real fresh butter and strawberry jam or dunked in turkey gravy, they were heavenly. I swear, I still dream about them.

We ate off the most beautiful china, which looked so authentic. I had seen pictures of 1800s dishes, and these had the same pattern but were brand new. Where on earth did they get them? "The Broadway," the prop men replied. I was amazed. "You mean you just went down to the department store and found these?" Turns out that the blue "Willow" pattern so popular in the 1870s had several revivals, and the company just kept coming out with new editions of the plates every few decades. They were apparently hot again in the '50s and had just had another comeback in the mid-'70s, so the prop guys were able to just pop out to the local mall and buy a whole set. They're back again. You can actually order them online today and eat in Nellie Oleson–style luxury in your own dining room this weekend.

The dinner scenes were also a hoot because you had all four Olesons in one scene. Rarely have such divergent personalities and schools of acting been thrown together at one dinner table. We had Richard Bull, playing my father, Mr. Oleson. A graduate of the Goodman Theatre in Chicago, he'd been on every TV show from *Ben Casey* to *Mannix*. Always very matter-of-fact and low-key, he is hands down the person I would vote for as being "Most Like Their Character on the Show in Real Life." He was the voice of reason at all times, sometimes rolling his eyes and letting out a Mr. Olesonesque long-suffering sigh when confronted with the continuously high-strung behavior of the one, the only, the often imitated but never equaled creator of the unforgettable character, whom the French call "La Belle Harriet," Katherine MacGregor.

I have had people ask me, "Just what *was* that woman on?" I don't know. She arrived in the morning like that, and that's how she went home at night. She is still alive at this writing, and she has not changed one iota. She was not actually Mrs. Oleson incarnate, but my God, she was close. Fortunately, Katherine does not share Mrs. Oleson's meanness—or her infamous prejudices against Jews, African Americans, circus fat ladies, poor people, and basically anyone who wasn't Mrs. Oleson. Unlike Mrs. Oleson and her pretense at great culture and education, Katherine actually did go to college and was an accomplished stage actress. Her most fabulous movie-trivia claim to fame is her appearance in *On the Waterfront.* Despite her enormous stage experience, she possessed relatively little experience with TV work. Hence, she could be counted on to play every scene to the back row of the theater, even when the camera was six inches from her face. The woman was *loud.*

But she was also a fascinating person to watch in action. She often had trouble with her lines. She studied them, of course; she even had an enormous leather-bound three-ring binder with her name in gold letters on the front to hold her script. It went everywhere with her, and in every dinner scene at the Mercantile, it was on her lap under the table for the entire meal. We rehearsed every scene before filming, and yet, it was not uncommon to hear, "Nels! How many times have I told you . . . Oh, FUCK!! What is that line again?" Whenever any of us had a scene with Katherine, we knew to make ourselves comfortable. We were going to be there awhile.

Sometimes, if she didn't care for the lines, she simply changed them. This drove Michael and Bill Claxton nearly insane, but she would not be swayed. They were also not terribly thrilled with her other little hobby: she greatly enjoyed directing the other actors. She had studied in New York with the famous acting coach Sanford Meisner, creator of the Meisner technique (who, ironically, was famous for telling actors, "Less is more"), and never ceased telling everyone within earshot. She would happily tell all the other actors—younger than her, older than her, less experienced, more experienced, it didn't matter—exactly how they should be doing the scene, right down to how they should stand, what props they should use, etc. She even gave us *s*pecific line readings, demonstrating the precise tone and emphasis we should place on a line.

No, most actors do not do this, certainly not unrequested. I've never seen anybody do it to this extent, not before or since. And it wasn't as if she was just tossing out a helpful suggestion. She was quite insistent and would tell people they were "doing it wrong." This behavior was greeted with varying degrees of resistance by the other actors. Richard Bull was strictly "no sale." He even spoke in an interview about how he loved her dearly, but that on the first day of shooting, he had to explain to her, "No, Katherine. You don't tell me how to act. You can do anything you want, except *that.*"

Some people didn't mind. Dean Butler, when he first started playing Almanzo, seemed to actively seek out her advice. Karen Grassle, Ma herself, even joined her at the acting class she was attending in the evenings. Katherine's advice wasn't bad, it was just constant and unsolicited. I sometimes took it, but many times I had already decided what I wanted to do in the scene, or the director had given specific instructions, and I was following them. When I would protest and try to explain this to her, she would shout, "He's only the director! What the hell does *he* know?!"

Now, in theory, Katherine should have been an utter disaster. One would think that, with all of this lunacy and forgetting and overacting and ordering people around, her performance would be awful, that she would be fired. Nothing could have been further from the truth. When she came on the screen, there was no one else there. Her performance was mesmerizing, hilarious, outrageous, and, on those occasions when Mrs. Oleson was in one of her pouting and wounded moments, even weirdly moving. Her acting was absolute genius. There was no denying it. No matter what she said or did, it simply *worked*. The show could not function without her. We would all have to just get used to being ordered about from time to time.

Katherine and Richard made an interesting couple, not just on screen, but off. They became great friends but were of such opposite personalities, well, sometimes I couldn't tell when they were rehearsing a scene or having an actual argument.

As if this wasn't a surreal enough TV family for me to join, there was my baby brother, Willie. Hollywood being the capital of nepotism, nearly everyone in *Little House on the Prairie* was related to someone else on the show. The most outrageous piece of casting was Melissa Gilbert's baby brother, Jonathan, as my little brother (and sometimes henchman), Willie. He apparently came along to her audition, and when the subject of Willie came up, their mother simply volunteered him for the job. He was six.

It was his first job ever and, other than again being shanghaied into one of his sister's other projects later on (he had a voice-over in her TV version of *The Miracle Worker*), his only appearance in TV or film of any kind. I never once heard him complain about this. He expressed no interest whatsoever in being in other movies or TV shows, the state of being famous, how much he was getting paid, the furthering of his career, or anything to do with Hollywood in any way, shape, or form. He was the living embodiment of "just along for the ride." He was, however, absolutely, utterly adorable. When stuffed into one of little Willie's "formal occasion" outfits, he was the cutest thing you ever laid eyes on: all floppy hair, grinning teeth, and huge eyes.

His one noticeable fault, if you could call it that, was that he was what is known as a mouth breather. Jonathan was one of those children who never quite figured out that you're supposed to close your mouth and breathe through your nose. But in these bizarre circumstances, it was all to his advantage. His wide-eyed, slack-mouthed stare became the trademark "Willie Oleson look" and made his character's antics, such as smoking cigars behind the Mercantile or playing pranks in the school yard, all the more hilarious. To this day, I have to wonder if he didn't really put on this act on purpose. Melissa was not impressed by any of it. To her, he was just her incredibly annoying kid brother. She frequently offered to let me keep him. I didn't have a baby brother, so the thought was a novelty. She said I was welcome to him as far as she was concerned.

He did come up with things to do just to drive people crazy. I particularly enjoyed his insistence in the show's later years that he couldn't read. He could, obviously, but he found it far more to his advantage to tell people he couldn't. I remember him driving our normally calm set teacher, Helen Minniear, practically to drink with this act when we first started the show. She was going over his reading workbook with him. The word in the sentence was *fez,* as in the hat. There was a picture of a man wearing what was unmistakably a red, tasseled fez. Jonathan dutifully read, "The man in the picture is wearing a fuzz." Over and over she said, "No, Jonathan, it's *fez*—see the *e*?"

"Oh, yeah, fez," he'd reply, smiling. Two seconds later: "The man in the picture is wearing a fuzz." He could keep this up for hours.

One day after school, I pulled him aside and said, "What the hell are you doing in there, anyway? I know perfectly well you know what a damn fez is! You can read! What was *that* all about?"

"Shhhh!" He looked around to make sure nobody overheard. "I can read, but it's better if they think I'm dumb. Melissa's smart, and she let them find out. Have you seen all the homework they give her? No way! I'm not doing all that!" I didn't rat him out, but I did tell him to please give poor Mrs. Minniear a break.

When he first started the show, he actually didn't read much, so his mother would read his lines to him, and he would learn them that way. But as he got older, he continued to learn his lines only without reading the rest of the script. If he wasn't sure what was happening, he'd just ask someone. That someone was usually his big sister, Melissa. She quickly got fed up with this nonsense.

I finally asked him, "All right, I give up. Tell me, why in the hell don't you just read the script?"

In all seriousness he said, "I like to be surprised when I see it on TV."

I nearly peed my pants laughing. But he wasn't kidding. I was at the Gilbert house one night to watch an episode, and I'll be damned if Jonathan wasn't shushing everyone in the room, saying, “Wait, wait, I gotta see this part!” He was the only one moved by the ending. He hadn’t seen it coming.

It did make working with him quite the experience. Once we were doing a funeral scene. We were gathered around the Walnut Grove graveyard, dressed all in black. Fake rain was falling gently. The Reverend Alden was giving his sermon. Little Jonathan stood next to me in his suit, with his hands folded and his head bowed solemnly, looking as if he might cry at any moment. Between takes, he turned to me and whispered, “Who died?”

I resolved to never tell him too much about an episode. Why interfere with brilliance?

Meanwhile, Melissa Sue Anderson continued to remain a mystery. The entire time I was on the show, I never went to her house, and she never came to mine. I had no idea where she lived. For all I know, she could have lived in a tree. She never spoke of her home life. I knew she had a mother who came to the set with her every day. I don’t know what Mrs. Anderson was like at home, but what we saw was a woman acting the part of the classic stage mother. She followed her daughter everywhere. Her every waking moment seemed to be focused on her daughter. The license plates on her car read MISSY. Was there a father? Siblings? Pets? These things were never discussed. Everyone else on the set, down to the last crew member, would at least give you a peek into their lives, if only by muttering something like, “My wife, Ethel, she sure drives me crazy.” But this was not the case with “Missy.” For all I know, the girl was hatched from an egg.

My aunt Marion seemed to know more. Always the one to befriend the friendless, and with a constant eye out for wounded sparrows of all species, Marion had picked up on the vibe surrounding Melissa Sue's mom. The other stage mothers and on-set guardians were clearly suspicious and prepared to dislike her. The only thing worse than being a child actor thrown into the boiling cauldron that is a TV series is to find yourself surrounded by the pack of ravenous vultures that are stage mothers.

Auntie Marion swooped in and made friends with her. How could she not? Melissa Sue's mother was also named Marion. From her I got bits and pieces of information that hinted at why Melissa Sue wasn't as eager to make friends as Melissa Gilbert. There was a father . . . somewhere. There had been a divorce. Things had not been easy for her and her mother. There were even whispers of a sibling—a sister perhaps?—but it was clearly just the two of them now, against the world.

Auntie Marion was very clear about one thing: if Missy ignored me, or refused to play with me, or even insulted me to my face, I was to just walk away and not attempt to escalate the situation in any way. I must try to be understanding or at the very least patient. "She's very unhappy at home," was all Auntie Marion had to whisper.

Well, I could certainly empathize with that. I hadn't the nerve to tell Auntie Marion what life was like at my house. As adolescence began to spread on the prairie, things only got weirder at home. My brother, who was now nineteen, had moved back in. He had been living in an apartment with several other people, but it didn't work out. Not only had they all run out of rent money, but when the police broke down the door and arrested them for possession of heroin, the landlord didn't want them back. My brother didn't go to jail. Even though he had been arrested for drugs before, he was still a minor, and also it seems that having your father right there with you when they raid the place does get you released sooner. It was a good plan, but I'm sure my father would have liked it better if they had told him about it in advance.

My father got a mysterious phone call from one of Stefan's then girlfriends who said that Stefan was very sick. He rushed over to the apartment without considering the potential for disaster. When he arrived, he found a man waiting on the doorstep as though he had just rung the bell. My father walked up and knocked anyway and waited with him. He thought the man looked very surprised to see him. He also thought there was something familiar about this man's appearance. He pondered his "look": longish hair, but not too long, mustache, jeans. He had that sort of '70s Burt Reynolds chic, like a porn star—or an undercover narcotics officer.

At the very moment that thought entered his brain, the door opened a crack, at which point, the rest of the narcotics officers leaped out of the bushes and went crashing through the door, and my father found himself lying on the floor underneath a pile of policemen and broken door parts.

They cuffed him, along with everyone else, and searched his car. When the raid was over, and he had produced ID showing that he was not, in fact, the dealer making the big delivery, as they had hoped, but an incredibly gullible father in the wrong place at the wrong time, the cops let him go and released my brother to his custody.

This led to a positively absurd encounter with my parents, when they attempted to "break the news" to me that my brother was on heroin. They actually took me to a park. I think perhaps they had seen this in a TV movie somewhere or read it in a brochure—"Try to break the bad news in pleasant surroundings." They made a very dramatic production out of telling me, "Your brother has been arrested."

I said, "Uh-huh. For what, now?" My brother being in trouble with the cops was not exactly an earth-shattering event.

"No, it's serious this time. He's on heroin."

"Uh-huh." My lack of amazement seemed to get a rise out of them.

"He's been using heroin," they repeated, as if I hadn't heard.

I sighed. "Well, yeah." I really thought they knew. They didn't.

"You mean, you knew about this?" they gasped.

Now I began rolling my eyes in earnest. Just how dense were these people? I explained to them that yes, I knew that he did heroin, and so did most of Los Angeles; that that's what all those people who came over to our house at all hours of the day and night to see him were doing: bringing him heroin, shooting heroin with him, reviving him after too much heroin. My mind reeled. Had they really not noticed? Why exactly did they think all the spoons in the house were bent and had burn marks on the bottom? What did they think was going on when they came home and found him in a bathtub of cold water with all his clothes on and his panic-stricken buddies running out the back door? A college prank? When he nodded off at the dinner table, did they think he'd been up all night cramming for the LSAT? He had done everything short of asking them to tie off his arm and help him find a vein. And they were absolutely clueless.

In a way, I took some comfort in seeing that my abuse wasn't the only thing in front of their noses they chose to ignore. This type of blindness apparently didn't discriminate. Just when I thought my parents couldn't be more frustrating, they asked the dumbest question on earth: "But if you knew this was going on, *why didn't you tell us*?"

Oh good Lord. I don't know which was worse, that they seriously thought that it was the job of their teenage daughter to keep them up to date on what was going on in their own house, or that they really hadn't noticed the other problem. When it came to my brother, they never believed a single, solitary word I told them. I had given up telling them anything years before.

Not being very popular with landlords and having no money left at all, my brother had now taken up semipermanent residence on the living room sofa. Well, it had been good enough for my parents all those years, I suppose it was his turn. He never let the fact that he was living with his parents and younger sister cramp his style, though. I frequently came home from school to find him and several other people of assorted genders sprawled nude and unconscious across the sofa bed and living room floor with bottles everywhere, ashtrays filled with cigarette and joint butts. I would just go to my room and watch TV.

He had the strangest girlfriends. One of them was always trying to pass on "secret" information to me. She attempted to convince me one day that if women washed their hair when they had their period, they would bleed from the scalp and drop dead. I had been to health class; I knew she was off her rocker. Then Stefan met a tall blonde at a party, and he immediately announced that "I just met my future wife." He wound up moving in with her, and they did get married. (She was his first of three wives.) I liked her. She was younger than Stefan, which made her closer to my age. She could have been my big sister. In fact, most people thought she was my sister, since we looked exactly, perfectly alike. People noticed, and remarks were made, but my family just laughed them off. There was nothing odd to them about a man marrying a much younger woman who just happened to look exactly like his sister. I was even a flower girl at their wedding, which was held in Auntie Marion's yard.

Really, they should have let me give him away.

CHAPTER EIGHT

MICHAEL: SINNER AND SAINT

> YOUNG CHARLES: I was a real dummy.
>
> YOUNG CAROLINE: What makes you say that?
>
> YOUNG CHARLES: My brother.

For me, work was a refuge. Oh, to be safely ensconced on something as wholesome as the set of *Little House on the Prairie*! Well, maybe the entire set wasn't completely wholesome by traditional standards, but in comparison to my family situation, it was heaven on earth.

With the early hours, hard work, and being a teenager, I was constantly in search of sleep. I craved sleep like other people craved drugs or booze. I would grab it wherever I could get it, in any form. Then and now I have always been able to nap in the back of the car, on trains, planes, practically standing up. On the way to and from Simi Valley, I often slept in the back of the car, and I sometimes grabbed a quick nap at lunch. But on some days, I just needed more. The challenge then was to find new places to sleep undisturbed without getting caught.

I soon discovered the prop truck. The prop truck was the great mecca, the paradise of the set. Everyone's vices could be indulged in the prop truck. It was where they kept the candy, cigarettes, and liquor. The two gorgeous and charming men who did props for *Little House* were Danny Bentley, the blue-eyed blond, and Ron Chiniquy, with the black hair and dark eyes, who was quickly nicknamed "The French Wrench," in contrast to the other Ronnie, key grip Ron Cardarelli, "The Italian Stallion." The prop guys had the keys to the *Little House* kingdom, and they knew it. In keeping with their function, they had become marvelously nonjudgmental about all of our needs. So when I asked, of course I was allowed to sneak a nap in the front seat of the truck without being ratted out.

I loved sleeping in the truck. It was warm on the freezing cold mornings and cool in the summer. I could hear what was going on outside as they filmed scenes I wasn't in, but it was all dreamily muffled. I can still close my eyes and feel the sensation of being bundled up in a borrowed down jacket over my frilly clothes, curled up in a ball on the front seat, hearing the distant repetitive shouting of the second assistant director's daily mantra, "Quiet, please!" "Speed?" "*Speed!*" "Rolling!" "Action!" and happily dozing off, breathing in the unforgettable smell of Simi, a combination of makeup, dust, horses, horseshit, human sweat, cigarette smoke . . . and alcohol.

One morning I awoke to the sound of footsteps and the creaking of the truck. We had a visitor. I didn't worry, as I knew whoever it was had come to see the boys, and catching lazy thirteen-year-olds copping a nap in the front seat would not be a priority. But when I heard the voice, I froze. It was Michael. I decided that not breathing or moving would be a good idea right then.

But he was there on business. Ron cheerily greeted him with

"The usual, sir?" I peeked around the seat to see Michael smiling in his Charles Ingalls boots and suspenders, extending a Styrofoam cup.

"Hit me."

Ron produced a bottle of Wild Turkey from one of the endless warrens of cupboards. No, not a bottle, a jug—the huge refill size. He began to pour.

"About four fingers," instructed Michael, wanting to leave some room for the coffee, I suppose. It was no later than ten-thirty in the morning.

I was not shocked to see Michael doing this. I knew by then that he drank. They all did. Most of the crew of *Little House on the Prairie* drank constantly, and a few actors as well. I have no idea how they did this and managed to finish the show every week. They not only filmed the show, but most episodes were completed ahead of schedule and under budget. From their performance, you would have thought Coors beer was some kind of miracle drug or performance-enhancing steroid.

Ron Housiaux explained the crew's drinking habits to me one day when I was about fourteen. Housiaux, appropriately nicknamed "Hooch," was one of the grips, second in command to Ronnie Cardarelli. (Yes, he was on a table tennis team with "The French Wrench." They were known as "the two Ronnies.") Housiaux was telling me that someone had been dispatched to go get more beer, as we were down to only one case. He explained that this was a major crisis because it took at least two and a half cases to get through a day of shooting. He talked about the beer supply with the same seriousness as he might about running out of film.

"Okay, yesterday wasn't so bad. That was a two-case day. Now, remember that day we had last week, with all those different setups that just never seemed to end?" I did and nodded solemnly.

"That was a three-case day! But now we're down to less than one case, and it's only nine a.m." He made sure I understood the serious nature of the problem. "If we run out of beer, this show comes to a grinding halt." The two or three cases of beer were just to get them through the day. Of course, they didn't take into account what happened at the end of the day, when work ended, and the prop men put a board up on sawhorses and set up the bar. Then the crew did some *real* drinking, joined by some of the more "manly men" in the cast, like Victor French.

Michael didn't seem to bother with the beer. Always one to cut to the chase, he simply went straight to the hard liquor and stayed there. I know no one will believe me, but I never saw him get drunk on set, just at the parties: the Christmas party, the big end-of-the-year wrap party, when there was food and wine and champagne and everyone was drinking. Under what would be called normal circumstances. Even then, he was only somewhat inebriated and still quite coherent.

As for work, you would never suspect he'd been swilling Wild Turkey all morning; on the contrary, he was so keyed up and energetic, and had such stamina, you'd think he was on an amphetamine IV. He positively bounced off the walls with energy. He was usually the first one to arrive and the last to leave. He oversaw everything, from the direction of the actors to the lighting to the camera angle. At lunch he would finish writing next week's episode. He never stopped working. Being just an actor could never be enough for him. He had to produce, write, and direct. And if another director was hired? Well, Michael never let that get in his way. No one but no one messed with Michael Landon. No one challenged his opinion or authority. No one told him he was wrong. This was understood—unless, of course, you were new to the *Little House* set.

Such was the case for Alf Kjellin, a popular TV director who had worked on everything from *Hawaii Five-O* to *The Man from U.N.C.L.E.* Kjellin was invited to direct the "Town Party, Country Party" episode, which involved Nellie throwing a party, then Laura throwing one to get even with her.

At her own bash, Nellie wrangles the other kids into teasing and taunting Olga Nordstrom, a sweet Swedish girl (played by Kim Richards of *Nanny and the Professor* and *Escape to Witch Mountain*). Olga has one leg that's shorter than the other, causing her to limp. (No running down the hills for Olga!) Laura hurts her ankle and is forced to sit out with her, and they bond. Laura gets a brilliant idea. She and Pa conspire to make Olga "magic shoes" (basically, one is higher than the other, eliminating her limp), and Laura saves the unveiling for her own party. Everyone sees that Olga can now run and play (it's a miracle!), and they begin suggesting other games so she can try out her new "feet."

Nellie, deciding this is a threat to her constant need for undivided attention, says, "I know, let's all take off our shoes and go wading in the creek." She might as well have said, "Hey, let's all leave our wheelchairs and other mobility aids here and go skiing" for all the subtlety involved. I am always amazed that neither Laura nor any of the other girls said, "No, if she takes off her shoes, she won't be able to walk; that's why she's wearing them, you dumbass bitch!" But it's hot, and the girls can't resist the creek, so they feebly go along with this, recrippling their friend at Nellie's request. Never fear; as on most *Little House* episodes, good ol' Laura has the last laugh and gets to teach that nasty Nellie a lesson.

The producers tossed around the idea originally presented in the books, of Laura luring Nellie into a pond inhabited by leeches. Thankfully, they dropped that one pretty quickly. For one, leeches are disgusting, and people ate dinner while watching this show; besides, in 1974, how many city-dwelling children even knew what a leech was? So the leech was replaced by a crab. Nellie gets freaked out by the crab and falls into the muddy pond. Take that!

When we began filming the "Town Party, Country Party" episode, it seemed we were going to all have a pleasant, if uneventful, week. I was happy because it was one of the episodes in which I got to wear the "party dress," which was purple-striped taffeta and made me look like a big piece of Christmas ribbon candy. To get everyone into the spirit of the episode, the director was a real-live authentic Swede. Alf Kjellin was doing a fine job; all was going quite smoothly, the real and imagined Swedes working together in harmony for several days. Then we got to the part where Nellie gets her comeuppance. I was to be spooked by the crab and run, falling face first into a pile of pond muck. For this, a stunt girl was brought in. It was only the seventh episode, and the producers were still going easy on me. In the near future, I would handle any falls, beatings, or dunkings on my own, and stunt girls would be used only in the most dire, life-threatening circumstances. But today, the stunt girl was to do the run and fall. I was to dunk my head under, then get up, spit water, and cry miserably. This eventually became my specialty.

Because I wanted my shot at doing the fall myself, Mr. Kjellin told me we would film two versions, one with the stunt girl running and doing the fall at full speed, and one with me, with less trajectory, but definitely splashing down. After lunch, Michael called me over to the pond. He said we were now going to shoot the "come up and spit" sequence. He told me that the stunt girl's fall was perfect (I had watched it, and it was fabulous), and we could just get on with the aftermath. It sounded reasonable, and, hell, I wasn't about to argue with him. I climbed into the pond and sat down.

Ewwww. It was cold and damp and very muddy, almost quicksand. I felt myself sink into the goo, and I knew right away I wasn't going to be getting up very soon, or very easily. Michael then began the process of "decorating" me. He had a bucket of that green, stringy algae that floats on top of ponds. He began carefully arranging hunks of it over my head and face, occasionally wetting it down by pouring some of the filthy pond water over my head. He grinned and giggled maniacally throughout this process. I sat there stone-faced; I didn't dare move.

Suddenly, Mr. Kjellin appeared. "What the hell are you doing?" he shouted at Michael. Michael, without putting down the bucket or getting up, or even so much as looking over his shoulder at him, said, "I'm getting her ready for the shot; what does it look like I'm doing?"

This enraged the visiting director. "But we were going to have her do the fall as well!" he shouted. Now Michael turned to him (still with a handful of algae) and said, "No, the fall was perfect.

Why shoot it twice?" This was a telling statement. Michael was very much a fan of the "If it ain't broke, don't fix it" philosophy, and if something worked well enough in the first take, don't bother tinkering with perfection—just say "print" and move on.

Mr. Kjellin came right up to him and began ranting furiously about how he was the director, not Michael, and so on. Michael replied with a crack about "having to do his job for him," and the two of them went on like this for several minutes. They left me helpless to get up and remove myself from the situation. I just sat and watched, openmouthed, my head moving back and forth like I was watching a tennis match as the two grown-ups yelled and swore at each other.

About me. Yes, I understood it wasn't really about me. I hadn't done anything wrong, but the argument was all about the scene I was in and what they were going to do with me. And now they appeared about to kill one another right in front of me.

It ended with a mutual "fuck off"—the gist was generally one of those "You can't quit, you're fired!" "You can't fire me, I quit!" situations. Alf Kjellin stomped off and called for his family. (Yes, to make all of this even more excruciatingly uncomfortable, his wife and children were visiting him on the set that day.) A car was summoned, and they were driven off.

I sat there aghast. I had never actually seen anyone fired before, certainly not eighteen inches from my nose and definitely not because of an argument concerning me. My mouth continued to hang open in shock.

Michael turned to me, still breathing through flared nostrils and red in the face. "What are you looking at?" he said coldly.

"Nothing. Nothing, sir. Nothing at all," I stammered. I tried to get up, to not much avail.

"Get. Back. In. The. Pond."

He then shifted gears and went back to happily applying algae to my head. During all of this, he had never put down the bucket.

When he cried, "Action!" I leaned forward and submerged my head in the pond. I felt water go up my nose and into my mouth. I gagged. I came up out of the water like the creature from the black lagoon, dripping and covered in muck. I screamed and spat and shrieked, in what was eventually to become the iconic Nellie howl of protest. "PRINT!" Michael shouted, grinning victoriously.

Michael Landon was one of the biggest walking bundles of contradictions I have ever met. He was a "family man" and talked endlessly about Lynn, his second wife, and his children, to whom he seemed utterly devoted. He had divorced his first wife, with whom he also had children, when he got caught having an affair on the set of *Bonanza* with Lynn (she was working as an extra and stand-in). He went on to divorce Lynn for Cindy (a *Little House* stand-in—and, even more bizarrely, my stand-in) when Lynn caught them at it. I can't imagine what must have gone through her mind then, after having gotten her start the same way.

Charles and Caroline Ingalls represented for all of America the ultimate perfect parents, and their brood had the happiest of childhoods. Yet Michael's own childhood had been utterly miserable. *Little House* was one of the most religious—and most specifically Christian—shows ever on television. Yet Michael was Jewish and had grown up in a home filled with religious conflict, including ugly battles over how he was to be raised. Michael's real name was Eugene Maurice Orowitz. His father was a well-known publicist in Hollywood. His mother, a former dancer and comedienne, was Christian. Well, let's just say "not Jewish," as her behavior was hardly what one thinks of as a definition of "Christian."

Michael wet the bed. His mother punished him viciously for this, even though it was a medical problem and not under his control. She would hang the soiled sheets out his bedroom window for the entire neighborhood to see, knowing that the school bus pulled up right in front of their house. Michael would try to wake up earlier and earlier each day to take the sheets down the street to the local Laundromat and wash them, then get back home without his mother knowing. If that wasn't possible, he would walk home rather than take the bus, then try to outrun it and get home to retrieve the sheets from the window before his friends saw them. Years later, he became a powerful runner and went on to become a track-and-field champion in high school. His specialty was the javelin throw. He eventually went public about his problems and the abuse and made an autobiographical TV movie called *The Loneliest Runner.*

A story that was not in the film, but that I heard on the set, was that in addition to the bed-wetting, his mother objected to Michael's adopting his father's religion, so much so that when he was finally allowed to have a bar mitzvah, his mother pulled him out of the room during the party and sneered, "I just want you to know that when you were a baby, I had you baptized. So this is all just a big joke!"

I remember that when I heard that story, I felt terrible for him. And now here he was, every week, standing up in church with the Reverend Alden, happily singing "Onward Christian Soldiers." What on earth could that have been like for him?

And, yes, he was gorgeous, absolutely breathtaking; all muscles and tanned skin, big white teeth, and a wild mane of shining, curly hair. He was like a male version of a Farrah Fawcett poster. I sometimes wondered what he would look like in that red swimsuit. He knew he was sexy, and he made sure everyone else knew it, too. I got the impression he had not been sexy or popular when he was a teenager, and this was the great payback of all time.

He was hard not to notice. He didn't walk. He strutted. He swaggered. Like a peacock. His aura annoyed some people in the cast. I remember Katherine MacGregor telling me she disliked him on sight, when, at her audition, he strutted into the room. "Like a baby bantam rooster!" she howled. I never minded it. I thought it was sort of cute. His somewhat overly macho posturing also struck me as dreadfully funny because he was so small. Michael Landon was short, really short. I don't know his actual height, because he was never without the enormous lifts he wore in his boots. I really think that much of his swagger was not to impress, but to keep from tipping over in those shoes.

In every scene with another male actor, he was always positioned on a staircase, up on a ladder, anything. They did everything but dig a hole for the rest of us to stand in. His image was of a big, protective father figure, but he was really more of a cute, cuddly, giggling little thing. And in the tightest pants you ever saw—with not a stitch of underwear.

This did give even me a shock the first day. It was the 1970s, so tight jeans and no underwear was a popular fashion statement in Hollywood. But no underwear beneath his Charles Ingalls homespun trousers? In the 1800s? What on earth was he thinking?

What he was thinking was that NBC had done research on the demographics of our show and determined that the largest part of our viewing audience at that point was women age forty-plus. And Michael knew exactly what they liked. So the pants remained tight, the underwear remained in the drawer, and the shirt stayed off, displaying his even, perfectly tan chest, totally hairless, with the wide suspenders crossing right next to each nipple (in case you hadn't noticed them and needed a hint where to look). Usually just a tiny rivulet of sweat, strategically placed, ran down his pectorals. *Sigh.*

Little House was a family show, but for a large part of our audience, it was also like one of those "bodice ripper" paperback romance novels. No actual sex, nothing dirty, but there was a handsome, sweaty, dashing hero who could scoop you up in his brawny arms and carry you into his rough-hewn cabin and . . . Then the moon went behind a cloud.

One of the most popular questions I get asked over and over again is "What was Michael Landon *really* like?" In truth, I'll never know. I was not married to him, I didn't date him, he wasn't my father; I didn't have to live with him day in and day out. Those who did know much more than I or anyone else ever will. And they have my sympathy. I loved him and loved every minute of working with him, but I have to think that being around someone that driven, that focused, that, well, just plain intense, on a regular, day-to-day basis would be enough to drive most people completely out of their minds.

Michael *was* like Charles Ingalls. Except when he wasn't. He believed in hard work for everyone. We child actors were expected to show up on time, know our lines, put in our best performance, and call our elders "sir" and "ma'am." When the AD called us to come do our scenes, we came running and said, "Yes, sir!" On location these requests were shouted over a megaphone, but always with the word *please*: "Alison, please!" "Melissa, please!" and so on. It was best if they only had to call you once. Because the location was huge (the ranch covered over 6,500 acres, and the Little House was a mile and a half from town), it was excusable, if you were very far away when called, to come dashing in by the second *please*. But you didn't want to wait for a third, because after that, the next voice coming though that megaphone would be Michael's. And he would *not* be a happy camper.

I recently met a young woman who plays a teenage daughter on a popular sitcom. She was telling me how much she enjoyed doing her show and asked about the conditions on our set. The people on her set were particularly nice to her, so she asked, "Did they treat you like little princesses, too?"

I couldn't help but laugh out loud. No, I had to tell her. We were not "princesses" on *Little House*. We were soldiers. None of us had our own trailers on location. I have been to sets where the lead actors in Michael's position and those playing the lead family, including the young girls, would each have enormous Winnebago-type trailers, lavishly furnished, complete with wet bars. Such a thing might easily be in someone's contract. But not on our show. We each had a place to change our clothes and go to the bathroom with barely enough room to turn around.

That's what we all got, including Michael. And on those days when we had a cast of thousands—those episodes involving ball games, Founder's Day picnics, etc.—we doubled up and shared, including Michael. Of course, we shared with people we liked: Melissa and I were always together, and Michael only shared with his best friends, either Victor French or his stunt man, Hal Burton, but double up he did, just like everyone else. We didn't need fancy dressing rooms. We all knew we wouldn't be spending that much time in there anyway, with the pace we worked at. There was an air of disdain for all "perks" in general. Hard work was its own reward. Well, that and your paycheck. This was true for us kids as well.

At one point there was an attempt to further motivate the children with rewards of gum and candy. This nonsense was brought to an abrupt halt by Michael. One of the ADs, a man who insisted on being called "Uncle Miles," a trait I always found disturbing, started handing out gum and candy at the end of the day if everyone was "good." It was mostly for the kids who were day players and background or extras, but some of the younger regulars got in on the action as well. I was a bit old for this, and gum chewing was at that time off the list for me, as I had braces. I also thought it was kind of lame, if not downright creepy.

"Okay, boys and girls; now, if everybody's good today, Uncle Miles will give you gum!"

Michael was not amused. I wasn't supposed to find out about his reaction, but between my aunt Marion and me, we had ears everywhere. Michael told Miles this gum business was to stop and stop immediately, that it was a horrible idea. "Gum if you're good? What if some kid says, 'Screw it, I don't feel like gum today; I don't have to be good'?" He said, "They don't need gum. They're here to do a job like everyone else. They're getting paid—they can go to the store and buy their own damn gum! They don't need to be given gum if they're good. If they're not good, *they're fired.*" The gum campaign was over. A few very young children complained briefly, but most didn't care that much.

I did. I thought it was one of the greatest things Michael ever said. I wanted to run up and hug him when I heard. He didn't want us treated as if we were stupid—or worse, like trained animals performing for treats. We were to be treated as thinking human beings, as actors, equal to anyone else on the set and just as accountable for our actions.

Everyone always asks if Michael was like a father to me, if he loved me. I have no idea if he loved me, but he went one better as far as I'm concerned. He respected me. Respect is something very hard to come by for child actors. They are often treated as dumb animals or props, objects to be moved about in service of the plot or the other actors. They're sometimes instructed to do no more than hit their mark and "act cute." Making silly faces and repeating inane catchphrases is encouraged. In these circumstances, not much is expected of them, and "not much" is exactly what you get.

I think this contributes to the rampant lack of self-respect we see so often in ex–child stars and the resulting self-destructive behavior. If you're never asked to meet a standard, never held accountable for anything, sure, nothing's ever your fault, but then nothing's ever to your credit, either. It's pretty much as if you were never even there. This was never the case for any child actor in *Little House on the Prairie.* Or as we like to say, "Cast of *Little House:* no arrests, no convictions."

And I do believe we owe that to Michael.

CHAPTER NINE

THE PUBLICITY-SEEKING MISSILE

> **WILLIE: I'm telling!**
>
> **NELLIE: You listen to me. You say anything, and I'll say you're lying. You know they'll believe me, because you lie more than I do. But if you don't say anything, I'll give you chocolate and gumdrops. Lots of them . . .**

Anyone who was anyone was there. It was a big, glitzy Hollywood party in 1974, thrown by a media organization to celebrate the new season's TV shows. The party was mainly for the "names" on the shows so they could hobnob with the press and get reporters and reviewers to write positive things. The only person on *Little House*'s cast who was deemed worthy of an invite was Michael—he knew how to charm the media. He had just come off *Bonanza,* and he was a bona fide star, while the rest of us cast members were still pretty unknown.

This, however, did not stop my dad. A friend of his, a French-Canadian gossip columnist, was going to the party, and he said he could get us in—in a backdoor, under the table sort of way. The party was a serious black-tie affair, and my dad insisted that for the occasion I was going to get my first seriously expensive dress. My father, normally a great lover of bargains, insisted we shop at the famously overpriced department store Neiman Marcus (there's a reason people call it "needless markup"). I was getting into this party, I was a star, and I deserved it, he explained to me. We ended up buying a beautiful gray dress, with little dark gray birds all over it. It was actually very *Little House on the Prairie,* and very Nellie Oleson in that it cost a fortune.

My father accompanied me in a tuxedo that he had bought for two dollars at a Catholic church rummage sale. But it wasn't as bad as it sounds. An actor had left his entire wardrobe to the church, including numerous designer suits. An elderly volunteer had been allowed to price everything, making it possible to purchase Ralph Lauren shirts for fifty cents—well, at least until lunchtime, when the other volunteers realized what she was doing and snatched the pen away from her in horror. But before they arrived and put a stop to the greatest designer clothes give-away in history, my father had grabbed up pants, shirts, ties, and several suits, including a tuxedo, and the sweet little old lady had sold him the entire lot for about fifty dollars, which in reality should have been the price of one of the ties.

So I, in my nearly thousand-dollar dress, and my father, in his two-dollar suit, sauntered into the hottest A-list party in town and tried to act like we belonged there. It was a great success. I was photographed with every star in the place—Karen Valentine, Barbara Eden, Will Geer, even Mary Tyler Moore. And then Michael showed up.

I have several beautiful pictures of him from that night, but

I would give anything for just one photo of the look on his face when he saw that my dad and I had gotten into that party. No one from the show was supposed to be there but him—not Laura Ingalls herself, not Mary, not even Ma. And here, of all the people on earth to show up, was the kid who played Nellie Oleson, a girl no one had ever heard of, just standing there in her little Neiman Marcus dress like she owned the place, and behind her, some crazy guy in a tux who ran a talent management company out of his dining room.

Michael's mouth opened in shock, as if he was about to say, "What in holy hell are you two idiots doing here?" But before he could say anything, the photographers were grabbing us and saying, "Oh, yes! Michael! Stand next to her!" and happily shooting away. He looked at me with a glint in his eye and shook his head, laughing. Then he assumed his official publicity grin with those big white teeth, and we posed for photo after photo. With one look he had said it all. *These two are going to be trouble. . . .*

Strangely, this outrageous act of defiance did not result in retaliation. Michael not only knew chutzpah when he saw it, I think he admired it. For the duration of *Little House,* every time my father pulled some outlandish publicity stunt (such as having me pose in a bikini with a killer whale at Sea World or go on a morning talk show with my pet snake), or I had some scandalous article in the *National Enquirer* claiming I was romantically linked to some actor I barely knew, others on the set would be appalled, but not Michael. He would just look at me with that twinkle in his eye, grin, and shake his head. My dad's abilities as a father are certainly in question, and his skills as a manager have received mixed reviews from different clients. But one thing was unquestionable: the man was a living, breathing, publicity-seeking missile. If there was an event, I was going to it.

The first year of the show, Katherine MacGregor and I received a request from a very exclusive girls' school to appear at their Easter-fair fund-raiser in full Nellie and Mrs. Oleson drag. We were to hold court and sign autographs at what was to be a charming, high-end event. This required coordination and logistical maneuvering on the part of many people. The costumes had to be brought in their entirety from wardrobe (I shudder to imagine the insurance issues). We had to be dressed, have our hair done in the full getup with bows by the set hairdressers, and arrive at the event along with all designated publicists and photographers—ours, theirs, NBC's, the invited press, and the uninvited press.

At first, it really did seem like a good idea. (I can't begin to tell you how many disasters in my life have started with those words.) The location was beautiful: a posh private school in the Coldwater Canyon area of Los Angeles with lush gardens and rolling lawns. The school's administrators had spared no expense for this event, bringing in a merry-go-round, filling the pond with baby ducks, and hosting an Easter egg hunt, complete with a guy in a bunny suit. Katherine and I looked fabulous. We posed for numerous pictures. There are shots of me with a baby duck and the two of us gaily cavorting on merry-go-rounds and the like. And then the school's publicity director introduced us to the children, both the students and the adorable overdressed young ones of the moneyed families who were attending in support. And that's when things began to go terribly wrong.

"Look, it's Mrs. Oleson and Nellie!" "Isn't that great, kids?"

Um, no. See, what the apparently delusional grown-ups had forgotten was, we played the villains. You know, the bad guys. The students didn't like us. At all. A few older kids and their parents got autographs. Then the playground got really quiet. A woman brought over her daughter, a girl of maybe four or five, to meet Mrs. Oleson. Katherine smiled warmly and said hello, and the child promptly burst into tears. And then started screaming. Really, really loudly. I honestly don't know who was more traumatized: the poor child being terrified by the spectacle of the actual evil Mrs. Oleson in person, or poor Katherine, realizing she'd just made a little girl cry by smiling at her. We were not entertaining anyone. We were just plain scaring people. No one in this transaction was having an even remotely good time. This was turning into a PR disaster.

Katherine and I decided to back off and just play the rest of the event low-key. We would be present but would not attempt to directly engage anyone. Those who actually wished to meet us or get an autograph could quietly do so on their own, but we would avoid any further public scenes. I decided now would be a good time to go get something to eat. I left the main hub of action and headed off to the area the school had set up as a food court. So there I was, walking down the sidewalk behind the main buildings, hoping to stay out of sight and enjoy my hot dog and grape slushee in peace, when, WHAM! A millisecond before, I had heard faint giggling and the sound of running footsteps behind me, but there just wasn't time to turn around. Suddenly, I felt the strange sensation of being kicked in the ass by not one, but two feet. Either someone had jumped straight up in the air and onto my butt, or I was being kicked simultaneously by two people. The sheer force knocked me to the ground. I fell to the cement and landed facedown. I closed my eyes before I hit, so I wouldn't get poked in the eye by anything, and my eyes were still shut tight when I heard my assailants giggle in triumph and run away.

As I lay there, feeling the cool cement against my cheek and hearing the footsteps fade in the distance, I thought, *Just how the hell did I get here? I mean, I don't even know these people, and they kicked me in the butt. Really hard. And now they're happy about it.* Between trying to determine if I'd fractured my wrist or cracked a tooth in the fall, I slowly pondered the meaning of all this. I had pretended to be someone else on TV. I had pretended to do things that I don't normally do and said a bunch of really awful things that I didn't make up and didn't really mean. I had pretended to hate a girl (Melissa Gilbert) I actually adored. I had pretended to be a fabulously rich and prissy girl in Mary Janes, when I was really dead broke and a tomboy in sneakers. I had pretended to be a confident, tough bully, when I was really an insecure, shy, frightened girl who got beat up a lot (like now, for instance). I had done these things because it was my job; they paid me to do it, and once again, it seemed like a good idea at the time.

And now, it seemed, I had done it so well, pretended so convincingly, that these two girls *really* hated me. They hated me so much, I made them so angry, that just the sight of me inspired them to beat me to the ground. Now, this is certainly some kind of achievement. I realized at that moment that even winning an Emmy could not provide more concrete proof of my ability to affect people as an actress. But then, it probably wouldn't hurt as much either.

I couldn't get up. I was relieved that at least all these damn petticoats and excessive costuming had broken my fall, but I was horrified when I realized that they also, once I was facedown, virtually turned me into a turtle on its back. I could not get up without assistance. I also wasn't really sure if I had injured myself. With that, and the sense of humiliation I felt having just been beaten up by small children in a public place, I decided to just stay down and wait for my dad to get there. I didn't even have the nerve to open my eyes.

"Are you all right?" he asked me minutes later when he arrived at the scene of the crime.

"Uh, I think so."

He helped me up, and that's when I saw that in addition to being attacked from behind and made to kiss pavement, I had been done out of a perfectly good hot dog and slushee, now splattered all over the ground. I managed not to start crying, as that would've just been too embarrassing on top of everything else, but my father said very sternly, "We're going home," and took me to get another hot dog and slushee on the way out.

When we got home, I heard him on the phone with the publicists who had arranged this debacle, saying, with huge, dramatic emphasis, "She was attacked, for God's sake!" It was agreed by all involved that I was never, ever, under any circumstances, to wear the dreaded costume in public again. It was simply too dangerous. It incited people.

I felt a little better. In a way, I was relieved. That getup was not something I wanted to wear more frequently than I had to. But I also knew this was not just about the dress anymore. My act, Nellie Oleson, had inadvertently unleashed something in people's psyches. The injustices that Laura faced on the prairie were too much like the injustices they faced in their own lives. They wanted to have someone to get mad at. And there I was, in all my smug, ringleted, smirking glory. Hell, *I* hated me.

I was going to need to toughen up, quick. The meek might inherit the earth, but if the meek are going to play Nellie Oleson on TV, the meek are going to get pummeled. Perhaps these circumstances could be turned to my advantage. I mean, what if instead of just wanting to deck me, they were actually afraid of me? *Hmmmm.*

Coming up with a way to avoid getting beaten up had always been a dream of mine. Between the school bullies and the frequent encounters with my psycho brother, I'd already perfected techniques like running, learning to take a punch without crying, and rolling into a ball and playing dead, but I couldn't keep that sort of thing up forever. At my new school, finding a way to avoid a beating was about to become a much more pressing matter, because Bancroft Junior High, which I entered in the seventh grade, didn't just have bullies; it had gangs—actual, real-live, weapon-toting, like you see on the eleven o'clock news, gangs. And in the early 1970s, Bancroft happened to be right smack in the middle of a major territorial gang dispute. The gang to beat was none other than the now world-famous West Side Crips.

Unlike some of my classmates whose parents drove them to school, I, in the spirit of social egalitarianism (or more likely because my parents were too busy to drive me anywhere), took the bus. The RTD is the mainstay of the L.A. public transportation system. It stands for Rapid Transit Department—which it really wasn't, but it was better than walking. I usually wound up on the same bus with some Crips members at the end of the day, when I was on my way home, and they were on their way to a fight. And that's how I met "Godfather Crip."

I had heard of the Godfather for some time and always assumed he was some sort of big *Scarface*-style drug kingpin in a fur coat and Rolls-Royce. So I was a little surprised when one day he pulled up at the bus stop across the street from school in a Toyota. There was a great deal of excitement among the young Crips at the bus stop. Jubilant cries of "Godfather! Godfather!" greeted the little orange Toyota with the dirty windows. A thin, gangly teenage boy got out and walked around to the passenger side.

"Dr. Scrooge!" someone yelled. This was apparently a high-ranking aide or bodyguard. He opened the door. Out stepped a boy no older than fifteen, in a full-length leather coat and high-top Converse sneakers. His face was almost completely concealed by a large leather hat. This was Godfather Crip. All five feet four of him.

Godfather Crip, his many fans, and I all got on the bus together. I didn't fully understand the sense of his taking the bus when he had a car and driver, but I think it had something to do with showing solidarity with his men before a fight. There were no seats left when I got on, so I headed to the back of the bus to stand. The Godfather asked me if I needed a seat. At this cue, Dr. Scrooge promptly threw a young gang member to the floor and offered me his now suddenly vacated seat.

I wasn't sure what the protocol was for turning down an offer like that, so I decided to take it. The Godfather asked if I wanted a cigarette. Dr. Scrooge started to violently remove one from the mouth of one of the gang's smokers, but I told him it was okay, I didn't smoke. The entire ride home continued like this, the Godfather's polite attempts at making conversation punctuated by Dr. Scrooge's outbursts of violently enforced chivalry.

Eventually, they all got off at Plummer Park in West Hollywood, where a number of rival gang members, Los Rebels, were waiting. Both sides were carrying various weapons, such as bats, chains, some knives here and there, but the Crips liked to battle with canes and walking sticks. They all seemed strangely happy about the whole thing. These were still the old days, when some still fought for sport or territory and mostly without guns. Not that they didn't sometimes kill each other; it just took longer. They also seemed to have little interest in killing anyone not directly involved in their disputes (like me). Now, anyone in range of an Uzi or an AK-47 is fair game. *Ah, for the good old days*. I wondered if any of these people had any idea just how really screwed up they were. Did they really think this was a normal, healthy way of life, or did they have some inkling that this behavior might be symptomatic of some kind of deep, inner disturbance?

I found that out when, along with several of my friends, I got thrown into detention. *For refusing to kill an earthworm.* Back then, even in a liberal California junior high, announcing that dissecting an earthworm was against your moral principles would still get you detention. The truth is, it wasn't really against my moral principles. I just couldn't do it without puking.

Some of the Crips were in detention with me, and we struck up a conversation. No one stopped us; there was no supervision.

(The idea of detention at Bancroft was to simply leave a bunch of strangers alone in a room for six or seven hours.) The young man I spoke to was so forthcoming about his affiliation, he even taught me a song:

I'm crippin'
And limpin'
And damn sure pimpin!

He explained that it was his ultimate ambition to be a pimp. He was thirteen years old. He went on to explain about "limpin'," and demonstrated his signature walk, enhanced by his standard-issue Crip cane. I finally asked him what Crip stood for, thinking it had to be an acronym for something: "Cool Rebels in Prison"? "Cruising Regally in Pontiacs"? I pondered.

"No," he said. "It's just Crip. It's short for 'crippled inside.'" Oh. I guess that answered that question. During our conversation, he did mention that the only thing that might dissuade him from being a gang member or a pimp would be if he could have his own show on television. I thought, *If this is what goes on in detention, this school must have a* very *interesting drama department.*

My brief experience in drama class was so horrible that I think I was better off in detention. At the beginning of each class, we would be given a scene to read, and the teacher would assign parts. It never progressed beyond a group cold reading. No instruction was given; and we engaged in no discussion about what anything meant. Not that it mattered, as far as I was concerned. I never got any parts, not due to any specific performance defect on my part, but because there was a girl in the class who decided she wanted first crack at any roles and wished to reduce the competition. She accomplished this by stuffing me into a broom closet every morning. It worked. She and a few friends would beat me into submission and stuff me in the closet and cover me with coats. By the time I crawled out of the closet and into the drama room, all the parts were assigned. (I don't know why I never thought to try this technique at auditions. Think of all the roles I could have gotten had I had the good sense to shove Jodie Foster into a cupboard!)

I did finally tell the teacher what was happening. She was a bored, listless type who didn't interact with the class much, but this time she did tell my captors that their behavior was going to cost them points off their final grade. They were very upset about this threat, and when class let out that day, they announced they were going to beat the crap out of me. Again.

I took off running and this time was lucky enough to run into a group of my friends. Unfortunately, they were my friends from the "gifted" algebra program: great if you needed to borrow a slide rule, but not the group you call to back you up in a fistfight. But what I didn't know was that with all this violence at my new school, some of their parents had packed them off to after-school self-defense and karate classes. I don't know if any of them really knew what they were doing, but they put on a hell of a show.

There was great yowling and shrieking, as the drama club diva and her friends found themselves set upon by a pack of future certified public accountants, all flailing about in their best Bruce Lee impersonations. Even if it was only the element of surprise, it worked and sent the drama bullies running. I was extremely touched that my friends were willing to jump up at a moment's notice, and even though fighting wasn't really their thing, they had been prepared to do their worst to protect me. I had been saved by geeks.

Then one day, the running, the hiding, and the pummeling came to an end. I was walking across the school grounds, when I was approached by a group of five girls, and I use the term loosely. They were very large teenagers, tall and muscular, and they looked like they had been in more than a couple of fights in their lives. In fact, they looked like they belonged to the Crips, or the "ladies auxiliary" thereof. They had these really fabulous 1970s' *Get Christie Love!*–style outfits, with big furry boots and miniskirts. I remember one girl had an enormous metal comb stuck in the top of her hair. It occurred to me that she probably used it as more than a decorative accessory.

They surrounded me.

"Your name Alison?" the tallest one asked. *Oh great,* I thought, *they have my name; it's a contract hit.*

"Yes." I didn't even bother to try to lie my way out of whatever was coming.

"Are you the one who's on *Little House on the Prairie*?" she continued, still in hostile interrogation mode.

"Uh, yes." *Now, this is taking an odd turn,* I thought.

"You play Nellie, right?" she asked.

Where the hell was this conversation going, I wondered. "Um, yes, I do," I answered, not sure if I was going to regret it or not.

"You're Nellie? You are *bad,* girlfriend! You beat the crap outta that stupid Laura Ingalls!" They were all smiles. In fact, they were positively thrilled. They laughed and giggled and told me how much they enjoyed my "badness."

I had been mistaken. These girls weren't my enemies. *They were my fans.* After that day, I never had any trouble with people wanting to beat me up at school. Ever.

There seemed no end to the confidence-building exercises. But I was still working on my shyness issues on the set. I sometimes had trouble talking to "new people" one on one, and I was now faced with a cast and crew of over a hundred, some of them with rather intimidating personalities, to say the least. I had hoped at first I could just show up, do my job, and lay low, but it was not to be. I would be forced into confronting my issues. First I had Bill Claxton asking me to stop looking at the ground when I talked to people, and now I was about to be totally blindsided.

Midway through the first season, my agent called my father to report that my shyness had been taken for "haughtiness" or unfriendliness. I was stunned. But then it occurred to me, if I'm playing a bitch on camera, and then off camera I just sit there and don't talk, what other information do my fellow cast mates have to go on? I could see where confusion could arise. But this was more than that. There were actually rumors that I was "difficult" or a diva. This was considered serious enough to possibly affect my employment. My parents told me that this was a serious situation that demanded immediate action. But what? I was going to have to try to be more outgoing.

I realize that to anyone who knows me now, this statement is possibly the most ludicrous request imaginable. But I really was shy back then. I asked my parents what on earth I was supposed to do. "Fake it," was the answer.

First off, I needed to dress more casually. I had been wearing a simple white button-down shirt to work, so I would have something that I didn't have to pull over my head, in case I had to put on the wig and makeup before dressing. I switched to something more colorful to make myself seem less stuck up.

My mother was not terribly helpful in this department. "Maybe you could a wear a hat?" she feebly suggested. I showed up the next day in a carefully selected cute outfit, complete with a spunky, tomboyish yet adorable baseball cap. Then I simply forced myself to talk to people. Auntie Marion was quite sympathetic to my plight. She had been terribly, almost pathologically shy growing up and had learned many tricks over the years to overcome it. She said the easiest one was to ask people questions. "Most people are perfectly happy to talk about themselves if you let them," she counseled me.

I also did my research. I started reading various celebrity tell-all autobiographies and discovered that many famous actresses, usually those known for being loud and brassy, were actually horribly shy and had simply learned to mask it with another personality. I found out that this list included the actress Nancy Walker and one of my heroes, Bette Midler. And that was how I learned to embrace what I still refer to as the "Bette Midler School of Overcompensation."

I took a deep breath, steeled myself, and simply did the opposite of what seemed instinctive. When I wanted to retreat, I barged up to people and started talking. When I wanted to look down, I looked up. When I wanted to cringe, I laughed. I even took to sitting on people's laps if they seemed so inclined. I kept thinking, *This can't possibly work. I feel like an idiot. Surely they will see through this ridiculous charade.*

No one did. Within two days my agent called to say how happy he was to hear I was "fitting in." My colleagues spoke about how nice it was I had "come out of my shell." I learned that people see what they want to see and believe what they want to believe. It takes very little to help them along.

I did, however, have an extra ace up my sleeve: Melissa Gilbert. She had found out about the rumors and, having been the first to befriend me, knew they weren't true. So what did she do about this at the age of nine? She called a meeting. One day, out in Simi, she went around the set and told all the little girls who were extras on the show, the ones who played the other girls in Miss Beadle's class, that they were to come to lunch in her dressing room. We all crammed ourselves into the tiny trailer, sitting on the couch, the desk, and the floor, anywhere there was space. After a few minutes of chatting, one of the girls remarked that she was surprised at how nice I was, that she had heard I wasn't any fun.

Melissa pounced on this statement. "I knew it! I already know someone's been spreading rumors about Alison! Where'd *you* hear it?" she demanded. The girl nervously pointed at one of the other girls. "She told me!" The accused girl backpedaled furiously. "I didn't start it!" They all seemed panic stricken at the thought of being interrogated by Melissa Gilbert. After an assortment of protests and cross-accusations, they finally narrowed it down to one of the girls who had not taken us up on the lunch invite. But then one of the older girls spoke up. "It wasn't really her, though. It was her mother."

Melissa was not surprised. She shook her head. She explained to the girls that in this sort of competitive environment, it would not be unheard of for a stage mother to start rumors about another girl in the hopes of getting her fired and furthering her own child's career. But, she cautioned, we must not let them get away with it. "We have to stick together, okay?" she said. The girls nodded.

"There's going to be a lot of stuff like this, people trying to turn us against each other," she continued. "From now on, if *any* of you hear *anything* about one of us—especially if it comes from one of the stage moms—you come to me first, okay?"

We all agreed. Her motion passed unanimously. She had just successfully organized a group of child actors against the stage mothers. There were no more incidents of this kind. And from then on, anything that happened on that set did not happen without her knowledge. She was now Don Corleone. For some of us, her growing up to be president of the Screen Actors Guild wasn't exactly a shock.

But then there was Melissa Sue. I tried to be nice to her; Auntie Marion insisted on it. It didn't seem to work, though. Eventually, being nice to Melissa Sue Anderson became a Zen meditative exercise. Waiting for her to respond was like waiting to hear the sound of one hand clapping. I always said, "Good morning," or, more accurately, a sickeningly cheerful "Good morning, Missy!" This was usually greeted with either a cold stare or a kind of "uh-huh" sound muttered under her breath. Often it was less than this. Sometimes she didn't even look up from what she was reading, as if I wasn't even there.

I did grow frustrated and sarcastic. I admit that, when one day, after what must have been months of this, she looked at me quizzically and said, "Uh, good morning?" I responded with "There! Now, *that* wasn't so hard, was it?" I know, this is not what we call positive reinforcement, but she was just so damn exasperating.

Constantly being compared to her was tiresome as well. All three of us girls were under a microscope, with the producers, the crew, and all the stage mothers constantly measuring and noting every stage of development, comparing us to each other as if we were sisters.

The funny thing was, we couldn't have been more different. Melissa Gilbert was a nice Jewish girl from a wealthy family in Encino, Melissa Sue Anderson was a devout Catholic in a single-parent home, and I was raised by an itinerant band of Canadian actors. The two Melissas and I were like some old joke about a priest, a minister, and a rabbi in a lifeboat. It was a wonder we spoke to each other at all.

And we were not the same age. I was the eldest, which confused many adults on the set. Melissa Sue looked older than I did, and so often when trying to excuse what was by then politely being referred to as her "aloofness," people would say, "It's a teenage phase. I'm sure Alison will be doing the same thing any minute." Auntie Marion was quick to correct them on this issue. "Alison is almost a year older than Missy. I do not recall her ever going through a phase quite like *this*." Although Auntie Marion stressed patience when dealing with "Missy," she wasn't past using her as an example. "Poor girl," she'd say, "if she doesn't change, that meanness will show up in her face.

Mom and Dad onstage in Canada in 1951. Yes, they were acting, but this scene could have been straight out of their real-life relationship.

Backstage with Liberace in 1969. Nah, he doesn't look gay at all. . . .

On the set of *Throw Out the Anchor* with Dina Merrill in 1972. I pay rapt attention as she explains how to be rich and fabulous.

Auntie Marion and I emerge from my trailer. I had to be very careful to hold my drink away from the dress . . . or else.

Katherine MacGregor and I relax between takes. (What am I reading? The *Racing Form*?!)

Gladys nails on the dreaded wig in the hair and makeup "demilitarized zone."

By the riverside in Sonora, California, while filming "The Camp Out" episode. Melissa (wearing Michael Landon's hat) and I were clearly up to no good . . . as usual!

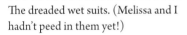

The dreaded wet suits. (Melissa and I hadn't peed in them yet!)

With my ever-ready henchman, Willie (Jonathan Gilbert), in front of the Mercantile.

The evil Oleson ladies' disastrous appearance at a school fair. This was shot moments before the crowd turned on us.

Conning our way into a Hollywood party in 1974. I wore a $1,000 gown while my publicity-machine dad donned a $2 tux.

What the hell are you doing here? Michael was shocked but happy to see me at the party.

Never wrestle with Melissa Gilbert. She'll put you in a headlock and make you eat dirt!

My all-time favorite picture of Melissa and me: She has that expression on her face because I have just shoved an ice cube down the front of her shirt. (She did it to me first!)
Photograph by John Wiltshire Photography

Since my boobs were the biggest of the teenagers' on *Little House* in 1977, I won Gladys's gold lame swimsuit. Here I show off the goods as Melissa stands by, green with envy.

BFFs celebrating my fifteenth birthday on the set at Paramount Studios.

Ever the prankster, Michael helps me cut my cake.

Palling around with "Percival." Celebrating with Steve Tracey at the *Little House* Christmas party in 1980.

With my mother and the late comedian John Deavon at a salute to Casper the Friendly Ghost (a.k.a. Mom) in Hollywood.

You can take the girl out of the prairie, but you can't take the prairie out of the girl. Post–*Little House*, I continued to be cast in period pieces, including the TV movie *I Married Wyatt Earp* with Marie Osmond.

Trying to shed my innocent *Little House* image by playing a tramp on *Fantasy Island* in 1980. Yes, that's Eve Plumb (a.k.a. Jan Brady) as my mom!

Visiting the real Walnut Grove in 1992.

J'adore the French . . . and they love me! A Nellie poster from 2009.

Not the blushing bride type, I wore a tux to match my husband, Bob, when we wed on November 6, 1993.

It always does, you know." She informed me that people's real selves always reveal themselves eventually; that those who are selfish, spoiled, and mean will age sooner and wrinkle earlier than those who are not. She said that if I was good and kind and patient, it would also show in my face; that I would age gracefully, and when I did get old, I would have laugh lines instead of deep furrows from frowning. I would have dismissed this as just a silly story to get young girls to be nice to each other, except that my aunt was in her seventies and looked years younger than all the other stage mothers on the set. The woman was clearly onto something.

I thought there must be something Melissa Sue liked to do. I was excited when I saw that she had taken up backgammon and thought this might be my opportunity to finally break through her impenetrable shell. I didn't know how to play at all, but I thought, *Even better! Not only is it a game she likes, but she can show off how good she is by teaching me to play it.* I marched up to her and expressed interest in the game. She looked bored. I said I didn't know how to play and asked if it was difficult. She looked at me in utter disgust and said, "No, it figures you wouldn't know how. You've always been a tad backwards."

I was surprised by such an open display of hostility. It had seemed an unspoken agreement that to keep peace on the set, all hatreds were to be expressed in a more covert, Victorian manner. Just coming right out and insulting people to their face seemed unusual, even for her. I decided to go with the possibility, however unlikely, that this was an attempt at humor. Who knows what this girl thought was a joke? Maybe "backwards" was just her way of saying "dizzy" or "silly." I laughed nervously.

"A tad backwards? Oh, I like that! Yeah, I'd say I'm sort of 'backwards'!"

She wasn't laughing. "No," she continued coldly, "actually, I'd say you're a lot backwards. In fact, you're quite stupid." Ah. So apparently she *didn't* feel like teaching me to play backgammon. And as I didn't feel like finding out what she was going to say next, I got the hell out of there.

Everyone assumed Missy's attitude had something to do with her mother, but we never knew for sure. I never even heard her raise her voice to Missy, but there just seemed to be something odd about their relationship. Some people weren't subtle about saying so, like Katherine MacGregor, who was never subtle about anything. One morning in makeup, Katherine was explaining how after years of therapy, she had realized that she hated her mother. Her mother had been extremely cruel to her, it turns out, and she had tried to pretend for years that it didn't bother her. She had felt great relief when she admitted she couldn't stand the woman. Melissa Sue walked in right in the middle of this, just as Katherine was saying, "And that's how I realized I hated my mother!"

Missy was horrified. She actually spoke up: "You can't do that. You can't hate your mother."

Katherine turned on her, like a dog smelling fear. "Yes, you can. Lots of people hate their mothers! No, it's not supposed to be that way, but sometimes mothers are horrible and hate their own children. And some people hate their mothers!"

"But you *can't* hate your own mother!" Missy protested.

"And just who told you THAT?" Katherine sneered ominously.

"My . . . my mother," the poor girl stammered.

"A-HA!" roared Katherine, pointing an accusing finger at her, like Mrs. Oleson cornering a shoplifter in the Mercantile. She had clearly hit a nerve. The poor girl turned and ran out of the makeup trailer. Auntie Marion would have never allowed me to do anything that mean.

To add to the Missy mystery, there was the legendary "one good day." It was during the first season, when Melissa Gilbert was having a birthday party. She invited me and a group of girls to go to Magic Mountain. Miraculously, she had invited Melissa Sue Anderson. It was early on in the evolution of our relationships, so perhaps she was still holding out hope.

Being one of the first parties with cast members I had been invited to, my father insisted I dress up. This meant a "dressy casual" print skirt and espadrilles. All the other girls arrived in overalls and sneakers. I was now officially a total dork. But to their credit, no one held it against me. We were driven out to Magic Mountain by Harold Abeleze, Melissa's lawyer stepdad. (Her parents divorced when she was young.) He was remarkably calm and patient for a man stuck driving a car full of twelve- and thirteen-year-old screaming girls for hours.

I have never been one for roller coasters, especially anything that goes upside down, so I spent most of the afternoon holding everyone's purses and sweaters as they went on the serious, hard-core rides. (Yes, my dork rating was through the roof at this point.) I had a good time, though, as we ate junk food and shrieked and gossiped and had a perfectly normal teenage-girl day. And to my and Melissa Gilbert's utter amazement, Melissa Sue was . . . happy. Really, genuinely, not-faking-it, smiling, laughing, and tossing her hair happy, all day long. We even sang songs in the car on the way back. (Poor Harold.)

Then her mother came to pick her up. It was like a dark cloud passed in front of the sun. She became quiet again, and her facial expression returned to its normal bored stare. Over the years, I saw her put on a show of smiling for people—no matter how hard she was scowling, she always threw on the smile whenever Michael showed up—but I will always remember that one time when she actually seemed . . . relaxed.

CHAPTER TEN

MELISSA AND ME . . . OR "TO PEE OR NOT TO PEE"

> **NELLIE: Half the time, you don't even SMELL like a girl! You're either sweaty, or you stink of fish!**
>
> **LAURA: Well . . . I sweat a lot, and I fish a lot!**

If you haven't been up to beautiful Sonora, California, or seen the majestic Stanislaus River, I will tell you, it's breathtaking. The river is also freezing cold and has incredibly strong currents. People drown in it regularly. So, of course, the producers decided in Season 2 that it would be a good idea to stick me and Melissa in this river and see if we lived long enough to finish the show. (And you thought the British invented *Survivor*?) The episode was called "The Campout" and involved the Olesons and the Ingallses going off into the woods on an ill-fated camping spree, resulting in Nellie's near drowning.

Now, the producers were not without mercy. First off, both Melissa and I were given wet suits to wear under our costumes. This not only provided an element of flotation but also kept the cold water from direct contact with our bodies. A lot of the people who fell into the river without wet suits or vests found that their chest muscles tended to seize up in the cold, making it even more difficult to breathe and/or swim, causing them to die quickly. In addition to being spared that, we had numerous safety measures in place. In the scene where we are floating downstream, clinging to what appears to be a clump of driftwood and old bushes, we are actually holding on to a large, black inflated inner tube covered in driftwood and old bushes (hard to sink).

Unfortunately, we were not tied to this craft in any way. It was our responsibility to hold on. Besides, there was that bit at the end of the episode where we had to abandon our clump and swim to shore (very dicey). At one point, William Claxton, who was directing this episode, briefly considered a sequence where we would have gone over some medium-size falls with the raft. (Well, not Melissa and me—professional stuntwomen pretending to be us.) Mercifully, someone suggested they first try a shot with dummies. On the first bump, the heads were torn from the bodies on impact. The rest was obliterated shortly thereafter. Needless to say, that sequence was removed from the script.

As it was, all we had to do was not be stupid enough to let go of the raft, and when we reached the one safe part of the river where we could realistically paddle to shore, we'd just have to remember not to stop paddling at any point, and we'd pretty much be okay. As we were preparing to shoot the scene, William Claxton explained the situation: "All right, all you have to do is go from here to over there. It's not that far, or that deep. If for some reason the current catches you, you slip, or you lose your footing or whatever, don't panic. Ron and a bunch of the guys are down there in the bushes, and they'll catch you."

Our attention was directed to a group of smiling grips in black wet suits, hiding in the shrubbery, looking like a Navy SEAL unit. "Now, should the guys be unable to catch you for some reason, you're too far out in the water, or the current's too strong, a few feet down from them we have a rope strung across the river. Grab it and hang on; we'll come pull you out. If you miss that rope, there's another rope about fifteen feet down. Grab that."

Melissa and I still felt a bit skittish. "Um, what if we miss the second rope?" I inquired.

"Well, honey, after that, we pick up your bodies in the next town," explained the stunt coordinator. He wasn't exactly kidding. About twenty yards after that last rope was that waterfall they tried the dummies out on.

Now, although Melissa and I both knew that our brave crew loved us and would gladly drown themselves to the last man trying to save us, we also realized that many big, strong professional rafters had indeed died in this river, so it might not be up to them. We knew that, as usual, our survival depended on remembering those valuable four little words from our stunt team: "Just don't fuck up."

So, on the first take, when our little pile of shrubbery beached on the rocks, and it was time to make a break for it to shore, did we ever. It wasn't far, but all I could think of, much like when you're climbing a ladder, and your mind keeps saying, "Don't look down!" was "DO NOT look downstream!" When my foot touched bottom without slipping, I breathed a sigh of relief and toppled forward onto the sand.

Of course, we found this sort of thing dreadfully exciting. What really bugged us was the cold. Well, that and the other issue. You see, Melissa and I were standing patiently, hip deep in water, waiting for the director and crew to set the shot and whatnot. Waiting and waiting and waiting . . . When Melissa said, “God, do I have to pee!”

“Me, too, now that you mention it.”

So off we trundled to AD Maury Dexter to tell him it was time for us to use the ladies’ room. “Now, girls, there’s a slight problem here,” Maury pointed out. “The bathrooms are all the way up the hill. If you go to the bathroom now, we have to put you in the car, drive you up the hill, *take off* the costumes, take off the wet suits, and have you go pee. Then you’ll have to put on the wet suits” (the now soggy and hard to put back on wet suits), “put the costumes back on” (ditto; actually, double ditto), “and we’ll have to drive you back down the hill. Do you have any idea how long this is all going to take?”

We groaned. We knew this would be a huge hassle, and we remembered what a pain these stupid suits were to put on that morning back when they were all nice and dry and full of talcum powder. We could only imagine what a total pain in the ass it would be to try to repeat the procedure soaking wet. “Look, it’s only an hour and a half till lunch. Why don’t you girls just hang on, and you’ll be done with this shot by then, okay?” We sighed and trudged off back to the river.

Time passed. And passed. Slowly. Water rushed by. Rushing, rushing, rushing. Splashing, trickling, sloshing. And the cold. We were standing waist high in freezing water; I realized I could no longer feel my feet. My lips had begun to go slightly blue, when I turned to look at Melissa. She was smiling. A little too much. Not a nice, natural smile, but an evil, satisfied, smirking smile of, shall we say, discovery. And her eyes were just a little too wide.

"Oh, God no, tell me you *didn't*!" I said.

"Do it. It'll keep you warm," she replied.

"Oh, yuck, that is sooo gross, Melissa!"

"No, listen, I'm telling you! Do it! Just a little at a time. It warms up the whole suit. Besides, it's still only twelve-thirty. You're not seriously going to hold out for another hour?"

She had a good point. Well, two good points, actually. I was freezing, and I really had to go. So with all the strength it took to overcome fourteen years of toilet training, I peed in my pants. God, she was right. I did feel better. I no longer felt like my kidneys were going to burst, and the wet suit heated up like, well, like someone had just taken a big hot piss in it, frankly, but there you are. It was better than freezing. And who would know? We were more than waist deep *in a river,* for God's sake. It wasn't like anyone was gonna hear the trickling.

So there the future president of the Screen Actors Guild and I stood for the next hour or so, happily pissing away in our wet suits (just a little at a time, we learned: the trick is to make it last). But it wasn't like no one ever found out. After all, the wardrobe women had to pick up the suits and costumes from our dressing rooms. I don't know exactly who screamed at whom, and I can only imagine what epithets were used, but all I know is, we were never denied bathroom privileges again.

Being with Melissa was never dull—which is why we loved spending time together away from *Little House.* You would think we'd have been sick of each other at the end of a long work week, but no, we made a habit of having slumber parties at each other's homes. Of course, sometimes we were the only guests. We didn't care. It was just an excuse to stay up all night and hang out together.

We had different living arrangements and families with totally different lifestyles and levels of wealth. Melissa's father, Paul Gilbert, was a successful actor, and her family already had money before she was on *Little House,* so they lived in a big house in Encino with a guest house and maids. My family lived in a two-bedroom apartment in West Hollywood, where my father ran his management office out of the dining room. We didn't have a guest house or a maid. We had a pullout sofa in the living room and my dad running around with a vacuum.

It was sort of like the "Town Party, Country Party" episode of the show, except Melissa lived in the Mercantile with all the dolls and the fancy furniture, and I was the one with the trundle bed and the creek (except, in my case, the creek we went to play in was Santa Monica Boulevard). Despite our differences in status, Melissa loved coming over to sleep at my place as much as, if not more than, I liked going to her house.

At my house, a big treat was going to the supermarket and buying all sorts of cake mixes and frostings to then make into elaborately decorated cakes. Of course, our idea of "elaborate" was a bit closer to "chaos," resulting in huge, sloppy purple-and-green things covered in silver and gold sprinkles. We didn't care, as long as chocolate was involved. We bought tons of stuff: soda, Twinkies, candy, cupcakes, and things like Screaming Yellow Zonkers. I later found out that part of the treat for Melissa was that in her world, she didn't go to the store. Groceries just sort of appeared at her house, bought by the help or delivered. Her house was way up in the hills and not in walking distance of a local store. She'd never been allowed to stroll out the front door and say, "Hey, I'm picking up a few things, I'll be back later."

And she wasn't allowed to have sugar. At all. No candy, no gum, no cookies, no cupcakes, no soda, none of it. It was all expressly forbidden by her mother, a minor detail that Melissa conveniently neglected to mention to me or my parents or anyone else for about fifteen years. Essentially she came to my house for the sugar and total lack of supervision. Who could blame her? She was like a dog off the leash.

One of the best parts of going to the store was freaking out people who recognized us. What on earth would Laura Ingalls and Nellie Oleson be doing in the local supermarket, but more importantly, what the hell were they doing *together*? Fans of the show really believed us to be mortal enemies. Melissa once had a woman come up to her and warn her that I was in the store. People were frightened for her safety and tried to protect her from me. We thought this the height of hilarity and went to as many stores as we could to see how often we could re-create this experience.

One time, I took her to the 7-Eleven for Slurpees (we loved to see who could get a brain freeze faster), and we decided to buy these interesting little cakes called BabaRums. They were based on the real dessert baba au rhum, which has lots of real rum in it. But since they looked like Twinkies, and the checkout person had no issue selling them to kids, we assumed they didn't have any real alcohol in them.

We assumed wrong. After we quickly scarfed down three or four, the rum kicked in. "Oh my God, I'm drunk!" whispered Melissa.

I realized that indeed she reeked of alcohol. These little cakes had been absolutely soaked in booze. We then decided that this was screamingly funny and ran back into the store and bought as many as we could carry out. Good call, as about a week later, someone noticed a bunch of eight-year-olds getting hammered at the school lunch table, and it soon hit the papers. BabaRums were revealed to be about forty proof and promptly taken off the market.

Years later, after Melissa recovered from a battle with alcoholism, she tried to pin it on me. "See? It's all your fault!" she joked. "You're the one who turned me onto BabaRums at the 7-Eleven!"

For Melissa, being with me was being free. She never mentioned to me or my parents the part about what TV shows she wasn't supposed to be watching or if there was something called a "bedtime" she was supposed to adhere to, or any nonsense like that. As a result, a typical weekend at my place always included staying up to watch *Saturday Night Live.* This was when the show was still new, fresh, politically oriented, and actually funny. These were the days of Chevy Chase, Gilda Radner, Garrett Morris, and John Belushi. We had a blast, eating huge piles of junk food washed down with punch and soda and watching not only *SNL* but all the late-night totally uncut movies shown on that new fabulous invention, cable TV.

And, of course, there was the thrill of danger. Real danger? No, not much. But to her, my neighborhood was really "slumming it." The first time she came to the front door of my apartment way back during our first year of the show (she and her whole family came to take me Christmas shopping), she stood in the doorway and actually said, no exaggeration: "Hurry up and let's get out of here, before we get stabbed!" The apartment was in West Hollywood at Hayworth and Fountain, not exactly a dangerous neighborhood. I found this hysterical and tried to imagine what she would do in South Central.

A couple of years later, in 1976, my family moved just down the street and wound up in the same apartment building as Gene LeBell, the famous wrestler and stuntman, whose mother owned the Olympic Auditorium. He made the news when he and a friend were arrested on suspicion of the murder of a business associate (though he was later acquitted of the charges). Everyone in the building was questioned by the FBI, and the atmosphere around the pool was rather awkward when he returned out on bail. Melissa absolutely begged to come over when he was released, and as soon as her mother dropped her off, she whispered with excited glee, "Which one's the murderer?"

Going to her house was very different, yet we managed to get up to a surprising amount of juvenile delinquency just the same. The place was huge. To me, it was like a hotel, with long halls with several rooms on each side. And there was that guest house, with a living room, a bedroom, its own bathroom, and a small kitchen. My entire family would have considered it reasonable living quarters. It was at one time the maid's quarters, then the pool house, and finally Melissa's first apartment when she turned eighteen. It made for great slumber parties, as it could accommodate huge numbers of girls, and, being separate from the house, you could make lots of noise without annoying Melissa's mom (which was something you really, really didn't want to do).

The Gilberts' kitchen was my favorite part. My family had lived in some places with big kitchens—some of the places we rented in the Hollywood hills were pretty impressive—but not like this. They had two refrigerators and an island, one of those huge structures in the middle of the kitchen that had its own stove burners and everything. I saw the caterers use it to heat up and arrange food when they had parties, but I never saw anyone cook on it, except Melissa and me, who used it to heat up pots of SpaghettiOs. I did not get the impression that Melissa's mother, Barbara, cooked. Over the years I got a lot of strange impressions about Melissa's mother. And not just from things Melissa said. Her mom did a swell job of being her own worst press agent all by herself.

I remember being there one day when she shouted across the house to her husband, Harold (husband number two out of a half dozen or so), that she wanted to go out to dinner. Well, what she actually said was, "Harrrrr-ooold! We gotta go out to dinner! The maid's been cooking again! The whole house smells like GARRRR-BAGE!" Apparently she was not a fan of Guatemalan cuisine.

One evening I was sitting at the table with Melissa, her brother, Jonathan, and her mom. We were seated in a strange arrangement with Barbara at the head of the table, me at the other head, and Jonathan and Melissa side by side to my right, as if we had left one side of the table open for the camera or perhaps the studio audience. It was chicken-and-rice night, and I was very hungry. Melissa and I had been running around all day, and I had worked up an appetite. Melissa was, as usual, playing with her food and not eating. Exercise only seemed to make her less hungry. And with Jonathan, who knows, he could have snuck out for a three-course meal at some point, and no one in that house would have even noticed.

Melissa's mom was becoming more and more upset. "Melissa! Eat your dinner! Jonathan, you, too!" She began to nag at the two of them, the usual rant about wasting food, don't-you-know-children-are-starving-in-China, when the conversation took an odd turn. She suddenly said, "Melissa, why can't you be more like Alison?"

What? I found out from Auntie Marion that she actually said this more than once. But then she really blew my mind. She was livid. "Melissa! Jonathan! IF YOU DON'T FINISH YOUR DINNER RIGHT NOW, I'M GOING TO GIVE IT TO ALISON!"

Give it to Alison? What was I now, *the dog*? I didn't say a word. I was floored. Melissa and Jonathan didn't say anything either. They both looked perfectly miserable.

"Fine! Alison, do you want this?"

Now, here was the rough part. I was really hungry. As I said, I had been running around all day (and I hadn't eaten anything earlier at my house since I knew was spending the night at the land of Unlimited Free Food and Two Refrigerators). And it *was* chicken and rice. And it was *really good.*

"Um . . . yes."

"Melissa! Jonathan! Give Alison your plates!" And she snatched up their plates of chicken and rice and forcefully slid them down the table to me. And I ate them. I proceeded to eat both their dinners, in front of them, while they sat there in silence, looking as if they were going to cry, as their mother continued to harangue and berate them. She finally felt she'd made her point or wore herself out, and it all mercifully ended.

Later, when Melissa and I were alone in her bedroom, I apologized. I said, "I'm sorry I ate your dinner." I felt that I should have protested somehow, but I can't imagine what I could possibly have said to Barbara that wouldn't have just gotten all of us in more trouble. "I didn't know what to do. She was just so mad, and I was really hungry."

Melissa said, "That's okay, it's not your fault. My mom pulls crap like that all the time. Are you still hungry? There's popsicles in the fridge." And then in the middle of the night, while her mother was fast asleep, we went into the magical giant kitchen and raided the two refrigerators to our hearts' content.

Despite her mother, we still had fun. Melissa and Jonathan were very creative. One afternoon, a whole group of kids, some fellow show biz brats and other rich kids from her Encino neighborhood, were over there, and they proudly announced that "there was a monster living in their garage." Now I, being the oldest, of course knew this was not a real monster, but I wondered what totally insane prank they had rigged, or what poor neighborhood dog or cat they had kidnapped and dressed up in costume. I figured I had better ask to see it right away so if it was really dangerous or involved some unsuspecting live animal, I could put an end to the prank quickly. (I also knew that, whatever it was, it would be a sight to behold and totally worth it.)

Jonathan kept swearing, on the Bible, on anything he could think of, cross his heart, that there was an actual monster in the garage. It was good to see that his total dedication to a performance was not confined to the set. The other kids and I gathered by the open garage door. Jonathan and Melissa explained that they had to put out "bait" to bring the monster out of its hiding place. "We feed it raw meat!" They proceeded to unwrap an enormous T-bone steak that they had pilfered from one of the infamous refrigerators. Now, this was the height of the 1970s' meat price inflation. People were actually boycotting beef in some places due to the high prices. This steak was top quality and looked big enough to have made dinner for four.

I was trying to calculate what ridiculous amount of money this thing had to have cost, when Jonathan, without so much as blinking, dropped it on the garage floor. Jonathan, not surprisingly, disappeared at that moment. Suddenly, Melissa shrieked, "There it is!"

I looked, and there, crawling out of the darkness at the back of the garage, was something large and furry. Slithering, really. It didn't seem to have any legs. Or a head. Just a large mass of lumbering, slithering shiny fur, inching across the floor toward its steak dinner. Really thick, shiny fur. Silvery, come to think of it. Kind of like a silver fox. Or a full-length silver fox fur coat. Melissa's aunt Stephanie's silver fox fur coat, to be exact. All $60,000 worth of it, on a fishing line, being dragged slowly across a filthy garage floor for the amusement of Melissa's slumber party guests.

I had to admit, this was pretty good. It was certainly the most expensively produced "monster in the garage" trick I'd ever seen, if not the most convincing. After we all finished shrieking and clapping, Melissa and Jonathan quickly got the coat off the floor, cut the fishing line, and simply hung it back up in the closet. I was relieved to see Jonathan at least rinse off the steak before rewrapping it and putting it back in the fridge. I shuddered to think what adventures the rest of the food in that house went through before it got to the table.

I was amazed at Melissa's and her family's attitude toward food. I couldn't imagine wasting food at our house. Like so many actors, we behaved as if every meal was our last, to the point that at "good" parties, my father would sometimes have to remind me, "Don't eat like an actor!" At least I hadn't resorted to carrying around Tupperware in my purse. I actually knew people who did that. They could be at a formal black-tie event, but when everyone turned their backs, they would snatch up as many hors d'oeuvres as they could grab and stuff them into the plastic container in their handbag.

I eventually saw the sense in this behavior when we ran out of money, which never happened permanently. Well, with actors, nothing is ever permanent, is it? My friend comedian Robin Tyler says, "Actors never say they're poor. They're always 'broke.' It's always just temporary. 'Broke' is 'poor with hope.' "

Then one day, when I was about fourteen, we went "broke." It was an accident. We had it all worked out. *Gumby* and *Underdog* had folded years earlier, and my mother's occasional guest spots on other cartoons were not frequent enough to pay the bills. So she was working downtown at a "straight job," playing executive secretary to the head of a big shipping company. She didn't like it, but she was good at it, and it paid well. At that time we needed the money. My father had left Seymour Heller and Associates to start his own management company, Arngrim and Associates, which, after squeezing out all of the other associates except his friend Jess, eventually turned into Arngrim and Petersen and became a perfectly viable business. A former actor and model, Jess was the taller, younger, good looking, and even more viciously sarcastic half of the management team. Whenever Arngrim and Petersen needed to play "good cop/bad cop" in a negotiation, Jess was the ultimate "bad cop."

But like most companies, in the beginning it barely made a dime. My parents had also spent insane amounts of money over the years on my brother: special schools, psychiatrists, lawyers, bail bondsmen. (When I was in junior high, my address book was from a bail bonds company. I was the only kid on my block with a little black book that read, "twenty-four hours' service—we'll get you OUT!") They had no savings to fall back on.

My mother's paycheck paid the rent and a few bills, but there wasn't much left over. My father was bringing in just enough to cover the car payment—a lease, of course (they still had yet to own anything). Where they came up short was on food. So my parents sat me down and explained the situation. It was temporary, they said. My father would be making more money in a few months, and they'd be out of debt soon. They weren't about to start charging me rent, but as *Little House* was now well into its second year, and I was making more money than anyone in the house (or probably half the people we knew), would it be possible for me to kick in some cash?

They suggested groceries. It seemed fair, since, being a teenager, I ate practically everything in the house anyway. I enjoyed cooking—why not take up shopping as well? I would be free to plan whatever menus I liked and make purchases accordingly. I would learn about comparison shopping and food prices. Plus, we wouldn't starve to death.

It worked perfectly for a while. I happily raced up and down the aisles of the grocery store, throwing in whatever I wanted. "Let's have steak! And ice cream! And king crab!" I'd cry. "You're buying!" replied my parents. At the checkout stand, they'd whisper to each other and then turn to me sheepishly and say, "Um, can we have some wine?"

"Sure!" I said. I was always happy to indulge them.

Paying for the food wasn't financial hardship for me. A chunk of my money was always sent off safely to the trust fund before I ever got my paycheck, and in the weeks I wasn't on the show, I actually received unemployment insurance. It wasn't enough for someone to support a whole family on, but it was a lot to a teenager. So spending a hundred bucks at the supermarket from time to time was hardly going to break the bank.

Until the accident. The show's accountants had made a mistake with my checks. They hadn't taken the correct amount out for the trust fund for several checks. They had to fix this at once. So they took the amount to make it up out of my next several checks, which, with taxes and agent commissions, left absolutely nothing. My checks were for one or two dollars, for about a month. And, as fate would have it, I was suddenly in every episode back to back for several weeks. No paycheck, no unemployment, which, under the newly established monetary system at our house, meant no groceries. *No food.*

"So now what the hell are were we going to do?" I asked.

"We'll find a way," said my mother.

It is amazing what you can do with leftovers. Other people's leftovers especially. I brought home food from the set. When we were on location, and it was catered, I brought back chicken, meat, and vegetables. When we were at Paramount, and there was no catering, I brought back the donuts, and we ate those. Somebody bought us a bucket of chicken. And the next day my mother made soup from the bones.

Let me make this clear: fast food–style fried chicken, such as KFC, is not—repeat, *not*—designed to be used for soup like fresh chicken. It was absolutely horrible. But we ate it.

After a week of this nonsense, my mother told my father that since her paycheck wasn't coming for a few days, it was on him to go get some cash and buy some real food. Now. Yes, she understood he was starting a new business, but tomorrow morning he was to go out and get additional employment or find some other source of immediate cash. *Or else.*

Both he and Jess Petersen dutifully went out the next day and tried their best. Although Jess had much more classic "office experience" than my father, if Jess had been cut out for normal work, he would have stayed at Seymour Heller's and not followed my dad. They tried some sort of phone sales gig, but it paid dismally, and they hated it. Determined not to return to the apartment empty-handed, they eventually went to a restaurant. They did not apply for jobs. They sat down and ordered coffee, about all they could pay for. Then, taking turns, one keeping watch while the other went from table to table, they stole every tip in the restaurant, and they used it to buy food.

That night, as we ate our delicious, much appreciated, if ill-gotten dinner, they solemnly promised to one day return to the restaurant and tip the staff heavily. Needless to say, I was ecstatic when about two months later my payment situation was resolved, and the money came pouring back into the house. My father was just not cut out for a life of crime.

CHAPTER ELEVEN

THE INFAMOUS WHEELCHAIR EPISODE

> **MRS. OLESON: Laura Ingalls! What have you done with that filthy animal?**
>
> **LAURA: Nellie, your mother wants you!**

There's something about "Bunny." Almost every single person I have ever spoken to about *Little House on the Prairie* has told me this episode, which aired October 18, 1976, during our third season, is their favorite. It's the case with men, women, children, straight people, gay people, everybody. It is the favorite episode in the United States; it is the favorite episode in France; and I have heard it is the favorite in Argentina, Bangladesh, Japan, and the Middle East. *Everybody* loves this episode. And it is, without a doubt, the most bizarre episode, not just of *Little House,* but of any 1970s "family" TV show.

The gist of the story is this: Nellie, while beating the crap out of the poor horse she took from Laura in the previous Christmas episode, causes the animal to bolt and throw her. While regaining consciousness (insert lots of "Quick, get Doc Baker!" and dramatic music here), she overhears her mother ranting on about it being Laura's fault. Never one to miss an opportunity to inflict misery on Laura, Nellie, of course, wakes up and announces that she can't feel her legs. Doc Baker, ever the genius, makes some bizarre statement about these things sometimes going away on their own (she's not paraplegic—it's just a phase!), but Mrs. Oleson is off on another bipolar fit of hysteria and screams that Laura has crippled her daughter. This sets off an elaborate chain of events, where not just Laura but the entire town is dragged into Nellie's narcissistic fantasy of the week. It's not just that she has Laura doing all her homework—Doc Baker is helpless, Mrs. Oleson is in full nervous breakdown mode, Pa has to drop what he's doing and fix up a wheelchair for Nellie, and even the normally rational Mr. Oleson is seen quietly weeping in a corner of the Mercantile. Sicker still, it appears that a large part of Nellie's motive is to prevent Laura from dating a boy at school whom she has a crush on. (As if Nellie ever had a hope in hell of getting him in the first place!)

Of course, during all this, Nellie makes a point of getting out of her chair whenever she can to have a good stretch, get more candy, or dance with her favorite doll. Ruining everyone's life is just all in a day's work. Laura eventually catches her at it, and on the pretense of "getting some fresh air," rolls her to the top of the highest hill in town near Hanson's mill and shoves her over the edge, sending her bouncing and screaming down into the mill creek. Mrs. Oleson arrives just in time to see her daughter drag herself up to her feet. Discovering that she can now walk, she shrieks, "It's a miracle!" faints, and falls off her horse onto her ass. The town is saved, and Laura gets her horse back and goes fishing with the boy from school. Nellie flips out, breaks a lot of stuff, and swears her revenge. And everyone lives happily ever after. Or until next week's show. But it gets weirder.

Right before we were scheduled to shoot this episode, I, like a complete idiot, managed to break my arm while skateboarding. I say like a complete idiot for several reasons: (1) People on TV shows aren't supposed to be skateboarding or skydiving or taking part in any other excessively dangerous sports. (2) I was not wearing a helmet or padding of any kind, not so much as a sweat band on my wrist. (3) I wasn't even doing an exciting, death-defying stunt. What was I doing when I fell? I was standing perfectly still on my skateboard contemplating what to do next. And I tipped over. Yes, tipped over—*like a cow.* I slammed my arm down to try to break my fall so my head wouldn't take all the weight. I managed to skin my knee, break my wrist, and give myself a huge purple lump on the side of my head. Very embarrassing. To make matters worse, when Jess Petersen scraped me off the pavement and drove me home, I was told my arm could not possibly be broken, and I most certainly did not need to go to a doctor. After all, everyone knew what a sissy I was: "If it was really broken, you'd be crying!"

A few hours later, when the swelling kicked in, and my wrist began to turn interesting colors and throb with pain, I did indeed start crying. This was solved by my brother (he was living with my parents *again*; over the years, he would often move back when his money ran out, bringing wife number one, two, or three with him), who cheerfully offered me a few samples from his pilfered stash of prescription drugs that had been randomly pulled from between the sofa cushions. I selected a pink pill (it looked pretty) and went to bed. I had no idea what it was, and for once I didn't care.

Come Monday morning, there was no getting around it. I had to see the doctor. The X-ray showed what is endearingly called a "green stick" break of the big bone in my wrist. This means it's not snapped all the way through, but half broken, like a green twig. That didn't make it hurt any less. I was sent off to an orthopedic specialist, who looked at my X-ray with disgust and demanded to know why the hell I had waited three days to come in. "What did you think you were going to do, wish it away?" he snarled sarcastically. I reminded him that I was a teenager and didn't have a car. It was up to my parents to take me to the doctor. I wasn't the one suffering from a permanent case of denial. ("You're fine!") He stopped giving me a hard time and went about putting on a cast.

The fun was just beginning. While I was at the doctor's, my agent, Lew Sherrill, called Michael Landon and Kent McCray, our other producer, to tell them that one of their lead actresses had had "a teeny little accident." Nothing serious, of course, but she's got "a tiny little cast on her arm." I, of course, had to report to the office so they could see the extent of the injury and reschedule episodes if necessary.

Now, remember, this was the 1970s, when they still used the big, plaster bandage casts. The fiberglass stuff had just come out; my second cast for the last three weeks of healing was one of the new small fiberglass numbers. But the first cast was huge. It went from the base of my fingers, past the elbow, almost to my shoulder, and it was big and white and puffy looking. Everyone was very nice to me at the meeting. Michael made lots of jokes about my being clumsy or having been injured in some sort of fight. He proudly autographed it in a prominent spot, then looked me in the eye and said very seriously, with just a touch of menace: "Okay, but you're not going skateboarding anymore . . . RIGHT?"

"Oh, *right.* No, no sir, no more skateboarding. No."

Then he was back to his grinning, giggling self, and I was slapped on the back and told I could go. As soon as the door closed behind me, I could hear Michael shouting: "JESUS CHRIST! HE SAID SHE HAD A TINY LITTLE CAST! DID YOU SEE THAT FUCKING THING?" I could hear what sounded like fists being pounded on desks, wastebaskets being kicked across the room. "WHAT THE HELL ARE WE GOING TO DO WITH THAT?" Then it quieted down to murmurs and whispers.

After a while the door opened again. Michael was all smiles, as if nothing had happened. I was invited back in and told that they had come up with a solution. Because the first part of the "Bunny" episode involved my being in an accident and faking a serious injury, they would write into the script that I did in fact have a minor injury. Nellie would break her arm and get bruised in the fall (lending some believability to her claims of paralysis), and the real cast would be covered in an 1800s version. The next episode would be delayed, by switching it out with one I wasn't in, and by that time I would be down to a small cast or something easily dealt with through camera angles. Again, Michael tousled my hair and said, "Remember, no more skateboards, right?" And then this gem: "If you ever break your arm skateboarding again . . ." He paused, flashing me a dimpled Charles Ingalls grin, which then suddenly disappeared. "I'll break the other one." This was followed by his high-pitched maniacal laughter. A joke, of course, but I decided that skateboarding might be bad for my health in more ways than one.

Shooting the episode was like making an action film. There were all kinds of stunt people and special effects involved. Who would be beating the horse? Not me! I couldn't ride to begin with, and in my current condition I was not going anywhere near a horse. I stood on a ladder, as the cameramen shot me from the chest up to avoid the cast, and using my good arm, I proceeded to whip the living daylights out of the side of the ladder. The editors crosscut this with footage of the professional stunt girl on a real horse pretending to beat him while he was doing all sorts of rearing and bucking maneuvers that would be utterly impossible for an amateur like me. She took off at a furious speed heading straight for a tree. Cut.

Now, how do you have someone ride face first into a tree branch at high speed and be knocked unconscious without killing them? You fake it. I sat on a box. Two grips held a piece of Plexiglas in front of my face. I bounced a little as if riding, and at the crucial moment, another grip swung a tree branch into the Plexiglas—slam! I simply rolled my eyes back into my head and fell off the box. I was good at falling over, and I was even better at playing dead or unconscious. I lay back in the nice, cool grass—a real treat, as usually in Simi we were stomping around in the hot sun, on the gravel road—and tried not to actually fall asleep. Here we were under the trees, and all I had to do was lie there with my eyes closed and look injured. And I was getting paid the same as I did for walking and talking. It was very relaxing. I nearly dozed off once or twice, as I listened to the two Melissas' frantic whispers take after take: "She's hurt bad!" "Quick! Get Doc Baker!" I greedily reveled in what it would be like to actually have anybody worry about me that much. (I sure as hell didn't hear anything like that when I was lying on my back in the parking lot with the real broken arm.) I could see how Nellie would think this was the start of something good.

Just as I was thinking this was really the life, and I might never open my eyes, I felt a strange sensation in my nose. It wasn't the blood—they had put a lovely cinematic trickle of fake blood running out of my nose for this shot. There was something else there now. In my nose! And then I heard "Shhh . . . keep it rolling and . . . cut!" followed by the infamous shrieking giggle. I opened my eyes. While I played dead, instead of just saying "cut" to end the scene, Michael had quietly reached over and stuck his finger up my nose and insisted that they get it all on film.

I got to spend most of the episode in bed. I liked the big Nellie brass bed I had on the show and developed quite a fixation on brass beds because of it. In fact, the first bed I owned when I had my own place was brass, and I insisted on nothing but brass beds for years. For my pretend injuries, the makeup artists did a good job re-creating my real skateboard-related wounds. I had a big bruise on my head in the same spot I had given myself the real one the week before. This was bigger and more purple and made out of a sort of waxy putty. At the end of the day, I could peel it off and stick it on the wall or on my bedpost like a piece of gum. The first day I wore it home and tried to convince my mother I'd fallen again and that it was real. (She didn't buy it.) After that, I stuck it on my notebook and took it to school.

They managed to turn my 1970s cast into an 1800s version with wood and cloth by covering it with boards and bandaging up the whole mess. It looked very sturdy, which was a good thing, because even if they didn't have to cover the cast, we certainly had to cover the autographs. After Michael, everyone on the show signed it. People wrote all sorts of rude things, drew pictures. It was great! And then came the wheelchair.

Propelling yourself in a nineteenth-century-era wicker wheelchair is not like pushing yourself around in an efficient streamlined chair. It requires a lot more effort, and steering is nearly impossible. In the scene where Doc Baker unveils the chair and lets Nellie try it out, he says, "It's all right; you can use your other arm." In the script, Nellie's arm injury didn't interfere with movement. But because of the way my arm was broken, and because the cast went up over my elbow, actually turning the wheel was extremely difficult. Every time he said that, I kept wanting to yell, "No, I can't!"

I particularly enjoyed the scene where Willie catches Nellie out of the chair, and she has to threaten him to keep silent. Jonathan was still quite small then. I could practically pick him up and sling him over my shoulder if I wanted to, and he would go along with anything that was thrown at him in a scene. If I was supposed to hit him, I only had to tap him, and he would throw himself across the room and collapse on the floor as if I had punched him full force. When he got up, he would grin with pride and ask, "How was that?"

In this scene, when he came into the room, I had to figure out how to grab him, blow out the candle he was carrying, turn him around, shut the door, and clap my hand over his mouth, all while only able to use one arm. I don't know how I did it, but it looked great. In one quick move, I wound up with my good arm wrapped around his throat, and my hand over his mouth like I was going to smother him. I held the candle in my other hand next to his face so I could hit him with it if I had to. I looked really menacing.

In later years, looking at this scene, I do get a slight case of the shudders. I watch how expertly I pin him, stifle his ability to scream, then threaten him and explain why we were going to do things *my* way. I would ask where on earth I'd ever seen anybody do anything so horrible to anyone, but I didn't have to. And my imitation had been perfect.

After an entire hour of tormenting everyone in Walnut Grove with my fake invalid act, things finally hit the fan. Mrs. Oleson goes to collect Laura's horse in order to have it killed. They even dressed her in an almost exact replica of the costume worn by the old lady who comes to take Toto in *The Wizard of Oz.* "You and your little dog, too," indeed. She had on a black-and-gray-checked dress and a straw hat—just like Elmira Gulch. But who could resist the chance to put Katherine MacGregor in Margaret Hamilton drag? And with Melissa doing her best Judy Garland choked sobs ("Please don't take my horse!")? Well, it was priceless.

I think that one of the reasons this episode became so popular is because it blatantly parodies classic films. Besides *The Wizard of Oz,* we have a definite homage to *What Ever Happened to Baby Jane?* When Melissa takes me out in the chair for my "fresh air" and begins pushing me up the hill, the imagery is unmistakable: the blond curls, the bitchy attitude versus the poor put-upon girl with the long brown hair. But now there's a twist. Which one is in the chair today? Oh my God! Blanche has finally put Jane in the wheelchair! I have had many people who saw this episode in adulthood tell me that they howl with laughter at the physical resemblance to a bizarre role reversal, with me as Bette Davis and Melissa as Joan Crawford. They smugly ask if I or anyone on the show had ever "made the connection." What they don't realize is, not only did we make the connection, but we got the joke while we were filming it. All the grown-ups on the set knew the film very well, and Melissa and I were fans of the pre-cable "midnight movies" that ran on weekends and so had seen most of the great creepy classics. Indeed, as we rehearsed pushing me to the top of the hill, giggles broke out here and there among the crew. And then the whispers. "Oh my God, it so is!" "Yeah, isn't it?" "Yeah, but the other one's in the chair!" "Oh my God! It's Blanche's revenge!" And what revenge! All the way down the hill into the water.

A lot of fans ask if I actually performed this stunt myself. The answer is yes. And no. First was the great push off, the launch. For this, a steel cable was attached to the back of the chair. Melissa pushed and let go, and I screamed as the chair began to tip over the edge . . . and stopped. The cable jerked taught, and the chair stayed put. But I almost didn't. You see, there was nothing holding me in the chair. I was just sitting there sliding around in my nightgown with no seat belt, nothing. If the chair jerked to a stop, and I didn't . . . Oh well. So I clutched the armrests as best I could with one hand not working that well.

Then came the big plunge. First thing I did was get out of the chair and walk away to let the stunt girl sit down. This was actually dangerous stuff, and Michael wouldn't have let me do it if I wanted to. Not only did the stunt girl manage to stay in the thing as it rattled and bounced down the rocky slope, when she hit the water, she shot out of the chair and did a full somersault into the air before splashing down. Without hurting herself. Or having the wig fly off. I was very impressed.

But I wasn't totally off the hook. They still needed footage of me in the chair. So they took me to another hill, down by the Little House itself. It was less steep, with no water at the bottom, but much, much longer. This was to give ample time to capture me on film, screaming my head off. The grips set up a dolly so that the camera was on wheels, and they laid down boards like temporary railroad tracks for it to roll down. The camera was kept secure, of course. Me, again, not so much. Ropes were attached to the chair, not for safety, really, but so that the crew could steer it a bit in order to get a good shot and to keep it from running into the camera. The priorities were clear: a good camera would cost a lot more to replace than a child actor.

I had no lines per se—all I had to do was go for a ride and scream. A lot. How hard could it be? Action! And the chair took off. Fast. Downhill. Over the rocks. Lots of rocks, large rocks, that caused the chair to buck and bounce sometimes right off the ground and tilt wildly from side to side. If you recall, this was not a wheelchair in the way we think of wheelchairs today—large, heavy, sturdily built things intended to navigate streets and curbs, something a disabled person could drive to work. This was a wheelchair designed back when the disabled were referred to as "invalids" and expected to go no farther than their carpeted front parlor. It was barely intended for outdoor use and certainly never meant to roll downhill at high speed. Which is why, among other things, there was no seat belt. So, every time it hit a bump, which was pretty much constantly, I felt my butt bounce right up off and nearly out of the chair. And every time it landed, I felt it slam into my tailbone. My teeth were rattling in my head. I was hanging on for dear life, hoping my hands wouldn't sweat too much and make me lose my grip.

After an excruciating and terrifying couple of minutes, the chair finally stopped, and they cut. It was agreed that we needed another take. Back up the hill the camera, chair, and I went.

I figured this wouldn't be so bad, now that I had the hang of it. Action! The chair went even faster this time. And now for kicks and dramatic effect, the crew members holding the ropes thought it would be a great idea to tell me that the rope had broken. They started yelling, "Oh no, the rope broke!" and simply let go of their end. On top of trying to scream loudly and convincingly for the scene, I was convinced I was going to fall out of the stupid chair, get my nightgown caught in the wheels, and get myself ripped to shreds. Besides that, the ride was now so bumpy I was starting to hear what sounded like the screws and bolts that held the chair together coming apart, combined with the sound of what seemed like my brain vibrating inside my head. And did anybody remember that I had a real broken arm? I screamed bloody murder.

In the end, I lived, and we got some really great footage, but this sequence definitely qualifies for the category of "Do Not Try This at Home." And we mustn't forget the water. Thankfully, I didn't have to do the back flip. I just had to "emerge" from the pond, adding a sound track of wailing and crying. But I had one teeny problem: the plaster cast. You can't get those things wet, or they'll disintegrate. At home, when I took a shower, I was told to put a plastic trash bag over it, so we removed my fake 1800s splint and put a plastic trash bag over my cast and secured it with rubber bands. The splint went back on over that. And into the pond I went.

This was not a natural pond. Nothing in Walnut Grove was. It was Simi Valley, where there was no water. It was a desert. There was no cute little brook by the Ingalls house, no stream to turn a mill wheel. The water was all fake, brought in from the outside, pumped in artificially. And not being a real running stream, it got a bit, shall we say, stagnant. Just like my first pond in "Country Girls," it was covered in thick, gunky algae. I have no idea what possible germs or parasites lived in it. I had to not just get in it, but put my face under the water and come up spitting. Again, total immersion.

Michael and I stood there in the stagnant, moss-covered pool of goo while the cameramen set up the shot. It seemed we were always standing around together in foul water. Was this man trying to drown me? Did he have some sort of fetish? Michael turned to me and asked, "Do you have a swimming pool at your house?" "No," I replied. "Well, good," he smiled brightly, "because after this you can swim in your toilet!"

I took a very deep breath, closed my eyes tight, and down I went. When I came up, there was just enough water up my nose and on my lips that I didn't have to get too big a drink of the stuff to spit it all over the place and sputter wildly. I heaved out all my breath in one of those great big, pitiful Nellie wails, and after the "Cut!" everyone hooted and cheered and clapped. As I climbed out, I saw that in addition to the slime and the algae, I now had several small snails on my nightgown and in my hair. Ah, the glamour of show business.

I think it was the huge success of this moment that prompted the large number of episodes over the years that involved dunking Nellie into ponds, rivers, and mud puddles and pouring things like water, dirt, eggs, and flour over my head. I apparently give my best performances when I have crap all over me. Because of this, I have developed a deep, lifelong appreciation of the joy and wonder of very hot baths and showers with lots of soap.

People often ask, "What the hell are you doing in there so long?" *Sigh.* Just trying to get clean, just trying to get clean.

CHAPTER TWELVE

BOOBS, BOYS, AND SATAN

NELLIE: What do you want to know?

LAURA: Well, what is it about you that attracts men?

NELLIE: Well, that's obvious, isn't it? My natural attributes.

LAURA: Like what?

NELLIE: Like my natural curly hair, and my smile. Mother says I'm beautiful, but I wouldn't go that far.

LAURA: Neither would I!

The set of *Little House* was an interesting place to go through puberty, especially as a girl. It was an insanely male-dominated, testosterone-fueled environment. Yet our crew was protective and territorial when it came to us girls. I have heard horror stories from other teenage actresses who had the misfortune to develop breasts in the presence of an all-male film crew: cat calls, obscene propositions, grabbing, and pinching. But this wasn't how it was done on our set and certainly not to me. The impression I was given in no uncertain terms was that if anyone bothered me, all I had to do was tell one of the guys on the crew, and the body would never be found.

I had huge crushes on both Ronnie, the prop man (and not just because he had all the peppermint sticks in the mercantile), and Ron Cardarelli, the key grip. Cardarelli was a classic New York Italian type, in the Fonzie/Vinnie Barbarino mold, complete with a cigarette behind his ear and a toothpick hanging out of his mouth. He even sometimes said, "Yo." I practically swooned.

I think it was the contrast that was such a turn-on. All of us actresses were covered from neck to ankle in our modest 1800s finery, all ruffles, lace petticoats, and pantaloons. Ours was different from the other shows on TV at the time. Shows like *Charlie's Angels* had plotlines filled with discos, strip clubs, and hookers, any excuse to get the female cast into skimpy outfits for what had even been officially referred to by the networks as "T&A": tits and ass. From what I've heard, executives routinely sent memos to show producers demanding "more T&A!" What on earth could the network demand from *Little House*? More bodice and bustle? Michael Landon and his sweaty chest were the closest thing to sex on the show. Even kissing was considered a big deal and usually followed by an immediate proposal of marriage. And with so many children present, nearly all the time, the actors and show personnel made at least an attempt to restrain themselves from any of the blatant sluttiness that was common on sets. This atmosphere, along with the costumes, gave the whole set a weird feeling of overheated, quasi-repressed Victorian sexuality. It was always there, simmering and bubbling under the surface.

And there in the sweltering heat of Simi, surrounding all the proper, corseted ladies, was the crew: all male, every one of them stripped to the waist, in jeans or shorts, covered in sweat and tattoos, reeking of beer and cigarettes, muscles rippling as they climbed ladders, hoisted heavy equipment, and reached up to adjust smoking-hot lights. There was something very *Lady Chatterley* about the whole thing. But despite their powerful position, the men on the crew did nothing but take care of me. They doted on me and told me to eat my vegetables and drink my milk. When I got braces, Cardarelli nicknamed me "Teeth" and kept reminding me how beautiful my smile would be when they came off.

Only once did I ever hear one of them make a remark indicating they had even noticed my development. I was wearing one of my usual lunchtime outfits. I didn't dare eat lunch in my costumes because I was a notorious spiller of food and drink, and one spot would be a disaster. So I always took off the dress and wore the petticoats, tights, and boots, but topped off with a T-shirt. Sometimes, I ditched the petticoats, too, and wore cut-off shorts over the tights. This was a particularly fetching look—revealing yet functional, like some sort of odd dance rehearsal outfit, combined with the ringlets and high-heeled boots. I looked a little like a girl superhero in a Japanese comic book. I was drinking a pint of milk. I was one of the only teenage girls I knew who drank milk regularly and actually preferred it to soda. I was leaning back, taking a long drag of milk, when I noticed two crew members staring at me. They just stared and didn't say a word. Finally, one turned to the other and said quietly, "I don't know. Must be all that milk." That is as close to a comment on my body as I got from any of them in my seven years on the show.

Some people, however, were another story. Poor Baby Carrie. Not only was she one of the most hapless, dopiest children in television history, but she was played by twins. It took two people to play someone that dumb. But they weren't dumb. They were just babies. Adorable babies. Rachel Lindsay and Robin Sidney Greenbush had already had what could be called a successful career before *Little House*. Together, they had played the baby in the movie *Sunshine*. They were also from a crazy show-business family, as their father was Billy Green Bush from *Five Easy Pieces* and that weird Robert Blake movie, *Electra Glide in Blue*. But we didn't really see much of him. We got Carol, their mother, instead.

People have often asked me, "Just what is wrong with Baby Carrie?" "Why can't Baby Carrie talk properly?" The girls seem to be perfectly nice, intelligent, articulate young women now, so how come on the show, every line of Baby Carrie's dialogue sounded like "Pah! Umma gumma boo gurble twee!" Well, if you ever met their mother, you'd understand. Even though she was a grown woman—an attractive, blond, heavily made-up woman, a twang-talkin', southern-fried, good ol' gal—a lot of what she said sounded very much like "Umma gumma boo gurble twee," thanks to her countrified accent. Why does Baby Carrie fall down the hill during the opening credits? Because she was stupid and clumsy? No. Here's what really happened.

They always switched the girls out every few hours, so they could take naps. It was the first season, the first episode, and when it was time to shoot the "Baby Carrie runs down the hill" scene, the director called for a "fresh twin." Mother Carol grabbed up the resting child and quickly put her little shoes back on. On the wrong feet. So the poor thing, who had only recently mastered walking, tried to run down a steep, rock-covered, gopher hole–scarred hill with her clunky high-button shoes on the opposite feet. Not surprisingly, she went down like a ton of bricks. But since Michael decided it was much too hilarious to reshoot, it now runs forever and ever, over and over again, at the beginning of every show.

To this day, I have no idea how Carol's daughters turned out as well adjusted as they did. She traumatized me, and I only had to be around her a few hours a day on the set. So there I was, during the taping of the fourth season, walking out of my dressing room in Simi Valley, wearing a T-shirt over my camisole. I had barely gotten the door open, when I heard a loud whoop. It sounded like some kind of waterbird coming in for a landing. It was the unmistakable voice of Carol Greenbush. As I stepped out onto the stairs of the trailer, she screamed in my general direction: "GET A LOAD OF THEM JUGS!" I froze in my tracks.

I was mortified. I was being screamed at, catcalled about my body parts in public, and it wasn't even by a guy. Not a crew member, not some hairy construction worker, but Baby Carrie's mother. I turned around, went back into my trailer, shut the door, and didn't come out until after lunch. My aunt tried to reason with Carol about her behavior, but I don't know that reason was possible with her. She never stopped coming up with gems like this.

Sometime later, when I was at least mercifully closer to eighteen, she marched into makeup and brayed at the top of her lungs, "Alison! Did you pose nude for *Playboy*?" It couldn't have been later than seven in the morning. I finished cringing and answered her.

"Uh, no. Not that I recall. Why?"

"Well, I heard that *somebody* from *Little House* had posed nude for *Playboy,* and I knew it couldn't be Melissa Gilbert cuz she's too young, and I figured it couldn't be Melissa Sue cuz who'd pay to see her? So I figured you being the only one with a good body, it had to be you!"

I sighed and tried to figure out through my morning haze if this outburst could possibly be construed as a compliment. I assured her that, however she felt about it, if she was looking for me to appear anywhere nude, *Playboy* or otherwise, she was in for a very long wait.

So I was the first one on the show to get boobs. What was strange for me was it wasn't like that at school. I was always one of the youngest in my class, and it seemed that all the girls I hung out with were Jewish or Italian. They had training bras in the fifth grade. I was a skinny Scotch-Irish girl who was still flat enough to go shirtless like a boy while they were all wearing C cups. But on the set of *Little House,* I was the oldest, and both Melissas were of similar genetic stock, so I won the race. It shouldn't have been a race, of course, but not only were we being compared all the time, there was the matter of the swimsuit.

Gladys had a swimsuit. It was from her glamour days, a genuine Schiaparelli gold lamé one-piece, Roman toga–style swimsuit. I couldn't imagine anyone actually swimming in it. But it was fabulous. Gladys told us that "whoever could fit into the suit first" would get it. Clearly, one had to have breasts that filled out the top.

Melissa Sue wasn't interested. It was me versus Melissa Gilbert in the battle of the boobs. Melissa wanted it so much, I actually caught her doing those isometric flexing exercises that are supposed to make your boobs bigger. They didn't work. The swimsuit still hangs in my closet.

I was also the first to get my period. Melissa got hers much later. I have no idea when Melissa Sue got hers. (As far as I know, Melissa Sue Anderson does not even go to the toilet.) Despite all the films and brochures, my period still came as a total shock. I was nearly fifteen and had probably given up looking for it. And although all the material warned about "some discomfort," it didn't really tell the truth. It didn't say it would hurt like hell.

I first noticed something was wrong after eating lunch one day at the infamously bad Paramount Studios commissary. They later redid the place, but at the time, it was well known as a good place to get food poisoning. So when on the way home from work I rolled into a ball in the backseat of the car and started moaning and complaining of violent cramping, all Auntie Marion could ask was, "Did you have the corned beef and cabbage?"

But I hadn't had the corned beef and cabbage. And when I got home, I felt much worse. My parents were ready to call a doctor, until I came out of the bathroom and announced what was really happening. My mother, wanting to be progressive, said that it should be a cause for celebration; it was a sign of growing up, young womanhood and all that. Periods were treated as something shameful when she was a girl, and she wasn't going to have any of that. She went to the corner liquor store and bought me a bottle of champagne and a box of Kotex pads, the kind with a belt.

I said, "Yeah, great. *Whatever.*" Taking the champagne, I used it to wash down a handful of Tylenol and locked myself in my room. I had never been in so much pain. I couldn't believe women did this every month. But I would soon become an expert on the subject. I got rid of the horrendous bulky pads—they were like wearing a sofa cushion between my legs—and learned how to use tampons.

And then, of course, being the sharing type, I taught everyone else. I was the hit of Melissa Gilbert's next slumber party, where I was the only girl who had started her period. All the other attendees were younger, like Melissa, or even later bloomers than me. I demonstrated the Playtex tampon versus a regular Tampax tampon in a glass of water like in the commercial. Everyone "oohed" and "aahed" as the Playtex showed its superior absorbency. But there was one thing I hadn't told them about: PMS. They had to find this out the hard way.

One night a few months later, the girls were staying up late talking, and I was exhausted. We were having the party in the "maid's quarters" and were all laid out on sleeping bags in the main room. This meant I could conveniently crawl off into the bedroom and shut the door to sleep. They decided to play a prank. While I was asleep (out cold, apparently), Melissa and the others snuck into the room and put things in my bed: a rock, some hair curlers, a brush, some—unused, thankfully—Kotex pads. Then they all snuck back out and waited for the fun to start. They got much more than they bargained for. I was a day and a half away from my period.

In the middle of the night, I rolled over onto a rock. *What the hell?!* Then I found the brush. And the Kotex. *What the fucking hell?* I don't wake up in the best of moods to begin with, but something about rolling over onto that rock really got me going. I wasn't completely awake, but I remember picking up every single thing in the bed, going to the door and opening it, and then throwing everything as hard as I could into the main room. I didn't look to see where any of it landed. I think my eyes were still closed. Then I stumbled back to the bed and fell asleep.

When I woke up, it was later, much later. Like noon. I walked out into the living room, which was empty. I went into the house and found the girls sitting around the kitchen table. They looked terrified at the sight of me.

"Hey, what time is it? How come nobody woke me up for breakfast?" I mumbled.

They just stared. Finally, Melissa recovered her composure and explained what happened. She said I had behaved like I was possessed, screaming at the top of my lungs—nothing in particular—just screaming. And throwing things. Rocks, curlers, everything. They had to dive for cover to keep from being hit. By the time I had gone back into the bedroom, they were all on the floor hiding under the furniture.

One of the girls had said, "Oh my God. What are we going to do? She *is* Nellie Oleson!"

Melissa told me they didn't wake me for breakfast because they thought I might kill them. I assured them I wouldn't but explained that it's very, very dangerous to put foreign objects into the bed of someone with major PMS.

Fortunately, I was able to benefit from my PMS. I don't know if the producers kept a calendar and charted my cycle, but miraculously, almost every one of the episodes where Nellie is at her most vicious, cruel, and obnoxious were shot while I was having my period. "Little Women," the episode where I demand that god-awful black wig with curls? Yup.

"The Music Box," where I make the little stuttering girl cry? You betcha. "The Cheaters," where I make my classmate Andy Garvey (played by Patrick Labyorteaux) steal the answer to the final exam from his own mother, who is subbing for Miss Beadle? Ouch. The one where Laura and I get into a fight over Almanzo and duke it out in the mud? That was a bad one. She's lucky she lived.

That was one of our best fights, and Melissa and I loved it. It was the episode called "Back to School Part II," in which Laura and Nellie fight over Almanzo. Laura, looking for a way to get out of her parents' house, sets out to take the teacher's exam and stupidly asks Nellie for advice on what to study. Nellie, not surprisingly, lies to her and almost totally ruins her chance at a teaching career. (Will Laura never learn?) Right before we started filming, the director told us, "There's no sound, so don't worry about saying anything." They were telling this to the wrong girls. When we realized that nobody in the viewing audience would be able to hear us, we instantly knew what we had to do. Melissa grabbed me, threw me down in the mud, and screamed, "Take *that,* you BITCH!" I came up yowling and thumped into her full force, shouting, "Oh yeah? *FUCK YOU!*" We screamed and swore and called each other every filthy name in the book and beat the crap out of each other. We were laughing so hard we couldn't breathe. And Melissa was strong! She was smaller than me, but a wiry little thing, and she tossed me around like I was a rag doll. At one point, she got me facedown in the mud in a headlock. Her other arm came around as I was screaming away, and as her hand came at my face, I saw too late that it was full of mud. She had grabbed a huge clot of filth and hit me with it square in the mouth.

People have actually asked me if that was "real mud." I am perplexed by this; I did not know there was such a thing as fake mud. If they have fake mud, we did not use it on *Little House on the Prairie*. We only used live, genuine, organic dirt on our show. In Simi, along the road into town, there was a large sunken area. In the summer, it was a popular grazing area for cattle, a cow pasture, and in the winter rainy season, it quickly became a duck pond. Occasionally, when Nellie required a dunking, a hose was used to turn the hole into a large muddy soup. That was what we were fighting in that day, and if you watch the episode closely, you can see it happen. And at the end, when I'm screaming at Almanzo, "Look at me! I'm covered in DIRT!" you can see that I have said dirt between my teeth.

The set doctor was very concerned. He asked us if we had gotten any in our eyes. "My eyes?" I replied. "No, but I just swallowed a quart of it!" He said that wasn't good. I did not get sick. I am apparently impervious to mud, duck shit, and cow shit. Melissa and I never worried about hurting each other during fights. We just had some kind of psychic choreography that allowed us to yell, "Go!" and start flailing away, without ever making real contact. Well, except once. It was this weird dream sequence in "The Fighter," where Laura dreams about boxing with Nellie. We were outfitted in 1800s boxing gear, including gloves. Thinking they were making it safer for us, the prop men padded the gloves so that our hands weren't really in them all the way. Instead, they were balled up at the base. Anyone who knows anything about fighting knows this is a terrible idea. We couldn't tell where the ends of the gloves were by feel. So, sure enough, Melissa swung, meaning to miss me, and punched me right in the nose.

I could feel my nose bend. I really thought it was broken for a second. But it was okay, and we opted to put our hands the rest of the way into the gloves to prevent further injury. We knew we would have been safer if they had just let us fight bare-knuckled.

Someone I never did get to take a swing at (and would have liked to) was Melissa Sue Anderson. We technically had a match scheduled, but it was canceled at the last minute. It was one of the few times Mary loses it. Nellie suggests that Ma is having an affair with the handyman. In the script, Mary was supposed to actually hit me with her metal lunch pail, which would have hurt. Thinking ahead, the prop guys brought in a rubber one for this occasion.

Missy and I were in makeup getting ready for the scene, and we started "trash talking," like a couple of TV wrestlers threatening their opponents. Melissa Sue turned to me and said, "I'm really going to hit you, you know." She wasn't smiling, and it appeared she might actually be threatening me. So I responded in kind: "That's okay, because when I pull your hair, *I'm going to rip it out by the roots.*" And then I looked right at her and grinned.

When we got all the way down the hill, I got the impression that perhaps someone had called down on the walkie-talkie and warned them of our little "chat." The director had dispensed with the entire lunch pail idea. Missy was now just to give me a simple slap, and I would take off. There would be no fight scene. Missy looked pissy that she missed the opportunity.

But *Little House* wasn't the only war zone in my life. There was also school. At this point, I was a student at Hollywood High.

Because of the demands of my job, I only attended classes sporadically, and eventually I managed to get into the "alternative school" program, which meant I didn't really have to show up at all. I was quite good in some subjects. I loved home economics. It was all about cooking, and if I could get it as my first-period class, it meant free breakfast. Weirdly, one of my worst classes was French. It shouldn't have been. I loved French and everything about France. But at Hollywood High, I had what may have been the worst French teacher on earth. He was an American, not a native French speaker, and it was a little unclear if he had ever actually been to France. Unlike my junior high teacher, who conducted the whole class in French, at least trying for a sense of immersion, Mr. Haig spoke English. And he didn't always talk about French either. He spoke a lot about his personal problems. Sometimes he discussed other subjects, like history and literature.

Mr. Haig seemed to have issues with my being on TV. I know that sounds like a line: "Oh, boo-hoo-hoo, my teacher hates me because I'm a child star," but this guy was a real character. I told him I would be out of school for a few days to film. I asked him for my assignments in advance, as was the rule, and about getting a make-up test for the exam that had been scheduled while I was working. He became very angry.

"Filming a TV show is not an excused absence," he sniffed.

I told him that it was and handed him the form from the State of California explaining the whole process, thinking maybe he wasn't familiar with it. That's when he went bananas.

"I *know* it's an excused absence in the State of California!" he shouted. "It is *not* an excused absence in *my* class. It is not an excused absence if you are *getting paid*."

I was slack jawed. What was he talking about?

"I am most certainly not going to give a make-up exam to someone who is out of school *making more money than I do.*"

And then he went into a bizarre tirade about teachers in France. "Do you know how much teachers are paid in France? Do you? Teachers are respected in France, you know!"

I didn't know what to do except back slowly out of the room. I went to the girls' dean, with whom I had been told to talk if I had "any problems." I didn't know what on earth she would do with this, but I thought I'd take a shot. She was very understanding. She assured me, "Don't worry about this. You just go on to your other class. I'll deal with him."

Then I ran into Radames Pera, who was not only a student at Hollywood High but was on *Little House on the Prairie* as well. He played John Jr., Mary's gorgeous boyfriend. Michael had decided to postpone the whole plotline about her blindness indefinitely and let her become a romantic lead. Radames was supposed to marry her. Unfortunately, Melissa Sue hated his guts, refused to kiss him, and eventually he left the show. So, of course, that meant Michael had to go back to the old plotline and make her blind. The logical consequences of one's actions or spiritual karma? You decide.

I, on the other hand, was crazy about Radames and could not believe Missy didn't like kissing him. I seriously thought about asking her if I could stunt double for her. I would have been quite happy to lighten that part of her workload. Radames had no romantic interest in me, of course. But he was still very helpful when it came to Mr. Haig.

"Oh, he did exactly the same thing to me when I was in his class," he said calmly.

"What?" I was amazed.

"He does that to all the actors. Did he give you the speech about 'teachers being respected in France'?"

It turned out Mr. Haig indeed had done this over and over to many students with acting careers. The girls' dean called him into her office, and the outcome was that he gave me my assignments and make-up tests. But no matter what I did in that class, good or bad, I never got a grade anywhere above a C–.

My other favorite class was "office service," a totally useless class where we learned to operate all manner of completely out-of-date office machinery that hardly anyone used in the late '70s—like a mimeograph machine and a switchboard. Only the biggest geeks took office service. That's how I met my friend Gertrude. She had the little pointy glasses, got straight A's, and was the only person I knew under sixty-five who wore sweater guards.

Gertrude was shy but very sweet. She didn't like to talk about her family. One day we were talking about religion, and one girl said she was Catholic. I said we didn't really have a religion at my house, and another girl explained the Jewish holidays. When we asked Gertrude what religion, if any, her family practiced, she seemed embarrassed and said, "Oh, we're kind of different." Everyone backed off and left her alone and went on to discuss another religion. The poor girl; we assumed they must be Jehovah's Witnesses or something.

She had a geeky mom, a geeky dad, a geeky brother whom I

already knew from school, and a geeky kid sister. They all wore trench coats and big, thick glasses, her dad's and brother's Buddy Holly–style black frames with masking tape on them.

While still in high school I had begun my foray into stand-up comedy. One night Gertrude came to see me and brought her entire oddball family with her. Afterward, while chatting in the parking lot, my mother asked Gertrude's dad what he did for a living. "Oh, I work at NASA," he said excitedly. "Oh, how nice," said my mother, trying to make conversation.

He went on about all the rocket ships and things he worked on, in very geeky detail. Then he added, "And I'm also high priest of my local Church of Satan."

Come again? I thought I hadn't heard him right, and my parents looked confused by this, too. He couldn't have really just said that, could he? But he had, and he kept going. "Yes, my whole family are Satanists."

And that's when he got out the pictures. So help me God, he had wallet-sized photos of them all posing and smiling in black robes. "In fact, my daughter is the youngest child ever to be inducted into the Church of Satan. Here she is at her first black mass."

My parents just kept glazed smiles through his spiel, not saying a word.

He finally wrapped up his happy tour of the underworld, and they all said good night and went home. There was the world's longest silence.

Finally, my mother slowly turned to me and said, "And you thought *your* parents were weird!"

LITTLE HOUSE SHOUT-OUTS

I remember the first time I realized that *Little House* had become part of the fabric of our culture. I was fifteen years old and had gone to see the movie *Network* with some "regular" (non–show biz) friends from school.

For about an hour, I felt like a regular teenager, enjoying the anonymity of the darkened movie theater. And then one of the characters on the screen began ranting and raving at Faye Dunaway about the scheduling of her show. She was furious about being opposite hit shows with which she couldn't compete in the ratings: " . . . and NBC's got *Little House on the Prairie*!" she spits in rage.

My friends all turned and stared at me. I was so embarrassed I wanted to pull up the floorboards of the theater and jump in. I slumped down in my seat and cringed.

But I eventually realized there was no escape. I now know that when I watch TV, go to the movies, listen to music, there's a pretty good chance someone will make a joke about *Little House on the Prairie* or Nellie Oleson. Once I finally gave in and accepted this phenomenon, I was able to beam with pride at the references—for example, while watching the episode of *Mystery Science Theater 3000* in which the show's cohosts send up Michael Landon's *I Was a Teenage Werewolf*, Servo says, "I think Nellie Oleson's behind the whole thing!"

Here are some of the other endless cracks that have been made about the *Prairie* in popular culture.

SANFORD AND SON, 1975

Fred's idea for a series about pioneer plumbers is titled *Little Outhouses on the Prairie*.

CREEPY CLASSICS, 1987

Vincent Price jokingly refers to Michael Landon's most famous show as *Little Howl on the Prairie,* while showing a clip of him as a werewolf in *Teenage Werewolf.*

FAMILY GUY, "FORE, FATHER" EPISODE, 2000

Father Charles Ingalls plays cruel pranks on his blind daughter, Mary.

THAT '70S SHOW, "RAMBLE ON" EPISODE, 2002

Eric tells Kelso that Hyde likes to watch *Little House on the Prairie*. Hyde admits it, because "the show reminds him of a simpler time."

LAW & ORDER: SPECIAL VICTIMS UNIT, "PHILADELPHIA" EPISODE, 2007

Benson's brother asks her which show she prefers: *Dukes of Hazzard* or *Little House.*

ROBOT CHICKEN, 2007

An episode is titled "Slaughterhouse on the Prairie."

CHAPTER THIRTEEN

BEING SOLD INTO MARRIAGE: THE ARRIVAL OF STEVE TRACY

> **NELLIE: But [Percival] likes my food; it doesn't make him sick!**
>
> **MRS. OLESON: Well, of course HE likes it; he's used to it! He's Jewish. A person can get used to ANYTHING! Look at the cannibals . . . they eat each other, and they think it's just dandy!**

We all had to be married off. That's what people did on the prairie. Laura's marriage was preordained in the books. The real Nellie married, too, and even got divorced (not as many times as Gladys). Mary got a lucky break on the show; she landed a hunky blind teacher (played by Linwood Boomer), thanks to some creative writing on the part of our TV team. In the books and in real life, she went blind at a young age and spent the remainder of her life tatting and crap like that.

At this stage, all bets were off on plotlines. When Michael and coproducer Ed Friendly split in the third year, it was like a bizarre, ugly divorce. They divided up the show and Laura Ingalls's life, like furniture. Michael kept the show, obviously, but Ed Friendly, thinking he might do something with this idea later, kept the rights to Laura's life story after sixteen. Michael, who always liked to see how far he could go from the books, now had an excuse to do just that.

Nobody was fighting for the rights to the marriage of Nellie Oleson. Most people didn't believe they would find anyone to marry her. I sure didn't. But one morning during the end of Season 6, I was in makeup when Michael came bounding in to break the news. "You're getting married! It's gonna be great!" he said. Then he ran out of the room. I figured he'd lost it for good this time. What horrible person would marry Nellie Oleson?

When he ran back in, I said, "Nellie Oleson can't get married. Hitler hasn't been born yet."

He snorted and said, "Oh, you'll love this! It's a short, little guy, but he won't take any crap! And *he's Jewish*!" He grinned triumphantly.

But how? Who? And wait, I was only seventeen. Oh, yes, but this was the prairie. Melissa Sue already had her TV husband, and Melissa Gilbert—although Laura was not old enough to marry yet—had already met her Almanzo. Getting married on TV is like living in a country where they have arranged marriages. You have no say whatsoever in the selection of your husband. You are told whom to marry and when. He may be older than you (all of our TV husbands, Dean Butler, Steve Tracy, and Linwood Boomer, were at least nine years our seniors), and you might not even meet him until right before the wedding.

I reminded myself this was just TV, not reality. It wasn't as if I was really walking down the aisle with a complete stranger. I would, however, be kissing him, hugging him, lying next to him in bed, and telling him how much I loved him . . . every day for the next few years . . . until death of our contracts or the show did us part. Sounded pretty real to me.

Melissa moped and complained about having to "marry" Dean Butler, who played Almanzo. He was blond, and she didn't like blonds, or the "hayseed" type. She liked them dark and mysterious. (Well, it turned out what she really liked was Rob Lowe, but there's no accounting for taste.) And she was young. She not only hadn't had sex yet, she hadn't even kissed a boy in real life, and here she was having to lock lips with a twenty-something-year-old dude on camera, in front of God and millions of viewers every week. Worse, in front of her mother. Of course she hated it.

I had kissed a boy before. A few of them. And I had gotten around to a few other things, too, with boys I actually wanted to be with. So I wasn't suffering from any fear of kissing, but I sure wanted to know who the heck I was going to be locking lips with. When Melissa and I heard that the role of my husband, Percival, had been cast, and the actor was due to arrive on the set, we sat vigil, as if I had been sold off into marriage, and we were awaiting the arrival of the husband to come take me away to his village. Every man who walked onto the set was suspect. *Is that him?* we wondered.

Well, not every man. You see, I had a disadvantage that Melissa and even Melissa Sue didn't have to contend with. Both of their husbands were supposed to be handsome and dashing. I was the comic relief, and my husband had already been written as a comedic character, which meant that, unlike theirs—who had been pulled from the list of actors marked "leading men"—mine was going to be what they called a "character actor." Translation?

An ugly guy. All I could do was hope he wasn't too hideous and that he at least had decent breath.

We also knew Percival was supposed to be short. So we watched for every short guy who entered. After an hour of this, I was peeking through my fingers. It was too horrible to contemplate. And then Steve Tracy walked in. He was indeed short, and he wore glasses. But he wasn't ugly; far from it. He had a big, beautiful mop of curly hair and sparkling eyes and freckles. He was *cute.* "Oh please, oh please, oh please let this be him!" I whispered, crossing my fingers so hard they hurt.

He introduced himself. His name was Steve Tracy, and, yes, he was The Man Who Would Be Percival. Melissa immediately began interrogating him: Favorite food? Favorite movie? Type of music? He liked pizza, enjoyed some of the same movies we did, and listened to cool stuff like Echo and the Bunnymen.

He did get awfully vague when she quizzed him about any possible girlfriends. Lucky for him, she didn't just come right out and ask if him if he was gay. Not the first day, anyway. It would take us a week or two to figure that one out. But he passed inspection. He also had a sense of humor and the ability to withstand being interrogated by Melissa Gilbert. And he made a point of always carrying a bottle of Binaca breath spray in his left breast pocket, so that he could spray right before every kiss. He actually told us this up front and showed us the bottle. This was a man who had done his homework.

Steve was fearless from day one. He had to be. He was walking into a hit show that had already been on for six years to play the husband of an established character, the villain, no less. As Percival, he had to be brave to stand up to Mrs. Oleson—and in real life he had to stand up to Katherine MacGregor. I wouldn't have wished such a job on anyone. But Steve relished every minute. His comic timing was impeccable, and it was clear from our very first scene that we had chemistry.

The episode was "He Loves Me, He Loves Me Not." In it, Mrs. Oleson buys a hotel/restaurant for Nellie as a graduation gift, but Nellie is burning the toast, scaring off customers, and running the place into the ground. Out of desperation, Harriet hires Percival Dalton to teach Nellie how to cook and be more "hospitable" in the hospitality business. In one hilarious scene, Percival pours eggs over Nellie's head; it's our *Taming of the Shrew* moment. For continuity, the crew had to keep my wig, with the eggshells on it, overnight and put it back on me, reeking, the next morning.

Steve had to look exactly as he had the day before, too. So they splashed some beaten egg on his tie and the fly of his pants, where it had been the day before. As the prop man was on his knees, painting the yolk onto Steve's crotch, Michael Landon walked up. He started cracking up and said: "You look like you just came out of the men's room at Studio One."

Steve went pale. He couldn't tell if Michael was screwing around or had just outed him on his second day of work.

Steve was a hit with the audience. When he marched into the Mercantile and told Mrs. Oleson to "be quiet!" he instantaneously became a national hero. And boy, could he kiss. When Nellie declares her love, and Percival asks her to marry him right there in the street, we both agreed to just go for it. It was a full, openmouthed lip lock. It made sense to me and Steve. Nellie clearly had a lot of pent-up emotions she'd been suppressing for a really long time, and Percival was a grown man, not a shy teenage boy. They were madly in love, so we figured these two would be the kind to kiss their brains out when given the chance.

Melissa watched from the wings and was scandalized. "Stop that!" she hissed at me between takes. "Stop what?" I laughed. "Stop kissing him like that! You look like a fish! It's disgusting! Close your mouth, for God's sake!"

I couldn't stop laughing. "We're supposed to be in love," I insisted. "And besides, I *like* kissing boys; it's fun!"

Melissa refused to watch the rest of the scene being shot. She was completely grossed out. So from then on, whenever she was around, Steve and I made a point of "overdoing it" just to drive her crazy.

Melissa wasn't the only one who noticed our gusto. A couple of months in, Steve and I found out about a "secret memo" discussing the various romantic couples on the show that was circulating among the producers. They were concerned that Laura and Almanzo didn't really look "passionate" enough. Melissa and her husband, played by Dean Butler, were sweet together, but she looked so young, and he was so delicate with her, that it didn't really generate what you would call sparks. It only became really noticeable that these two were mismatched when the next scene showed me and Steve happily slobbering all over each other. "Can't they turn it up a bit?" the execs wanted to know. "Now, Nellie and Percival—*those* two look like they fuck *like crazed weasels*!"

I nearly died. Steve joked, "Well, technically, we do. Just not each other." We were sorry we couldn't tell everyone about this wonderful "review," but it was supposed to be top secret. We really wanted to show up to work in T-shirts reading "Crazed Weasel 1" and "Crazed Weasel 2," but we figured the producers would kill us.

It didn't take that long to work out the "Steve is gay" bit. Melissa turned to me one day and said, "Alison, your husband's ears are pierced." It was 1980, and ear piercing wasn't as common as it is now, but I reasoned, "Lots of guys have a pierced ear."

"Both of them?" she asked. That was definitely not common.

So we asked him. Steve hemmed and hawed and told some story about having them pierced years ago as a hippie. "They grow back," was all Melissa said.

Back then gay actors, especially actors on shows like *Little House on the Prairie,* didn't come out of the closet. They often went to absurd lengths to make up cover relationships. But Steve didn't have to worry about covering because everyone thought he was sleeping with me. It helped our performance enormously. There's a wonderful scene in Season 7 in "Come, Let Us Reason Together" where Percival and Nellie are lying in bed laughing. Steve and I weren't acting. We were actually hysterically cracking up under the covers.

To begin with, we both had on funny underwear. I had blue panties that said "Friends Forever" on them, and he had briefs with some kind of cartoon pattern. We thought doing a bed scene might be difficult, and bringing our silliest panties would help break the ice. It did. In the scene, we talk about our insane parents and the fight they've been having over our soon-to-arrive baby. Percival's parents are Orthodox Jews, and the Olesons, since they go to Reverend Alden's church, are Christian, some kind of Protestants. The agreed solution was that if the baby was a boy, he would be raised Jewish; if a girl, Christian. Of course, Nellie winds up having twins, one of each, and each religious faction gets a baby.

In real life, neither of them would be Jewish, unless their mother, Nellie, had specifically converted, and no, you cannot in an Orthodox home say one baby is a Jew and the other isn't. It simply does not work that way. But you go try telling Michael Eugene Orowitz Landon that. His mother wasn't Jewish, but he said he was, and if he had to rewrite the entire Torah on national television to make it so, he would. (It's probably why for *Highway to Heaven* he just went the rest of the way and became an angel.)

So Steve and I had to lie there and laugh at all this religious confusion, which wasn't that hard, given that we'd already seen each other's underwear. We were in fits. We giggled and snorted all over the place. We laughed so hard, that Michael began to wonder what we were up to. He came up close to the bed and said, "What have you two been . . . Wait, are you guys . . . ?" He wouldn't complete the question. We weren't sure if he was about to ask if we were sleeping together in real life, or if we were stoned, both of which must have seemed like reasonable possibilities at the time.

This sent us into further hysterics. Steve looked at me, and I looked at him. We realized from the looks we'd been getting from the crew over the last few weeks that I was the only one (except for Melissa, who suspected) who truly knew for sure that he was gay. And not only did none of these people have a clue, they even believed that he and I were a romantic couple—that we were having sex. We burst out laughing. *And could not stop.* We howled until we were out of breath, then cracked up all over again as soon as we looked at each other.

Michael gave up even trying to get us to shut up between takes. He just sighed and said, "Keep it rolling."

We knew we would be, like my panties said, "Friends Forever."

CHAPTER FOURTEEN

ON MY OWN

> **NELLIE: You know, it's not easy being the richest girl in town.**

I'm pretty good at endings—the result, perhaps, of my constant upheaval as a kid. I don't usually let myself get too attached to material stuff; I don't pine away for exes or scour Facebook for long-lost friends. I'm practical: I know that nothing lasts forever (unless you're in syndication). There's no sense in clinging to the past; it's in the past. You let go, you move on. Life is about having the rug pulled out from under you, over and over again—or at least my life is.

So when it came time for the end of my years on *Little House,* I thought I would be relatively comfortable kissing this phase good-bye. I reasoned with myself: Hey, it was a great gig, and there would be others. I'd had a long run—seven years is an incredibly long time to do anything. Most actors are not that lucky, not even close. So I should be thankful that it lasted as long as it did. Onward and upward!

But what I didn't figure into the equation was one small but important fact. These people that I had worked with day after day for seven years weren't just my colleagues or even my friends. They were my *family*. And *Little House* was not just a show, it was my home for almost my entire adolescence.

It was the end of the seventh season, and I was shooting the episode "Blind Justice," where I wasn't heavily featured. I had two scenes, most of which involved walking out of the kitchen in Nellie's restaurant/hotel and saying, "Who had the lamb stew?" It seemed like a bit of a letdown. I knew lots of people who had been waitresses for seven years and ultimately became TV stars, but I had been a TV star for seven years and had somehow morphed into a glorified waitress.

Nellie, now "reformed" by her marriage to Percival, had become bland and boring. I didn't seem to have much to do. I loved having Steve as a TV husband, but I secretly hoped that perhaps Nellie would have a terrible relapse, some sort of postpartum depression, with wild mood swings causing her to scream at Percival, hurl things, have a few more mud fights with Laura. Some terrifying drama where she becomes a danger to the twins? "Quick, get Doc Baker!" But no such luck. I had become a tame prairie wife, happily serving up pie and coffee.

So when my seven-year contract ended, and NBC and my agent, Lew Sherrill, began renegotiating, I felt a distinct lack of excitement. Was I really going to sign up for another several years of this? How many would they want? Two? Four? I hoped not another seven. That would make it a fourteen-year run! I would be nearly thirty years old before I got off this thing! When I mentioned that to my father, he snorted and said, "My God, you'll be like Amanda Blake, who spent nineteen years as Miss Kitty on *Gunsmoke*!" I felt sick to my stomach at the thought.

Apparently, NBC wasn't that keen on the idea either. The network refused all requests from my agent for raises, extra episodes, or any type of concession he suggested, no matter how small. Their offer was four years, same money, same conditions—take it or leave it. Of course, both my agent and my father were appalled. For decades they had both prided themselves on being able to "broker a hot deal" with anybody, under any circumstances. But the lawyers at NBC simply refused to negotiate. It was unfair: I was loyal to the network for seven years, yet there was no loyalty being shown to me. My agent and dad were enraged, but despite their pride and anger, they told me the final call was up to me. I thought about how much of my life had been spent on *Little House*. I was nineteen now and had been on this show since I was twelve. I had gone all through junior high and high school, gotten braces on my teeth, had them removed, learned to drive, grown up, and I was still on this show. It didn't take me very long to make up my mind: I was ready to take a chance on a career beyond the prairie. I said no to NBC's last offer.

But this meant there was no real "good-bye." I had left on hiatus, at the end of Season 7, not knowing if I would be coming back for Season 8, and now I wasn't. I was just . . . gone. The writers were able to build it into the plot seamlessly: Nellie, Percival, and their twins had simply moved to New York City to take over Percival's father's store upon his death. In case fans were missing Nellie, they added a whole new bitch. They called the first episode of Season 8 "The Reincarnation of Nellie." And they weren't kidding. In it, the Olesons adopt a new daughter from an orphanage. Little Allison Balson (yes, we even shared the same first name) was cast as Nancy Oleson, and she was a mini-me—ringlets and all, poor thing.

I wasn't the only one who had passed on a contract renewal. Melissa Sue Anderson had opted to leave as well. The writers took care of her sudden departure: Mary and her husband, Adam, moved to New York, too, so Adam could work at his father's law firm.

So that was it: no more Nellie. But my decision didn't affect only me. No Nellie meant no more Percival. Steve Tracy had just started to become established on the show after two years, and now his time was up. He'd even gotten a phone call from the lawyers at NBC—they'd hoped to use him to pressure me into staying.

Steve and I had become very close during our TV marriage. We had decided to capitalize on the rumors of our "affair" and used it to foil the tabloids in their attempts to find out if he was gay. We shamelessly lied to the *National Enquirer* ("Yes, we are deeply in love!") and wound up becoming a "Hollywood couple," appearing together at every charity event, red carpet, and photo op our publicists could get us into. We stuck it out through thick and thin, even marching the picket lines together during the long, terrible actors' strike of 1980. In truth, we probably got along better and had more interests in common than many couples in Hollywood who actually slept with each other.

So when we went to lunch to discuss my decision, I poured my heart out. I told Steve everything—the whole chapter and verse of the negotiations, who said what to whom, what was offered, what wasn't. I told him how I felt after spending what was more than a third of my life playing one character and why I felt I was done.

He listened patiently, then said, "Yeah, I freaked out when I first heard. I mean, of course I'd rather keep getting paid! But if I was in your shoes, I would have done exactly the same thing." I was so relieved he was still my friend. Going out into the world without *Little House,* I was going to need all the help I could get.

After it all went down, I also called Melissa. She didn't sound shocked by my news—but then again, the girl is a rock, and she knew *everything* on the set. She probably even knew before I did that I wasn't coming back. She said that she had argued and held out as well—practically threatening to blow up the joint—just to get a nominal increase in her salary. But in the end, the network conceded. Hey, how could you have *Little House* without Half-Pint?

"I don't blame you," she said, "but life is going to be pretty boring here without you." Then she sent me a present for my birthday in January: a cute little gold charm of a screaming baby. She said it reminded her of me (well, there is *some* resemblance), and she wrapped the box in the want ads from the *L.A. Times.* On the wrapping she wrote, "You probably will need these now."

Right after I left, I felt a sense of wonder and excitement that I hadn't felt in years. What would I do first? To listen to my dad or my agent, one would think producers would be banging on my door, asking me to star in this movie or that one. I could just picture it in my head: "Nellie Oleson is available? Get me her agent!" But I was delusional. Hollywood is all about sex and glamour, and *Little House on the Prairie* was considered decidedly not sexy or glamorous. I tried my best to convince them otherwise: I even played a teenage prostitute on *Fantasy Island.* (A truly horrifying experience that resulted in me being chased around by Hervé Villechaize. Yikes!) But no one was jumping up and down to hire me.

It was a tough time for all us girls from the prairie. We were no longer children, we were young women, but people had a hard time visualizing us that way. We all felt this enormous pressure to "break out" of our "wholesome" image. Melissa Sue Anderson was playing an ax murderess in the lurid 1981 slasher flick *Happy Birthday to Me,* Melissa Gilbert was wearing twelve pounds of eyeliner and running all over town with Rob Lowe on her arm (among other body parts), and I was popping up in the *National Enquirer* every other week in a bikini. We were all doing our best to prove we were modern, sexy girls.

But I guess I wasn't sexy enough—not for the Farrah Fawcettized early '80s. When I finally did land a role in a movie of the week, it was in *I Married Wyatt Earp,* an 1800s period piece costarring Marie Osmond, which didn't exactly cast me in a different light.

Between these intermittent gigs, I was doing stand-up at The Laugh Factory on Sunset Boulevard. I had first tried stand-up when I was sixteen. I was hanging out at The Comedy Store, where my dad was managing a comedy troupe called The Village Idiots, when one night a stand-up onstage dared me to try it, and I did. I told jokes about braces and puberty. ("I wear a training bra. See, you can tell." And then gazing down at my boobs: "Sit!") I was a hit, and they had me back. I added in a dead-on impression of then president Jimmy Carter's young blond, slightly geeky daughter, Amy. I wound up playing every single coffeehouse and comedy club in L.A., most of the time four nights a week, while I was still working on *Little House.* Stand-up was always a rush—but at nineteen, I was still trying to be an actress. So I ran all the way to Edmonton, the capital of Canada's Alberta Province, to do dinner theater for three months. I appeared in a French bedroom farce every night in my underwear (the poster for the show had a warning label: "Adults Only!"). If that isn't challenging your wholesome image, I don't know what is.

When I came back to Hollywood, it was time for "the conversation." This conversation has happened to almost every even remotely attractive actress in history, and it's usually initiated by an agent or a manager. Sometimes the idea is relayed to the parents first, who then broach the issue directly with their daughter. In my case, my agent made a suggestion to my manager, who was my father. So it was his duty to tell me the ugly truth: that I would be much more "marketable" if I had surgery to make my nose smaller and my breasts larger.

I believe my response was, "You're fucking kidding me, right?" But no, he and my mother were serious. They even quoted me prices: the nose job would be fairly reasonable, the boobs would be more, of course, but considering the difference they would make, they could reasonably be expected to pay for themselves in a very short period of time. I sat there, stunned, appalled. My parents—my own parents—were essentially telling me I was ugly. It seemed particularly outrageous to me that my father of all people would complain about my nose. He had the exact same one! Yet I remained weirdly calm. I guess I just didn't know how to respond. I asked if I could take some time and "get back to them on this one."

"No problem," my father assured me. "It's totally up to you." I didn't believe that for a minute. I knew they'd be sorely disappointed if I didn't listen to their valuable career advice. But I was an adult. This was my decision and no one else's to make. It was my body, my boobs. I was kind of attached to them.

I went off to the only place truly appropriate to consider such a decision, the Hollywood Memorial Park Cemetery (now the Hollywood Forever Cemetery), where I often ventured when I needed a quiet spot to be alone with my thoughts. It wasn't in a great neighborhood at the time, so tourists steered clear, and I had the place mostly to myself. I sat cross-legged on the stairs across from Douglas Fairbanks's dark, weed-choked reflecting pool. I prayed to God for some sort of wisdom, but what category of wisdom is required to determine whether or not to get plastic surgery? So I broke it down mathematically, binary code, if you will. There were two possible decisions and therefore actually only four possible outcomes to consider.

DECISIONS?

1. Get the surgery
2. Don't get the surgery

OUTCOMES?

1. You get work and become rich and famous.
2. You don't get any more work. Ixnay on the rich and famous.

Therefore, the four possible combinations were: 1A, 1B, 2A, and 2B. I would simply work out how I felt about these possible scenarios, and the decision would be simple. Say I got the surgery, and it worked: I'd look fabulous, everyone would love the new nose and boobs, and I'd work like mad and get rich. Hooray! But what if I got the surgery, and my new look didn't work? I'd have spent a fortune, undergone a major medical procedure, and . . . nothing. I'd still shuttle fruitlessly from audition to audition, year after year, finally throwing in the towel and getting some other kind of employment—but now with *someone else's nose and boobs.*

What if I didn't get the surgery at all and, as a result, didn't become a millionaire starlet? Would I be worse off than I was now? And what about that other possibility? That I not touch my nose one bit and still have a successful career? Can anyone say, "Barbra Streisand"?

There was absolutely no way anyone could predict with any accuracy the likelihood of any of these outcomes. The variables were too great. There were thousands of women out there with perfect noses and huge racks who couldn't get an acting job to save their lives. And there were famous actresses with flat chests and great, terrifying honkers, several times the size of mine, who worked all the time. I wasn't getting anywhere.

So I asked myself: How will I feel every time I look in the mirror and see my altered looks staring back? I am the only one who will have to live with this decision. The doctors, the agents, the managers, the producers, my parents will all go home at the end of the day. I will be left alone with my nose and my boobs for the rest of my life. And even if my new looks helped me achieve the career of my dreams, would I spend my life worrying about whether I was popular for my acting or for my plastic boobs? Here's a dark thought: imagine people telling you that you're beautiful and fabulous and that they love you, but you know that they've never seen the *real* you.

Suddenly, I was overcome with a feeling of peace. I had made a decision and wasn't the least bit confused about it anymore. I thanked Mr. Fairbanks and God and went home. I told my parents I'd thought about it, and I wasn't going to do it; if I had to starve to death with this nose and these boobs, so be it. They didn't put up much of a fuss. They may have privately fantasized about having a perfect sex-symbol daughter with a perfect nose and perfect tits, but they were not prepared to drag me to a surgeon against my will. They had taken their best shot, and it was simply no sale.

While I was trying to figure out my future, I moved out of my parents' house and bought my own two-bedroom condo in West Hollywood, just above the Sunset Strip. I had cashed in my trust fund, and money was burning a hole in my pocket. I had an interior decorator fill the rooms with all this absurdly fancy Queen Anne furniture. I don't know what I was thinking. The show was being rerun both in prime time and in syndication at this point, so the residuals checks were pouring in. I was a thousandaire! I had money and, for the first time in my life, no family to feed or share the bathroom with.

I loved the idea of being "on my own," but, frankly, I was never alone. I was surrounded by not only the occasional kooky live-in boyfriend but a never-ending parade of out-of-work actors, trust-fund brats, and assorted visiting Canadians and Euro trash. They all seemed to be trying to "find themselves," and for some reason they all decided to begin their search from the comfort of my living room couch. I invited them, of course. It was actually a great system. True, none of them ever paid rent or a phone bill or anything like that (hence, my pad became known as "Auntie

Alison's Home for Wayward Boys"), but they fulfilled a number of important functions. First off, it was very difficult for me to find friends my own age who were not completely weirded out by the fact that I had money. I know everyone thinks that if you become rich and famous you'll have more friends. It's not true. Getting a lot of money, especially very suddenly, actually alienates most people, who worry that you won't want to be their friend anymore, or who feel like failures by comparison. Not knowing quite what to say, they start to drift away. For the first few months after buying my own place, I couldn't tell if I'd cashed in on my trust fund or caught a contagious disease.

So gradually, these other people appeared. Most were nineteen or twenty and didn't have jobs. Those who did worked part time as waiters or movie ushers. But they all owned new cars and nice clothes and seemed utterly unconcerned about money—mine or theirs. They had apartments but preferred hanging out at my place. But they never commented on the size of the place, the furniture, or asked how much it cost or how I paid for it. They didn't care. For them, money was something people simply *had.* They were trust-fund kids.

It was the most blessed relief to sit around all night (well, all night, all day, all the next night—we didn't have a lot to do) with people who didn't give a flying one that I had more money than any kid my age should or that I was on TV. Actually, we didn't care about much. We became the Condo of Lost Souls. We had a schedule of sorts: *Twilight Zone* reruns started at eleven a.m., *Alfred Hitchcock Presents* was later, pizza was ordered in between. We were on a first-name basis with the manager of every pizza place in Hollywood and began inviting them to parties. We also made a lot of Jell-O, those big, solid Knox Blox. We didn't eat all of it; some of it was for throwing. If we decided that a particular TV personality was annoying, we would throw blocks of Jell-O at the screen. We even had a color-coding system signifying which shade of Jell-O was appropriate for which celebrity.

My new friends stayed at my apartment on and off, in droves. The record was eight at once: one person sleeping with me in my bed, two people in the spare bedroom, three on the pullout sofa, one on the floor in the living room next to them, and one on the balcony. (The one on the balcony was not there by choice; he had annoyed us and was in exile.) Some came to my house to get sane, others to go crazy.

At first, I rejoiced in my newfound free time. I was giddy with the idea that I had nowhere to be. I could sleep, I could party, I could do whatever I damn pleased because I had no daily grind, no set to report to, no lines to memorize. My life was like a never-ending vacation. But then, all of a sudden, one day about a year after I left *Little House,* my past hit me like a ton of bricks. I had time to think, and all of the issues that I had willfully avoided came flooding over me in a tidal wave of fear, dread, and anxiety. *Little House* had been such a great escape for seven years; I had been blissfully distracted. I had had no time to think about what my brother had done to me, or even to allow those feelings to bubble close to the surface.

But now I had plenty of time to think about it. I hit a period around age twenty when I had not a single job on the horizon. I was auditioning for all kinds of nonsense, but it seemed that every part I read for required me to play a cheerleader, someone naked, someone dead, or a ghastly combination of all three. Yet not even these bleak prospects came to fruition. I was suddenly confronted full force with my old demons. The feelings not only bubbled up, they drowned me. I had trouble sleeping at night: my heart raced for no reason, I broke out in a mysterious rash, and I often felt so anxious I thought I might pass out from the stress.

I had blocked out my emotions for so long, I'd assumed they had gone away. But when you're abused, the pain doesn't just "go away." It sinks down under the surface, invisible to casual observers. You might even convince your best friends that you're okay, but the pain is still there, growing like a seething tumor. Abuse lives on in the very cells of your body, carved into the neural pathways of your brain. Your friends can't see the scars, but they are present every minute of every day.

Now I found myself in a very dark place, and I didn't know how to deal with it. I didn't cry. I didn't scream. But I was depressed and scared. I felt like I wanted to die. I was throwing up all the time. It wasn't bulimia; I knew I wasn't fat, and I wasn't putting my finger down my throat. If anything, at 102 pounds, I was emaciated. When I heard on the news that Karen Carpenter had died from anorexia, I was taken aback to hear that she had outweighed me by six pounds. I knew I had to do something.

I was a little skittish about going to a doctor, so I went to one of the few physicians who I knew for sure wasn't nuts—my gynecologist. Being a Hollywood doctor, she did have an immediate prepared response. As soon as I said I was unhappy, had trouble sleeping, and was feeling anxious all the time, she chirped brightly, "I can get you some Valium!" I realized that a bottle of pills was probably what most of her patients really wanted. But it was just what I was trying to avoid, and I told her so.

"Yes, I'm sure you could. And I'm sure I could take them. Lots and lots and lots of them, every day for the rest of my life. Which is exactly the road I am trying not to go down."

"*Ohhh,*" she said, understanding perfectly, "you actually want to *do* something about your problems!

"In that case," she continued, "take this number. She's a therapist, her office is upstairs from me. She's great." I did. And she was.

I had heard about how people spent years in therapy and never got around to telling the therapist what was really going on in their lives. I always thought that was a strange thing to do, especially at those prices. I couldn't imagine shelling out a couple of hundred dollars to sit around for an hour and lie to a total stranger. Maybe I'm just cheap, but it seemed like a waste.

So I walked in for my first appointment, sat down, and said, "Hi. My-name-is-Alison-my-father's-gay-and-I-was-sexually-molested-as-a-child. Can you do anything for me?" She stared at me for a minute and said, "Can you come in three times a week?"

"That bad?" I asked.

"Yeah," she said.

With the trust fund and the residuals, I had the money. I certainly had the time for intensive therapy, and unlike some people, I really did have the inclination. I was only too happy to go in three days a week and spill my guts psychologically. I was spilling them physically several times a day anyway, so what the hell did I have to lose?

And the treatment worked. I didn't miraculously get better overnight, but even within days of just talking about what was bothering me, I stopped throwing up. My therapist asked me to promise not to kill myself, which wasn't a difficult promise for me to make. I didn't want to actually kill myself. I just wanted to stop feeling like I *should.*

She said that many people don't start dealing with the things I was talking about until they're in their forties. To show up all by myself at twenty—without being sent or hospitalized—was an accomplishment on its own. She didn't insist that I talk to my parents, but suggested, since I was so young, and they did live just down the street, that maybe asking about "the gay thing" and seeing how much they knew about the sexual abuse would be useful in my therapy.

I didn't like the idea at first, but suddenly, the issue came up in a context my parents could grasp: an audition. I was asked to try out for a movie about a girl who was sexually abused as a child. The script was terrible, and the film never did get made. But my parents thought it was a meaty role and insisted that I audition for it. I didn't want to—and I told them why.

I talked to my mom first. She came over to my condo, no doubt thinking it was just some sort of stage fright, or lack of confidence, fully prepared to give me a pep talk on why I would be great in this film and had nothing to worry about. I explained I didn't want to get up and perform this scenario on screen because I already had experienced it in real life. I told her what Stefan had done. I reminded her that I had repeatedly begged not to be left alone with him.

She was silent for a few seconds. Then she said simply, "*Oh, shit.*"

Well, I gotta give credit where credit is due: at least my mother believed me. In fact, she was suitably appalled and upset.

I had for years questioned whether, at worst, she knew what was going on and condoned it, or suspected and actively chose to ignore it, or, at best, really was in the dark. But when I heard and saw her reaction that day, I knew she'd been clueless. Nobody is that good an actress; she was in shock. She assured me I could simply forget about this entire audition nonsense at once and that she would tell my father immediately. Since we were on the subject, I had to ask, "Oh, by the way, he *is* gay, right?"

She explained that indeed he was, but it was all on the up and up, as far as she was concerned. He'd never lied about it, and she didn't mind. I told her that the endless denials on this subject had been rather confusing, to say the least, and she said she was sorry about that, but they had been told back in the old days that they shouldn't tell the kids. They thought they were doing me a favor.

My therapist was pleased with my conversation with my parents and saw it as progress, but she wasn't done. She wanted me to now confront Stefan. It was the '80s, and everyone was so full of "forgiveness" and "healing" and "reconciliation," it had become a downright fashion statement. I didn't think we were exactly going to "kiss and make up," but I didn't like the idea that my brother could do all those horrible things to me every day for years and expect me just to forget about it and let him get away with it. Did he really think his behavior was acceptable? Had he blocked it all out? My curiosity overrode my fear, and I decided there was only one way to find out. I had to talk to him.

Stefan was sober now, or so he said. Well, he was changed. He had recently fallen—or jumped, or was thrown?—out of a third-story window and woken up in the hospital in traction with metal pins in his body. That would definitely kill anyone's buzz. He was clearly no longer doing the mountains of drugs he had been doing in his teen years and early twenties, so I figured maybe there was hope. To break the ice, my mother talked to him first so he knew what was coming. I didn't initiate the conversation in person. With his long history of physical violence toward anyone who even so much as contradicted him, I wasn't taking that chance. Over the years, he'd beaten most of his girlfriends black and blue, and he wasn't above fighting his own mother—he'd even caused her to break her arm once by shoving her during an altercation. So I played it safe and called him on the phone.

At first, I thought I had gotten lucky. I expected denial, loss of memory, threats, yelling. I wasn't getting any of that. Stefan remembered the abuse, all right, and he admitted to everything. He said he was "very sick," and he blamed the drugs and alcohol. He even said he understood if I never wanted anything to do with him.

Just when I thought I had witnessed a miracle of reconciliation, that he understood how much he had hurt me, would never do anything like this to anyone again, and maybe even felt bad about his behavior, he had to go and keep talking. He didn't say he was sorry. He said: "Sexually molesting you was the greatest sexual experience of my life, and everything else has been downhill from there."

Really, that's what he said. He was dead, cold sober. As totally aghast as I was at this statement, I had the presence of mind to reply: "Wow. You *really* need to get out more."

On that note, I ended the conversation. I had had enough.

I felt some relief, though. At least no one had denied what had happened to me—not even Stefan. But there was denial of another kind. My parents thought I should put it all behind me. We should go back to "the way things were." They didn't seem to realize that the good old days never existed; my childhood was a living hell. Besides, once you've announced that your entire relationship with your brother was a lie, that he beat and raped you for years, it's a little hard to go back to playing "happy family." It's like trying to put toothpaste back in the tube.

The day I confronted my brother was just one of the many moments in my post *Little House* life when I questioned my wisdom in leaving the show. I missed it terribly; I missed my "family," the people I had grown up with, who had always been such an integral part of my existence. I didn't miss that awful wig, but I missed Gladys putting it on in the morning. I can't say I missed the sweltering heat of Simi, but I missed the ritual of going to the set. I didn't miss getting into those stifling costumes and undergarments, but I missed being Nellie in all her glory.

No, I didn't want to spend the rest of my life on *Little House,* but my leaving had been so sudden, it felt incomplete. There had been no official good-bye. One day, it was January, and I was taking off on our annual hiatus; the next day, poof! There had been no wrap party, no hugs, no kisses, no sobbing cast and crew members saying they'd miss me.

The story felt unfinished, too: Mrs. Oleson held up a letter from Nellie stating that she and Percival were now in New York. That was it. After all those years of campy drama, and that's how the writers ended it. They hadn't even pushed me down a cliff in a wheelchair or dumped me in a leech-infested lake. It was simply not enough—considering the seven long years of blood, sweat, and tears (on camera and off) I had given to this show. I needed some kind of closure.

Well, it took Michael a year, but he gave it to me. Out of the blue, I got a phone call from my father saying that my agent, Lew Sherrill, had just called him in a state of joyous disbelief. They wanted me back on the prairie. Michael had an idea for a show in which Nellie returns to face off with her rival, her newly adopted sister, Nancy. Lew had been so disgusted with the previous year's negotiations, that when the call came, he snorted and harrumphed in disdain and boldly asked for a ridiculous amount of money. He though the network would never meet it. It was four times their top offer for an episode the year before.

Then the producers said, "Okay."

"What? How in the hell . . . ?" Lew sputtered.

The producers didn't specify why they had such a sudden change of heart, but we knew. The network's biggest concern was the bottom line. They were not thinking about the characters or the plotline. They were simply going to the store with a grocery list and a budget. I meant no more to them than a head of lettuce or a can of soup. But now, Michael had given one of his "decrees." He had decided that the episode needed Nellie, and he barked, "Get her!" When Michael gave a decree, he didn't care what it cost. He didn't take no for an answer.

So, miraculously, I was back on the show—but just for this one episode. And it was at a rate of pay I could not have ever dreamed of. I was going to get to see all my friends again, to say good-bye, to have the hugs and tears and ending I thought Nellie deserved. My poor Percival (Steve) didn't get to join me, though, which would have made it all the more wonderful—I guess the producers didn't want to cut two paychecks. Still, "The Return of Nellie" was a very satisfying episode for everyone. Nellie comes back for a visit and meets her hideous new adopted sister, Nancy. Nancy flies into a jealous rage and runs away from home. In the tradition of Laura Ingalls and all the other girls who run away on the prairie, she runs all the way to the mountains and gets lost in the forest. Mr. Oleson and Nellie have to go out and find her.

I got to go up to Sonora, California, and shoot the outdoor scenes. I loved going there as a child, running through the woods, fishing for trout, and so on. Of course, this time I was twenty years old, and instead of being chaperoned by Auntie Marion, I brought my crazy boyfriend of the minute, who proceeded to get drunk with the crew and make a total fool of himself. Then again, how many of the crew could remember that the next morning?

I also got to work with my "replacement," Allison Balson, who played the psychotic Nancy. Now, let me set the record straight: we were not rivals in real life. I get complaints from die-hard Nellie fans all the time: "We hated the new Nellie!" "She's not as good as you!" and my favorite, "You are the only true Nellie!" As if this was some sort of religious cult, and this little girl and I were fighting over the role of Messiah. I think this is all perfectly ridiculous. I loved how Allison Balson played Nancy.

She got the role at age eleven, the same age I was when I first played Nellie, but she had the advantage of growing up watching the show and watching me. A conscientious young actress, she worked hard to avoid anything resembling an imitation. She became determined to create her own brand of bitch. She had done her research and decided not to make Nancy the proud, imperious type. Instead, she played Nancy as a deeply disturbed, miserable little wretch. While Nellie believed everyone loved her (or should, if they had any taste), Nancy was a ball of hysterical neurosis, prone to cries of "you hate me, you hate me, you ALL HATE ME!" I thought she was fantastic. My favorite scene with Allison was the one in which Nancy and Nellie shared a bed. Little Nancy snored, and I put a stop to this by holding her nose and nearly suffocating her. It was proof that, no matter how nice Nellie got after she got married, she still had some bitchiness left in her.

But clearly, Allison the Second won over me in one respect: she got my hair. I was cheerfully informed upon my return that I couldn't have my old wig back. It was now firmly planted on the head of my successor. I had literally passed the crown! So I was given a new wig, a whole new hairdo, one that was apparently the height of fashion for wealthy New York shopkeepers' wives in the early 1880s. Unfortunately, this meant a gigantic "Gibson Girl" blond pouf on top of my head, making me look as if I were wearing an exploded container of Jiffy Pop as a hat. I still get questions from fans who ask, between sobs of laughter, "What the hell was THAT?!"

But what really surprised me was what happened in the scenes with the rest of the cast. Melissa, Katherine MacGregor, Richard Bull, and Jonathan Gilbert, my little baby-bro Willie, who was now a grown-up, handsome man, even choked up for real to see me. Many of the scenes felt like real life, not like acting at all. When Nellie is at the hotel with practically the whole cast, and everyone is carrying on about how much they missed her, no one was pretending. It turns out everyone did miss me, and I missed them. There were a lot of new people now: Pamela Roylance and

Stan Ivar (who played Sarah and John Carter, the new inhabitants of the Ingalls house) and all the new children. It was as if a whole new generation of freckle-faced child actors had come to replace us.

Melissa was the happiest, of course; she had her partner in crime back. At one point, she pulled me aside and whispered, "Things are really tense here without you." She explained that until I left, she and the others didn't realize the function I unknowingly performed on the set. I was not just comic relief in the series; I was the comic relief in real life. I remember that I made people laugh and enjoyed doing it, but Melissa said it was more than that.

"You were, well, sort of a 'buffer,'" she said. "Just when people would start getting really uptight, you'd do or say something silly, and everybody would start laughing and forget all about it."

"So you're saying I was the 'court jester'?" I didn't think this sounded like a compliment.

She insisted it was. "Believe me, it is a total drag around here without you!"

I realize this "skill," if you can call it that, is a psychological defense mechanism. In my own family, I knew that a well-placed gag could diffuse the tensest of situations—even save my life. Sometimes, I could make my brother laugh so hard I could momentarily distract him from what he was about to do next. (A hell of a way to learn comedy, but it does make the toughest audience seem like a breeze by comparison, doesn't it?)

"The Return of Nellie" was the reunion and homecoming I had hoped for, both on and off camera. I could finally let go of *Little House* and move on. The episode aired on November 15,

1982. It was very strange to watch. It was Nellie, but then again it wasn't. Who this new girl really resembled, aside from the popcorn-shaped bouffant, was, well, *me*. It was as if, in a bizarre plot twist, instead of Nellie coming back, they decided to have Alison Arngrim just magically appear in the 1800s. I had never played myself before, and it gave me an eerie feeling to watch it. Seeing all the people of Walnut Grove so happy to see me was even stranger. I think in all those years of desperately trying to overcome my shyness, it hadn't really sunk in that it was possible that most of these people just genuinely liked me.

At the end, when Nellie boards the stage coach to go back to New York, and everybody starts tearing up, there wasn't a faker in the bunch. Not even me.

I'LL BE SEEING YOU. . . .

Over the years, the cast of *Little House* has reunited several times—often because a fan group or an event planner wants to fly us all out to speak and sign autographs (most of us are happy to oblige, hang out, reminisce, and catch up on our lives). The first was in Sonora, California, in September 1998, fifteen years after the show went off the air. Some of us hadn't even seen each other since—so it was an emotional get-together with tears and hugs as we suddenly caught sight of each other at the airport. I hadn't seen Kevin Hagen (Doc Baker) in forever and I went all to pieces. And I couldn't get over how gorgeous Karen Grassle's skin was; she hadn't aged a day! I remember also that I was wearing a hat from the musical *Peter Pan* that said "Never Grow Up,"

and everyone teased me that I obviously hadn't and declared that it must be my secret to looking young.

Melissa Gilbert and I, inseparable as always, went together. We decided it would be a blast and were thrilled to see not just Karen Grassle and Kevin Hagen but also Charlotte Stewart; Matt Laborteaux; Rachel Lindsay and Robin Sidney Greenbush, who brought their mom (we voted her "least changed"); and absolutely everybody else. The winner of "Most Changed" would be the the Carrie twins' brother, Clay Greenbush. As a child, he'd been an extra on the show and was famous for being a real Bart Simpson–style brat, always in trouble. He has grown up to be an absolutely *gorgeous* big strapping man: smart, charming, and an accomplished actor and photographer.

A few years later, much of this group, along with Dean Butler, would reunite in Beatrice, Nebraska, in June 2005 at the Homestead National Museum. A month later, Melissa brought her entire brood to the Tombstone, Arizona, Western Film Festival. (Her hubby, Bruce Boxleitner, had actually turned her on to it, and she had convinced the rest of us.) This one was a huge party: the Carrie twins, the Baby Grace twins, Charlotte, Dean, Hersha Parady, Pam Roylance, Stan Ivar, Brian Part, and even Allison Balson. Allison and I did a lunch presentation together where fans could finally see Nellie and Nancy settle their differences in a civilized manner. We even took turns trying on the Nellie wig!

In May 2007 the *Today* show with Lester Holt gathered us together on national television. The call came completely out of the blue, and we all joked that the network was trying to make up for being so late on their residual payments. I was joined by Michael's daughter Leslie Landon, who played Etta Plum on the show; Charlotte; Karen; Dean;

Rachel; and my dear ol' mom and dad from the Mercantile, Richard Bull and Katherine MacGregor! (Katherine said this was the last time she'd ever do anything like this, but between you and me . . . she loved it.)

Just about every year since, someone has put together an event for us to congregate, and we're all very grateful and look forward to it. Our last big event took place in Keystone, South Dakota, in September 2009. This one was called, of all things, "Holy Terror Days." (I thought it was dedicated to me.) At this reunion, it was me, Karen, Charlotte, Hersha, Rachel, Robyn, Wendi, Brenda, and Patrick Labyorteaux. With Patrick and Hersha there, it turned into the Garvey mother and son reunion! We had a parade, autograph sessions, parties, and then we all went to see Mount Rushmore. It was like a family vacation!

The only one who has never come to a reunion? Melissa Sue Anderson. Big surprise there.

CHAPTER FIFTEEN

A CHANGE IN THE RELATIONSHIP

> **NELLIE: What will I say to him?**
>
> **MR. OLESON: Try "I love you." It's easy to say, and it's right to the point.**
>
> **NELLIE: All right. I will. I'll do it.**
>
> **MRS. OLESON: I'll go with you, honey.**
>
> **MR. OLESON: No, Harriet. Now, let them be alone. Maybe Percival won't stop to think who his new mother-in-law is going to be!**

I couldn't marry Steve Tracy (that gay thing kind of got in the way), but I did marry a friend of his sister. I met Donald Spencer in December 1984. He was twenty-two, like me. He told me a friend of his back in Florida, a girl named Cindy, had a brother, Steve, who married a TV character named Nellie Oleson. *Small world,* I thought. But Don claimed to have never once watched an episode of *Little House.*

Getting married seemed like a good idea at the time. I had gone through a whole parade of boyfriends, none of whom were exactly marriage material. With my childhood, I thought any guy who didn't hit me was "a good catch," and I tended to overlook things—things like huge age differences, boozing, drugs, chronic unemployment, severe mental illness. Then suddenly it dawned on me that I wasn't a teenager anymore. My friends, like Melissa, were getting married. (She married Bo Brinkman after knowing him a mere six weeks.) I thought maybe I should at least consider it. Don seemed like a good possibility—a guy who was classically tall, dark, and attractive, who didn't smoke, drink, take drugs, or run around with other women. He was an actor and a writer. He was hilariously funny. He could both cook and sew. He had lived through a terrible childhood but was getting his life together. And he was definitely looking to settle down. In fact, Don asked me to marry him on our third date.

I had to talk him out of it and urge him to slow down. Looking back on it now, the fact that I was dragging my feet should have told me something wasn't quite right. It all sounded a bit too good to be true. I should have listened to my instincts. But we married in the spring of 1989 in a big Episcopal church. I even wore white. Well, whitish. I didn't want my pals to fall out of the pews laughing and hurt themselves. So I went with a nice ivory, a shade slightly off of virginal white.

The whole time I was dating and engaged to Don, I always referred to Steve Tracy as my "other husband." In the years after we both left *Little House,* we stayed incredibly tight. It was as if our relationship picked up where *Little House* left off. We kidded around and told each other dirty jokes. We still could finish each other's sentences—without a script. It was as if we never stopped being Nellie and Percival. Steve was my friend, my teacher, the confidant I ran to if I had a fight with a boyfriend. I needed him. He was the only constant in my crazy life, and I clung to him when everything else was spinning out of control.

I came home one day in 1986, and Steve had left a message on my answering machine: "Um, hi, it's Steve. Uh . . . call me." Then he hung up.

I felt the hair on the back of my neck stand on end. It wasn't what he had said, it was the way he said it. He sounded like someone who was being held hostage with a gun to his head. It was the scariest message I had ever heard. Frantically, I tried to reach him. I called and called until I finally tracked him down. But when he answered, he said in a hushed voice, "I can't talk right now."

"Okay, fine," I replied. "Then we're going to play twenty questions, and you just say yes or no, okay?"

"Okay."

"Are you okay?"

"No."

My heart was now leaping out of my chest. "Are you being held hostage?" (I thought I ought to get that one out of the way.)

"No."

"Are you in some kind of trouble?"

"Yes."

"Physical, financial, or legal?" (I know. That wasn't really a yes or no question, but this was taking too long.)

"The first one."

"Shit! Are you sick?"

"Yes."

"Very sick?"

"Yes."

"Do you have cancer?"

"Sort of."

"What? Who the hell 'sort of' has cancer?"

Then he said, "I have to get off the phone now."

I knew this was bad. Really bad. I was on pins and needles, waiting for Steve to call and fill me in. But he didn't. I knew he wasn't playing games or purposely trying to give me a nervous breakdown. Steve wouldn't hold out on me. So I figured he was sorting it all out, and I gave him some time, although it was torture. He finally surfaced a few days later and explained that he had been diagnosed with cancer and had freaked out. He assured me it would be all right; he was getting treatment. But I knew he was lying his face off. I knew him too well and loved him too much not to know.

Yet he desperately wanted me to believe everything was going to be fine; he needed me to believe so he could believe it, too. So I never contradicted him—if he smiled and cheerfully told me the radiation treatment was working, I replied, "You betcha!" But deep down, I knew that wasn't so. He was a great actor, but it killed me every time I saw through it.

Finally, a year later, Steve fessed up. He had AIDS, and he was going on *AM Los Angeles,* a popular morning news program, to go public with his diagnosis.

"I wanted you to hear it from me, not on the news. I'm really sorry I lied to you," he said softly. He explained that he was trying to spare me the worry and the pain. He admitted he had known it was AIDS for some time, before most of his doctors, in fact. In the early 1980s, few doctors were very knowledgeable about AIDS, whereas Steve had kept up with all the medical research from the first moment the disease was even whispered about in the gay community. In fact, when he initially got sick, he had a sinking suspicion what it was. There was no blood test yet, so he went to doctor after doctor until he got a proper diagnosis.

I cried like a maniac at the news. He went on about fighting it and experimental treatments. He tried to reassure me, telling me not to be so upset, that "it wasn't really a death sentence." But the reality was that the average life expectancy for someone diagnosed with AIDS in 1986 was nine months. There was no "drug cocktail" to suppress the virus, no combination therapy, no protease inhibitors or any of the medical advances we take for granted today. Good Lord, there wasn't even AZT yet. People with AIDS didn't get better. I was going to have to watch my friend die.

I told him I would be brave, but when I hung up the phone, I lay on the bed, facedown in the pillow, and screamed and screamed.

I was twenty-four years old. Both of my parents were still alive, I wasn't old enough to have lost friends in Vietnam, and I was born in an age when epidemics like diphtheria and polio were distant memories. Death was something that happened to very, very old people. Not your friends. Not people you depended on. And I was already in mourning—I had lost Auntie Marion the summer before.

Marion had liver cancer. She remained very brave and dignified, right up until the end. When the medical transportation service came to take her to the convalescent home, she sighed and said, "Well, I guess I'd better go shave my legs." She had already done her hair and didn't want any part of her looking unkempt when the nice men loaded her into the ambulance. She refused to have a private room. She though it presumptuous, and, besides, she loved to talk to people. She remained beautiful; her skin was so perfect that staff at the facility would ask why this much younger woman was sharing a room with those two old ladies. She was seventy-seven.

Ever polite and considerate, on the day she died she waited until the senior nurse came on duty in the morning. She looked up, smiled, and said, "Oh, good. You're here." She then closed her eyes and stopped breathing. She wouldn't have thought it right to die in front of young trainees; it might upset them.

As much as Marion had tried to prepare us, I was devastated. The person I could count on to know right from wrong, who had taken such good care of me all those years on the *Little House* set, was gone.

Now Steve. He was more than my friend. He was also a mentor and protector. He gave me great confidence as an actress. Like Katherine MacGregor, he, too, had studied acting extensively, but rather than telling people what they were doing wrong, Steve took great pleasure in letting me know when I had it right. He was nine years older, but he treated me as an equal. When he was just starting out on *Little House,* a reporter asked him how it felt to play opposite a girl of no more than seventeen. The guy was digging for dirt. But Steve had nothing but good things to say about me: I was a breeze to work with, and I had impeccable comedic timing. He didn't have to say that. Neither I nor my publicist was in the room, and I wasn't going to get him fired. But he said it anyway, and he told me he really meant it.

Steve was thirty-two when he was diagnosed with AIDS. The idea of anyone dying at thirty-two struck me as obscene. And for it to be my friend was downright unforgivable. He kept telling me not to, but I cried every day.

Steve didn't cry—at least not in front of me. He was not just brave, he was noble. He let the doctors experiment on him, and he agreed to be part of a radical new study, which required him to jam needles filled with experimental drugs into his thigh. He told me that most people had quit this study because the treatments were so excruciatingly painful. But he said he didn't mind the pain. The doctors might find a cure, and even if it was too late for him, he could be saving someone else's life down the road. His courage and compassion floored me. If the tables were turned, I don't know that I would have the strength, stamina, or stomach to do what he was doing.

And then the *National Enquirer* called—they had gotten wind of what was going on. Was it true about Steve Tracy having AIDS? How long did he have to live? How'd he get it? And the best one: *Did I have it?* After all, I had kissed him on TV. I was now in the "Linda Evans position": When actor Rock Hudson's AIDS diagnosis was revealed, people thought Linda Evans—who was kissing him constantly on the soap opera *Dynasty*—was in danger. I couldn't believe how ignorant most people were about AIDS. You couldn't contract it from kissing; you couldn't catch it if someone sneezed or coughed on you. It was blood borne through sex, needles, and transfusions.

Steve educated me day by day. Just as he had been my mentor and teacher in life, he was going to keep up the job while he was dying. At first, I was afraid to be around him if I had a cold. I thought his immune system was so fragile, he would pick up any germ—and that it could be fatal.

"Relax, will ya?" he said and laughed. "I'm not the Boy in the Plastic Bubble."

I went with him to the doctors, to "healing workshops," to candlelight vigils. We even checked out a Louise Hay workshop. Louise Hay was a cancer survivor who had written the book *Heal Your Body* about how positive thought patterns and meditation could affect one's health. The AIDS community embraced her teachings. They were faced with a terrifying disease that the doctors barely understood and could offer no cure for. Happy thoughts had worked for Louise; she was cured. People with AIDS wanted to believe this course of treatment could cure them as well.

Louise Hay's meetings were usually held in church basements or public recreation rooms in West Hollywood. They were insanely popular, and the attendees quickly dubbed them "Hay-Rides" for their cheery, upbeat atmosphere. I was highly skeptical of such things and feared they might only offer a big dose of bogus "faith healing" nonsense. Steve insisted I go with him. "I promise, you'll be surprised," he said.

The recreation room at Plummer Park in West Hollywood was packed. There was a giddy feeling in the room like before a revival tent meeting, so my skepticism continued. It didn't help that many of the longtime attendees were desperately ill. I was surrounded by people in wheelchairs, people whose friends had carried them in on stretchers. Some were even walking around with Hickman ports, the permanently attached tubes that deliver medicine through a hole cut in the patient's chest. What on earth did these people think Louise Hay could do for them?

When Louise walked onto the stage, the crowd went wild. She was a beautiful woman, with blond, almost white hair and porcelain skin. The meeting began with a lot of very churchlike meditation, repeating of affirmations, and whatnot—all stuff that confirmed my suspicion that this lady was really full of it.

And then she spoke. After a few opening remarks, her beatific smile disappeared, and she became serious. "I have to talk to you about something," she said quite sternly. She explained that, to her great disappointment, people were claiming that she could magically "cure AIDS" and other diseases; that they no longer needed anything from their doctors; that they could throw away their meds and just read her book. "Nothing could be further from the truth," she said.

She explained that she had, in fact, during her cancer, done everything the doctors asked her to do, even surgery. It was only when these attempts began to fail that she knew she needed something more. Meditation and beliefs by themselves were not sufficient, she warned. One must also take care of one's body in a concrete fashion. She explained that the instructions she was giving in her meetings were not just intended for the hour, but were meant to be used all the time—in their diets, their medical treatment, their living conditions. Getting happily blissed out for an hour a week was not going to produce a miracle. Fighting diseases like AIDS and cancer was just plain old-fashioned hard work. In other words, the sweet, beautiful, sainted healer stood there and read us the riot act.

I turned to Steve and said, "She's fabulous! Why didn't you tell me she was like this?" He replied, "Well, I did say you'd be surprised, didn't I?" We gave her a standing ovation.

For the record, Louise Hay is still alive and well, and so are some of the people who went to her workshops. Just not Steve.

No matter how bad the disease got, Steve insisted on being self-sufficient. Even though his mother and sister flew in to be by his side (a rare occurrence back in the 1980s, when parents routinely abandoned their sick and dying children out of fear or prejudice), he would only let them do so much. I asked him what I could do. He explained the "volunteer schedule" he had worked out: "Well, I've got a guy from the AIDS Project Los Angeles Buddy Program coming over. He helps me with a whole bunch of stuff and even takes me to the doctor. The maid's still coming to clean, and what with APLA and Project Angel Food, I've got no problem getting food delivered. Oh, then there's this poor guy they sent over from Shanti, but he's a complete idiot. So I make him do my laundry."

What was left for me? Steve thought about it for a few minutes, then decreed I would be "the goodtime girl." I would hang out with him; we'd go to dinner and the movies. My job was to continue to help him enjoy life. I liked my assignment.

Through it all, Steve never lost his sense of humor. He even taught me a few AIDS jokes, including this one:

So this woman goes to a nutritionist and says, "Can you help me? My son has leprosy, bubonic plague, and AIDS. Is there any diet that will help?' "

"Leprosy, bubonic plague, and AIDS?" says the nutritionist. "Let me see . . . Okay, we're going to start him on a diet of pizza and pancakes."

"Pizza and pancakes?" asks the mother. "How interesting! Will that help?"

"I don't know," says the nutritionist, "but it's the only thing we can slide under the door."

Though it was meant to be funny—and it was—this joke accurately captured where people's heads were at when it came to AIDS. Fear and misinformation were rampant, and AIDS patients were looked upon as lepers. I couldn't believe the stuff people were asking me—about toilet seats, mosquitoes, all sorts of silliness. And they were people who should know better: not just other actors, but everyone from my best friend's aunt in Boston, to tabloid reporters, to reporters from so-called legitimate newspapers, even friends. For some reason, I was suddenly a noted authority on the subject. But why me? Who cared what *I* had to say about it? I was an actress, not an epidemiologist, for Christ's sake. And then I remembered the scene from one of my all-time favorite movies, *Network*. TV news anchor Howard Beale, played by Peter Finch, has cracked up and thinks he's hearing the voice of God when Ned Beatty's character tells him why he wants him to carry his message. He says, "Why me, Lord?" And the answer is: *"Because you're on television, dummy."*

So, I thought, *all right, if everyone's going to insist on getting their medical news from somebody on TV—namely, me—what if I did something totally crazy, like providing correct, possibly life-saving information?* So I went to AIDS Project Los Angeles and signed up for hotline training, which consisted of weeks of classes with homework and a five-page final exam. I had hated school, but now I was finally studying for a reason.

I more than passed the final exam; I got the highest score anyone had gotten on it. I not only worked the phones but also wound up at the food bank, the hospice, and ultimately the speakers' bureau. I was sent all over Los Angeles to speak on AIDS and HIV—schools, offices, even prisons. Many of these had turned away AIDS speakers before. They didn't know them, they were strangers, and they worried—crazy as it was—that they'd bring AIDS with them. But they knew me. I had been in their living rooms. I wasn't a threat; I was a TV star. I'd sign autographs, I'd quote Nellie-isms, I'd do whatever they wanted—as long as they listened to me and wised up about AIDS.

Skeptics said I wouldn't keep up my activism for long. "They always quit when the friend dies," the old-timers at the organization said. I didn't even allow that thought to enter my mind. I wasn't blind—I saw that Steve was getting worse. He looked so pale and gaunt, as if a strong breeze might blow him away. We both knew the end was coming, though we never discussed it. Good-time girls don't talk about dying. That wasn't in my job description.

Then one night in November 1986, Steve called. He told me what I had been dreading for several months: he had very little time left, and his mother and sister were coming to take him home to Florida. He wanted to die at home. I was inconsolable. I wanted to rush to his side and keep him here with me. I thought if I could just hold on to him, I could stop death in its tracks.

But then Steve said, "Don't worry, this isn't the end; it's just a change in the relationship."

Less than a week later, on Thanksgiving Day, Steve Tracy died. I didn't get the call from his family until a few days later. But I already knew. I was heading home from Thanksgiving dinner at my parents' house, when Donald and I stopped for gas. It wasn't terribly late, and we weren't in a particularly bad neighborhood, and yet I was suddenly hit by the most overwhelming sense of danger.

When Don got back in the car, I said, "I think something's happened." He didn't dismiss this feeling. He sensed it, too. We drove home in silence. So when the call came from Steve's family, it wasn't a surprise.

Steve's death was very hard on his mother and sister, who had stood by him through his illness, even though they lived in Tampa, Florida, a city that was not exactly what you would call enlightened about the AIDS crisis. When he died, their local funeral home refused to cremate him. They wouldn't take the body. Nor would the next place his mother called. Or the next one.

We'd had trouble like this in Los Angles, too. The AIDS hotline even made a list of funeral homes you could call that knew that you didn't get AIDS from preparing a dead person for cremation. But Steve's mom wasn't in Los Angeles. She finally found a funeral home that would help her: the one funeral home that took people who had died of AIDS was the only African-American-owned funeral home in town. Having been the target of discrimination and hatred for so many years, back to the days when white-owned funeral homes wouldn't touch the body of a black person, its owners understood what it was like to have someone tell you that you can't bury your loved one, because "we don't serve your kind."

After they got him cremated, Steve's mom and sister brought him back to L.A. They fulfilled his final wish and scattered his ashes under the Hollywood sign. If you're ever looking up at it, that's Steve, right there under the *D*.

There was a small memorial for Steve at the home of a friend of his. His mom and sister got to meet their now famous son's Hollywood friends. Melissa Gilbert and I stood in the kitchen drinking wine from plastic cups and toasting Steve's memory. He was the first of our *Little House* cast to die before his time. We didn't know then how many more we would lose.

Despite the old-timers at AIDS Project Los Angeles' predictions, I didn't quit when Steve died, and I still haven't. Instead, I've spent the past decades working with different AIDS organizations all over the country. I eventually met my soul mate, my second husband, Bob, through my activism, and I made a couple of hundred best friends along the way. Of course, I lost most of them to the disease, but I still see all of their faces—and hear all of their voices—clear as day. Steve's is the brightest and loudest among them. And he has all the best lines.

CHAPTER SIXTEEN

MICHAEL GETS THE LAST LAUGH

MRS. OLESON: You have to learn about men, Nellie dear—they're all as fickle as weathervanes!

"Michael Landon just died."

It was July 1, 1991. I was volunteering at Tuesday's Child, an AIDS organization that provides services to children and families dealing with HIV. Even with the plethora of AIDS organizations in Los Angeles, babies and little kids had managed to fall through the cracks. At Tuesday's Child, we did our best to catch them. A fellow volunteer heard the news from her mother, who'd just seen a report on TV. My stomach was churning, and I felt that awful chill I had felt when Steve died.

Michael had battled cancer for three months now, since April. But not just any cancer; it was pancreatic, the worst, inoperable kind. Brave and crazy as always, he made his final appearance on the *Tonight Show* with his old buddy, Johnny Carson, on May 8. He joked with Johnny that he'd been told he could cure his cancer with coffee enemas. When Johnny grimaced, Michael roared, “Then I guess I won’t ask you to come to my house to pour the cream!”

When I watched him on TV that night, he was a shadow of the man I knew on *Little House.* He looked awful, pale, thin as a rail, but acted like having terminal cancer was the funniest thing that ever happened. It gave me terrible flashbacks to Steve Tracy and his unstoppable bravery in the face of death. What was it with guys from *Little House*? They all greeted death like mad Viking warriors.

It was months since I had last seen Michael. I never did have the fun of working with him again, and I regret that. I ran into him once in a while if I was auditioning for something out at the MGM lot, and he was always glad to see me, full of his usual grins and hugs. He knew I was making fun of him in my stand-up act almost every night and thought it was the world’s greatest compliment.

I didn’t have the strength to go visit him when he was sick. Melissa did, but I couldn’t bear the thought of seeing the one man I truly believed to be indestructible lying on his death bed. Over the last couple of years I had watched dozens of friends die of AIDS. I was at the point where I could look at someone’s face and know exactly how many days they had left. I wasn’t going to stare into Michael’s eyes and start counting.

The day Michael died, I was booked to do an interview with *Entertainment Tonight* about Tuesday’s Child. I knew what was going to happen now. The interview would be only about Michael. There was not going to be time for any sort of “private” grieving; just moments after I heard the news, the *ET* crew was in the elevator coming up to my office.

Knowing I had only few seconds before the media onslaught, I grabbed the phone and quickly dialed Melissa. She had just heard also via the television and was utterly hysterical. I tried to say something comforting, but what was there to say? We both knew Michael was the only real father she ever had. All I wanted to do was hang up, jump in my car, drive to her house, and bring her a Slurpee.

But by the time I hung up, the *ET* crew was already in my office setting up. "I'm sorry," said the producer, "but you realize what part of the interview we have to do first." I knew perfectly well this meant "instead" and, as sad as I was about Michael's passing, I felt disappointed not to be able to impart the message I had intended about Tuesday's Child. I already understood that the purpose of TV shows is not to inform the public or perform some sort of educational service but rather to make audiences stay tuned long enough to see the commercials. And people don't generally stay tuned to hear about sick and dying children. They do, however, stay tuned to hear about sick and dying celebrities. If we were lucky, Tuesday's Child might get mentioned. But Michael Landon's death was going to be the lead story everywhere, and this crew would be able to say they had interviewed Nellie Oleson within seconds of Michael's death.

The questions were the same ones interviewers always asked—"What was he really like?" "Was he fun to work with?"—except now, for the first time, they were being asked in the past tense. It was a little too quick for me. I stopped the reporter at one point and said, "You know, he's only been gone for thirty minutes." It was almost impossible to imagine someone who'd been that almost alarmingly alive just not being here anymore. It seemed very wrong, incomprehensible.

Then the phone began to ring. Every other news crew in town was coming to pick up where *Entertainment Tonight* left off. In general, I was happy to talk about my experience working with Michael, because he meant so much to me, but one reporter in particular really got under my skin. My Tuesday's Child coworkers who were still in the room were horrified at this woman's lack of tact. The body wasn't cold yet, and she was swooping in like a vulture to get a trashy tabloid sound bite. She had already made up her mind exactly what she wanted me to say and was going to keep asking the same stupid questions several different ways until I told her what she wanted to hear. Finally, she asked, "Was he like a father to you?"

I found this to be an utterly perplexing question. Perhaps she got her notes mixed up, and this was meant for Melissa Gilbert's or Melissa Sue Anderson's interview. Michael didn't play my father; he played the father of my mortal enemy. And unlike the two Melissas, I had a real, live—if crazy—actual father in my house the entire time.

"Why would he be like a 'father' to me?" I said. "Um . . . no."

She hated this answer. "Did you not get along then?" Yikes! In this woman's universe, were there only two possible types of relationship? "Substitute father" or "intensely disliked"?

"No, no, I liked him very much," I tried to explain.

She seemed genuinely excited by the possibility of a down-and-dirty negative angle. "Were you afraid of him?" she asked, arching an eyebrow.

At this point I just burst out laughing. "Hardly!" I snorted. I then tried to explain his wonderfully outrageous sense of humor and how much we had all enjoyed that. She seemed terribly disappointed by this. My remarks were cut almost entirely from the interview.

When this interview wrapped up, I headed straight for my car. I had to get out of there and decided to drop off some supplies at PAWS (Pets Are Wonderful Support), the volunteer group who took care of pets for people too sick from AIDS to manage. PAWS was founded and run by the famously eccentric Nadia Sutton, a woman who loved animals and people with a fierce passion. She had a wonderfully exotic foreign accent and personality to match.

She had heard the news as well. “Dahling, come in and sit down!” she cried when I walked into PAWS’ office. She took the bag of cans from me and hugged me. I slumped into a chair and blurted out the whole awful story, how the press was asking all these ridiculous questions and nobody seemed to understand how I felt about Michael, and how all I wanted was to be able to hear that crazy, hysterical laugh of his one more time. I told her the media were trying to mourn the image of the Michael they had known, Pa Ingalls and Little Joe. Nobody wanted to hear about the real flesh-and-blood person I had known.

“Oh, dahling!” Nadia cried. “I understand perfectly.” And she did. “Your friend was a real person; he was good, and he was bad, and you loved him anyway. And they want to make him a saint! But that’s not the person you loved!

“Look at me,” she continued. “Everyone says I am so nice, I help all these people and animals, yes? But I am also sometimes the bitch, yes?” She understood. Of course she did. She was *French*. And that was just it. I wondered to myself: Why is it that when people die, we make such an effort to turn them into saints? Especially when the entire reason we loved them so much in the first place is because they weren't.

I didn't feel like I could tell the interviewers about the seven years I spent working for a guy who smoked, drank, swore, told horrible jokes, never wore underwear, and celebrated the end of the season by taking us all to the racetrack. And I certainly couldn't tell them I enjoyed every minute of it. Or that even at his most erratic, Michael taught me valuable lessons that have served me all of my life. Michael Landon was not really Charles Ingalls, and the world is a much better place as a result. "Pa" might have been the world's greatest dad, but he would have been a terrible producer. *Little House on the Prairie* would likely have never made it to the screen. And where would I be, quite frankly, without *Little House*?

Michael's funeral was to be at a secret location. Enormous subterfuge and expense had been employed to keep the ceremony private so as not to let the press get wind of it. Naturally, it was the *National Enquirer* that called to give me the address. They always knew everything first. But the reporter did have one question for me since he had me on the line. The *Enquirer* had taken photos over the fence of Michael's house when his body was carried out to the mortuary's hearse. They wanted to know why the body bag was red. Did that mean Michael Landon had died of AIDS? They had heard this rumor and wanted me to clear it up before it spread nationwide. I told him they were a bunch of idiots and immediately called my mortician friend, who was appalled, but explained the situation, which I later relayed to the *Enquirer.*

"Different mortuaries use different brands and colors of bags.

I know his mortuary. The bag wasn't red, it was burgundy. It's one of your better body bags."

If you're famous, don't expect any peace, even when you're dead.

The funeral at Hillside Memorial Park in Culver City was beautiful, even with the five helicopters whirring furiously over the building during the entire service. Don and my father came along with me. Ronald and Nancy Reagan were there. As Nancy walked in, she gave my father a strange look. There were so many celebrities in the room, she may have thought she recognized him and was trying figure out who he was. My father turned to me and in a very loud stage whisper said, "Help! I'm being cruised by Nancy Reagan!"

Almost the whole cast was in attendance. We filed in and wandered around uncomfortably for a minute before sitting down. When we settled and looked around, we all noticed it. We had taken our seats in exactly the same positions we sat in when we did church scenes on the show. The women sat down in the same pew as their TV husbands (except for me, of course—though Steve was there in spirit), and we all sat the same number of rows back from the front. It was as if Michael had called us with his old megaphone, and we'd all gone on autopilot and gotten into formation. My God, he had us well trained.

It was good to see my old friends and colleagues, even under these circumstances. Some of us hadn't seen each other since the show ended in 1983, and nearly went to pieces.

And then there was Melissa Sue Anderson, looking absolutely beatific and holding her beautiful new baby. I thought,

She's married and has a baby now, so she must finally be happy. I approached her cautiously and said, "What a beautiful baby!" (No lie there.) "How old is she?" All mothers like to talk about their babies. Give them a chance, and they'll talk your ear off about every single cute thing their kid has done since birth.

"Six months," she said curtly and turned away. And she never said another word to me.

The eulogy was given by Merlin Olsen, who was a famous football player back when Los Angeles actually had a pro football team, the Rams. He had also played Jonathan Garvey on the show and was most famous at this point for his FTD flower commercials. His speech was absolutely brilliant, moving and funny at the same time. He started by saying, perfectly deadpan, "Hello, I'm Merlin Olsen. I sell flowers." He then went on to do a virtual stand-up routine about Michael. Michael had insisted his funeral be funny, and he got his wish.

Some people had wondered if Michael would have a religious funeral when he died. He did. It was Jewish. But even the rabbi made fun of him: "Michael was not religious, in the traditional sense of the word. . . ." He spoke of Michael's response when the doctors told him that the chemo treatments would destroy his beautiful mane of hair. He said, "I'm rich, I'll buy a hat."

Friend after friend, story after story, people cried and laughed their heads off at the same time. I worried that poor Melissa wouldn't get through her speech. She looked as if she'd locked her knees to keep from shaking, and I feared she'd pass out. She invoked the poem from the episode in which Academy Award–winner Patricia Neal guest stars as a character who finds out she's dying and has to find a home for her children. It was an episode that Michael had written:

Remember me with smiles and laughter,
Because that's how I'll remember you all.
If you can only remember me with tears,
Then don't remember me at all.

Afterward, when we were walking to the car, the paparazzi were taking pictures from across the lawn. They were at least being quiet about it and staying reasonably far away. Everyone just kept their head down and walked straight to their cars. Until I walked by. They started yelling. "Hey, Alison! Yoo-hoo! Over here!"

My dad, Don, and I ducked our heads and walked more quickly, but then we started to laugh. They didn't harass anyone else like this, but for some reason they thought it was perfectly okay in my case. It had somehow been decided, for better or worse, that I wasn't like the "other" celebrities. I was glad that I wasn't seen as "too precious" or overly sensitive. Besides, I was with my father, the infamous Thor Arngrim. He wasn't going to get upset about the threat of possible publicity, planned or not.

At least I knew one thing: Michael would have thought it was hysterical. There she goes again, that girl who crashed the party and her crazy old man. I'm dead, and they're still hogging the camera!

CHAPTER SEVENTEEN

DIVORCE VIA FAX

> **MRS. OLESON: Well, in my case, Nellie and Willie were *more* than enough.**
>
> **CAROLINE: In the case of Nellie and Willie, Mrs. Oleson, I'd have to agree with you.**

My marriage to Don fell apart—maybe because I didn't have Steve to vent to anymore. Perhaps if Steve had been around to talk to, I'd have left sooner. Four years into our marriage, I realized that Don and I were having the exact same arguments over and over. It was like being on some sort of emotional treadmill, where you run and run and never go forward. I was dizzy and exhausted from going in circles.

I don't know how many things he actually lied about. I just know he started telling these ridiculous stories to cover up stuff I didn't care about in the first place. He hid food wrappers and lied about what he ate. He lied about where he'd been even if he'd really been shopping or doing something totally innocent. I couldn't trust him, and I knew it was time to go.

I went to my best friend Sharon's house; she had been maid of honor at our wedding. She was happy to take me in. But before

I could come in the house, I had to let her husband stand on the porch and say, "I told you so."

I couldn't believe I was getting divorced. Melissa Gilbert took me to lunch. She had just divorced her first husband, Bo Brinkman, and was prepared to offer any assistance necessary. I noticed that we had done so many things at the same time. We had gotten married around the same time, to writers, and we were both getting divorced the same year. We compared notes on our failed marriages, and I suggested that perhaps we were both picking the same kind of wrong guy.

She said, "No, silly, *I* just go for sexual compulsives. *You* marry gay guys."

She offered to help me find a lawyer, but I had found out you could do the whole thing by fax. I called this service, 1-800-DUMP-HIM, and divorced my husband by fax. I know it was pretty harsh. I guess I can't very well make fun of young people who break up via text. To this day, my friends still joke, "Don't piss her off! You'll get a fax!" But truthfully, Don would have had to be blind not to see it coming. We did go to counseling for several months, and even the shrink told him I was going to leave him.

I didn't know what or who to believe anymore. Worst of all, I'd discovered a real whopper: Don *had* watched *Little House on the Prairie*—maybe more than *Mary Tyler Moore*. He knew exactly who I was when we met. In fact, the day after we met, he had gone to a friend of his, an entertainment writer who had interviewed me years before. He got the tape of the interview and went home and listened to it for "tips." *Creepy.*

Don had some sort of fantasy that if he moved to Hollywood and married a blond actress, this would solve all his problems.

But wait, who better, than, well, Nellie Oleson herself! Lesson learned: never, ever, get romantically involved with anyone who has watched *Little House on the Prairie.*

By contrast, among many of his refreshing characteristics was the fact that Bob Schoonover hadn't the slightest idea who I was and, even when people told him, didn't care. Bob was the director of the Southern California AIDS Hotline, where I had volunteered back in 1986 when Steve was diagnosed. When we met, he did ask for an autograph—my mother's. He was a huge fan of *Underdog* and wanted to meet Sweet Polly Purebred.

Bob was an unusual person. When most people still didn't know what AIDS was, he was applying for work at the AIDS Project Los Angeles. He was the sixth person they hired and the first straight man. When he started there, they gave him an office, a remodeled broom closet, and took great glee in ragging him about being "in the closet."

We became great friends. We were often booked to speak on the same panels and hung out together so often that one volunteer took to calling me "the ever lovely *Mrs.* Schoonover." At the time, I was married, and Bob had a girlfriend. Besides, he wasn't my type. For starters, he was much too nice: intelligent, polite, well educated. And employed!

I knew Bob was twelve years older than I was, but that didn't concern me. He was obviously an "ex-hippie," complete with beard and ponytail. But not just any ponytail; Bob's was curled into one, great, black ringlet. People at APLA actually used to whisper behind his back, "How the hell does he get it to do that?" He was a man of many mysteries. I called his home number one day and got his answering machine. I was greeted with a terrible, high-pitched grinding sound, a screaming roar from the pit of hell. I later asked him what on earth it was.

"Oh, that's my guitar solo," he replied.

"A guitar solo?" I asked incredulously. I didn't even know he played guitar.

"Yes. It's from a song I've been working on. It's called 'Godzilla Christmas.' " He said this as if it was the most normal thing in the world.

"I swear when I heard it, I thought it was a blender."

Strangely, he seemed to take this as a compliment.

When I got divorced, Bob and I went to lunch to commiserate. The same month I was getting divorced, he was breaking up with his girlfriend of many years. We compared notes on all the awful things that had gone on at our respective houses.

I said, "You wouldn't want to go out with *me,* would you?"

Bob looked as if he'd just bitten through his fork. He stammered out, "In a New York minute."

Our first date was March 31, 1993, Bob's last day as director of the hotline. After nine years of dealing with death, disease, and bureaucracy, he was starting to burn out. The staff threw him a send-off party after an AIDS seminar, and we planned to go get coffee after it. Bob was presented with a huge cake, and our colleagues made speeches about how much they would miss him. I was the only one in the room who wasn't saying good-bye. Afterward, we headed to a coffeehouse in Hollywood, just a few blocks from the AIDS Project. We sat uncomfortably on high stools with our lattes and muffins, in the deafening din of the coffeehouse, trying to think what on earth we should say to each other now that we were on a "date." We kept getting the giggles.

We never had any lack of topics to discuss before, but now we felt sort of silly and on display.

Nevertheless, we went on another date, and many more after that. All my friends told me it was a terrible idea to rush into a new relationship so soon after a divorce—and with someone I'd been friends with for nearly seven years. A former coworker, no less. They insisted it was a rebound and doomed from the start. But they didn't know Bob. They hadn't looked into those brown eyes of his, and, well, they certainly hadn't kissed him.

One day Bob was out of town at some AIDS conference. He called me late that night from his hotel room, and in the middle of telling me how much he missed me, he said, "I was watching this movie, and, well, the interaction between the man and the woman reminded me of us."

My mind reeled. What on earth was he watching? *Casablanca? Wuthering Heights?* What famous film couple did he see as us?

"It was just something the man said to the woman that got to me," he continued.

" 'The world's a much more interesting place with you in it.' "

I slumped off the sofa onto the floor still clutching the phone. Yes, he had just quoted me the last line from my favorite movie of all time, but not one I had ever thought of as a romance. He had just uttered Dr. Hannibal Lecter's last words to FBI agent Clarice Starling in *The Silence of the Lambs.* In that scene, the evil doc is admitting that, in Clarice, he has finally met his match. And I knew I had finally met mine.

Bob and I were living together by June. In November we got married in the beautiful backyard of a friend's house, a woman who had also been a hotline volunteer. Bob announced that he was going to wear a tuxedo. This was quite a surprise to those who knew him as someone who favored torn jeans and a T-shirt on an almost daily basis. I tried to explain to him that it was a small, daytime wedding, and that tuxedoes were for huge weddings, with dozens of bridesmaids and groomsmen. I explained also that, since it was my second wedding, I would not be wearing anything resembling a gown, so a tuxedo would not be appropriate. Bob was not swayed by this kind of reasoning in the slightest.

He insisted, "I don't care how many times you've been married! It's my first wedding, and I'm wearing a tuxedo!"

I protested, "But then, what on earth am I going to wear?"

"Why don't you wear a tuxedo, too? You always look so cute in a dark suit," he answered with a smile.

So I did. And I went barefoot, too. The wedding was in a garden, after all.

Bob had one more helpful suggestion: "Why not paint your toenails black to match your tuxedo?"

"Black toenails? Are you nuts?" I said. "You seriously expect me to paint my toenails black?"

And that's when Bob looked at me with that grin and said, "I will if you will."

For the walk down the aisle, I carried no bouquet. Bob and I both had on rose boutonnieres and red AIDS ribbons pinned to our lapels. Both the best man, Bob's best friend, Timmy, and the matron of honor, my best friend, Sharon, wore tuxedos and had black toenails as well. Our friend David Taylor, a professional magician, was the ring bearer. Our rings appeared in a ball of fire and then sailed up into the air and floated over our heads. The Reverend Stephen Pieters, a friend and long-term survivor of AIDS, snatched them out of the air laughing and proceeded to marry us.

Months later, Bob and I went to a party where we ran into the volunteer who called me the "ever lovely Mrs. Schoonover." He hadn't heard about the wedding. He was standing by the swimming pool when we walked in. He smiled to see us and said, "Oh, look! If it isn't Bob Schoonover and the ever lovely Mrs. Schoonover!"

We smiled and held up our hands with the matching rings and simply said, "Yes, actually." He was so shocked, we nearly had to fish him out of the pool.

CHAPTER EIGHTEEN

THEY LOVE ME—THEY REALLY, REALLY *LOVE ME*

NELLIE: I'll fix you, Laura Ingalls!

January 18, 2002, my fortieth birthday, should have been a horrible day for me. This particular milestone is not a good day for a lot of women, and usually a bad day for actresses, particularly former child actresses. To top it off, I spent the day working at a temp job because, although *Little House on the Prairie* paid residuals, it wasn't *Friends* money. *Little House* was a good gig for its day, but it wasn't a free ride for life. And since I wasn't going to go out and steal tips off tables like my father, I had long since adopted my mom's outlook on being an unemployed actress: whenever she needed money, she did the honorable thing—she temped.

My mom had passed away less than a year before. Her death was very sudden. It was September 2001, and my father called from Vancouver. My mother had just been rushed to the hospital, something about an intestinal blockage. "It's very bad," he told me.

After I got off the phone, I began to make arrangements to fly up. Five minutes later, the phone rang again. It was my father. "She's gone."

Over the sound of the blood pounding in my ears, I heard him say in a broken voice, "Can you come up?" I remember I was so worried about his heart condition at that point, I made him promise not to leave the hospital alone. Bob and I flew up that night. We arranged a huge beautiful funeral, and hundreds turned out to pay their respects to Gumby, as well as to Norma. The place was packed. But because of the terrorist acts of September 11, the scattering of her ashes had been postponed, and I now had the cold comfort of knowing that she was at rest in a plastic Tupperware container in my father's closet.

As if my mother's death wasn't depressing enough, after a couple of years of trying to have a baby with Bob to no avail, the doctors had officially informed me that the chances of my producing a child through the usual means were essentially slim to none.

Yet despite all these circumstances, I was strangely happy on my fortieth. Not exactly dance-in-the-streets happy, but I knew things could be worse, and I felt grateful for all I had.

Then the phone rang. It was my manager, Thomas DeLorenzo. After my dad retired, I had managed to find someone nearly as nutty and definitely as gay—if possibly gayer—to take over the job. He snarled into the phone, "Pack your shit. You're going to France."

I was booked to appear on the French talk show *Les Enfants de Tele (The Children of Television)*. I would be getting paid, and I would be staying at the George V Hotel, possibly the most expensive place in Paris. And there were two tickets in first class. But I wouldn't even get a chance to ask Bob.

"I'm going!" my manager barked.

The plane was nearly empty. It was only January, just four months after September 11, and people weren't running down to the airport to jump back on a plane yet. We were the only people in first class, and the only other passengers on the entire flight were six soldiers. We were booked on a wonderful airline called Air Liberté that went out of business during the post-9/11 travel-industry collapse. Too bad; they had a hell of a cheese cart.

Going to Paris for the first time was like going to Mars. Never having been on a transatlantic flight, when I looked out the window at night and saw this huge black nothingness populated by just the moon and a few stars, I felt as if I was traveling to outer space. This sensation only increased when I landed.

We were met by two absolutely gorgeous Frenchmen. One was working with the TV station, and the other was our chauffeur/bodyguard. As Thom and I climbed into the back of the black Peugeot, I laughed, "I'll take the blond, you can have the brunette." Always one for the blue-collar, rough-trade type, I, of course, preferred the bodyguard.

We checked into the hotel, and Thom insisted we must go out immediately for chocolate mousse. He was always insisting on things, but he was right this time. He had been to Paris before, and I deferred to him on what were the "must sees" and the "must eats." Now, I had eaten a lot of chocolate mousse in my time, and I knew a good mousse when I tasted it. But this was orgasmic. Maybe they just use more cream, or maybe it's something they feed the cows—I don't know. But I took one bite, and my eyes bugged out of my head. I had been in France for only a few hours, and I knew my life was about to change radically.

And then there was the show. I had been told I would be

interviewed, but I didn't find out until I arrived on the set that the talk show was over three hours long and broadcast live. Who in their right mind does a live three-hour talk show? What the hell was this, the Jerry Lewis telethon? No, it was France. Three hours is a perfectly reasonable amount of time for a talk show, as far as they're concerned. It just means you can have more guests.

The green room was filled with people drinking champagne and eating gourmet hors d'oeuvres, and the hair and makeup folks were extraordinary. They seemed happy to give us anything we wanted. Thom wasn't even going on camera, and he was able to get a haircut while he was hanging out backstage.

On the show, the producers just kept bringing on guests from various French TV series and films. One group would get tired, leave, and a new set would be brought out. Every now and then a group of belly dancers would come out, and confetti would drop from the ceiling. The girls all had something written across their stomachs and backs. I asked what on earth this was about. I was told that since the show was live, the producers knew that people watching shows on other stations were going to switch over to them at the commercial break. So every time the other stations went to commercial, the confetti rained, and the girls came out. The message on their stomachs said, "Welcome, Channel 3 Viewers!"

The show kept presenting random clips of things, including an uncensored segment from an American newscast of Mike Tyson threatening another fighter on TV. Thom and I watched aghast as Mike Tyson was projected onto a giant screen screaming at his opponent, "I'm gonna fuck you till you love me!!" The

French thought this was absolutely hilarious. Then the stage manager turned to me and said, "Okay, you're next."

The other guests on the set at this point were popular French comedians and actors, mostly from the new live-action movie based on the famous French comic book *Asterix.* It was just about to open, and its studio was doing a huge press campaign like we would have for the next *Batman* or *Spider-Man* film. One of the actors was a young man named Jamel Debbouze, a hugely famous star in France. I recognized him as the grocery boy from *Amélie,* the one with the crush on "Lady Di."

The show's host, another famous Frenchman who, like Madonna, went only by the name Arthur, had been teasing the audience for the last couple of hours with the promise of an upcoming special guest who had traveled all the way from the United States. He had been dropping hints, and Jamel had been trying increasingly hilarious bad guesswork to figure out who it was.

But now Arthur dropped the big hint: *"La Petite Maison dans la Prairie!"* The studio audience oohed and aahed. The screen began to display a slide show of pictures of various cast members. Karen Grassle had been a previous guest on the show, so they knew it wasn't her. As each cast member's picture appeared, the audience yelled out his or her name in unison. "Charles Ingalls!" "Doc Baker!" "Laura!" (pronounced "Lohr-rah!") "Marie!" "Monsieur Edwards!" Finally, the screen showed a picture of Nellie. The crowd went berserk. The host told Jamel who the guest was. He roared in protest that it was not possible.

As the *Little House* theme music swelled, the audience began to sing. I was backstage about to enter when I heard the entire studio audience singing—chanting—the theme to *Little House on the Prairie.* And there aren't any words to the theme from *Little House.* People don't just start singing it spontaneously in America, but they do in France. Loudly, slowly, reverently, in unison, "Laaa la la laaa, la la lalala. Laaa, laa la la, la la la la laaa . . ." *My God,* I thought. *It's a religious cult.*

I walked out onstage, and everyone rose to their feet. I never got a standing ovation for walking out onto the set of *Geraldo* or *Sally Jessy Raphael* back in the States. I sat down on a high stool between Arthur and Jamel at an enormous triangular table that made the set look like a giant Ouija board. It was all so brightly lit and science-fictiony, I thought the whole room was going to take off at any minute. An assistant plugged the translation headset into my ear.

"Is it you? It is really you?" Jamel demanded in English.

"Yes, yes, it's me," I replied nervously.

He then tried to speak English. "Why you? Why!" he sputtered, searching for words. "*Why YOU SO MEAN TO LAURA?*" he screamed in my face. The audience howled with laughter. He breathlessly continued, "Why? Laura is nice, she's pretty, but *you* . . ." He then said something that didn't translate, something about *"why the footing of the girl?!"*

I was afraid to even ask what that meant. He finally resorted to screaming and sign language. "You're always, ARRRGGGHHHH!" And he mimed me hitting Laura. "In my room, I cry and I cry! Why?" I wasn't sure if this was a rhetorical question or if I was actually supposed to answer him.

I tried to explain, slowly, so the translator could broadcast my statements to the television audience. "Nellie was jealous. I had this horrible mother, and my stupid brother, Willie, and my poor father, who couldn't stand up to my mother. And here was Laura with her perfect family. I was jealous."

The famous comedian Alain Chabat leaned over and in English said, "I am with you." This sent him and the others into a frenzied discussion. The translator did her best to keep up, but I was getting bits and pieces of sentences, like it was coming in over an old radio. "Jealous." "Poor thing." "Unhappy."

Finally, one of the actors made an impassioned speech that began with something like "Nellie, who was a child without a smile . . ." and everyone went "Ahhh!" The audience applauded wildly. They had analyzed Nellie's situation and agreed she was a poor, unhappy, friendless little thing. It was as if they had just put Nellie on trial on national television and determined that her actions against Laura were motivated by jealousy, making them crimes of passion and therefore forgivable under French law.

Later I was hugged and kissed by a group of French fans backstage. For the next several days these encounters continued, until it was clear: things were different in France. They didn't hate me here. They *loved* me. All those years of reading about France, all those years as a child living in the Hollywood version of a French castle, all the stories about all the talking mice and rats who lived there, all the drooling over French menus, all the dreaming about this mythical, romantic place with better food and prettier people—and all this time, they had been dreaming of me. Hell, they didn't even think Nellie Oleson was "mean." They thought she was French. When I left a few days later, I assured them, "Oh, don't worry, I'll be back. . . ."

While France had granted me a birthday wish beyond my wildest imagination, New York was still wild, uncharted territory. For years I had been doing stand-up comedy, but I had yet to appear in New York. All the Los Angeles comedians I knew were terrified to play there. They all thought the audiences were "much tougher" than in L.A. I met Chip Duckett in Texas in the summer of 2001 at a bizarre promotion for Alizé liqueur, where different celebrities played hostess and introduced the evening's entertainment. Chip booked a lot more than just celebrity booze busts, so we met for lunch a year later, and he explained the plan. He booked talent for Club Fez, a small but popular venue in Greenwich Village where Joan Rivers was doing shows at the time. Chip didn't have to say much more; if this place was good enough for Joan, it was certainly good enough for me. And then he dropped the bomb.

"Okay, you'll need to do at least an hour and a half, give or take a few minutes."

What? My brain locked up. I didn't have an hour and a half of material to save my life. I had been playing so many clubs where the standard was fifteen to twenty minutes—if you were lucky. I probably had thirty minutes max of anything remotely useful. Then, just to make matters worse, he said, "Oh, and if you're not already, you should be *really* dirty. You would not believe the things Joan Rivers says up there."

So not only was I being asked to run a comedy marathon, but because old Joan was coming in a couple nights before me to curse the air blue, I would need to completely alter my material and amp up the profanity. I sometimes said the word *bitch,* as in, "Yes, I am commonly known as the Prairie Bitch." But that was about it. I did not say *fuck*. I did not say *shit*. I didn't even say *goddamn*. I had an almost totally clean act.

For this new show, I was going to have to come out of the closet as a person who swears. Fortunately, I had some material at my disposal to choose from in that arena: a pop-culture magazine called *Detour* had recently done an article about me. It was a lovely, complimentary piece with a great picture. But at the top of the page under my photo was an unexpected little poem:

When she was good, she was very, very good.
When she was bad, she was a cunt.

My agent nearly had a seizure when he saw the article. He sputtered and stammered over the phone, "I can't send *this* out to people! It's . . . it's got . . . the . . . *the C-WORD* all over it!" I read it to my father. He didn't stop laughing for a week. I decided the magazine article was going into the act. Let's see Joan Rivers top *that*!

A comedian friend of mine once told me, "You know, I love your act, but the stories you tell in the bar afterward are ten times as funny!" I decided he was right, so I incorporated all of the crazy stories that made everyone, especially the critic in my head, say, "Oh, no! You can't possibly tell people *that*!" into the show.

I had also noticed for years that no matter what I was talking about onstage, someone in the audience always had to ask a question about *Little House on the Prairie.* Usually, it was annoying and broke my rhythm, but now I thought, *Well, there's another solution. I can answer questions. That ought to kill some time as well.* So I set aside a portion of my act for Q and A. I would hand out index cards and pens before the show and tell the audience to ask absolutely anything they wanted. What the hell, I'd even bring the wig! I didn't have the real one, of course, but I had a fake one from a party. I called this part of my act "The Wig: A Psychological Experiment (Is It Me or My Hair)?" We could try to see if I was evil or if the evil was a result of the blond ringlets. Then perhaps we could see if it worked on the audience as well. That's it! I'd let them try on the wig.

Armed with a whole bag of totally new, insane, and profane material, I prepared to make my New York comedy debut at the Fez. But I was shocked by what I saw when I climbed down into the small basement club/restaurant under the Time Cafe in the Village: my manager escorting his mother and aunt to their seats. Thom hadn't paid much attention to the details of my act, since he was just interested in ticket sales. I hadn't told him about the new material, and he hadn't asked.

I was horrified to see his guests. I said, "Thom, you brought your mom? What the hell were you thinking? Do you have any idea what this show is going to be like?"

I showed him the magazine to give him a taste of what was to come. He went pale.

"Well, too late now!" he cackled. He said it would probably be good for the old girls to get their blood flowing anyway.

The place was packed with about two hundred people, mostly gay men, and several clearly crazed *Little House* fans, women who had even braided their hair and brought *Little House* lunch boxes with them. These people were ready for anything. I went onstage, and I didn't say, "Good evening" or even "Hi there." I said, "Tonight we're going to answer some questions, starting with, why am I such a bitch? You people want to know why I'm a bitch? I'll tell you why. Do you have any idea the shit I have had to put up with?"

I didn't address the audience so much as rail at them. I complained to them. I chastised them. I gave them all manner of shit—and called it shit to boot. And I confessed to every insane, embarrassing thing I could think of. I told them about Michael Landon's not wearing any underwear; I told them about my gay father and Liberace; I told them about my ridiculous appearance on *Fantasy Island.*

They loved it. They laughed, they screamed, they spilled their drinks. And then I pulled out the stack of index cards and answered their questions. I didn't have written answers to any of them. I just read the question on the cards and answered them truthfully.

The crowd went berserk. Thom's mother and aunt looked as if they could hardly breathe, they were laughing so hard. I didn't do an hour and a half. I was onstage for over two hours, and when I was done, Chip came out and made me go back out onstage and answer more questions. I had to do an encore.

It was a complete smash. Nothing like this had ever happened to me before. I knew I would never do my old act again. I would never again lie or have to make anything up onstage. I was free. All I had to do was tell them the fucking truth.

CHAPTER NINETEEN

FIGHTING FOR CHILDREN . . . AND LARRY "F-ING" KING

> **CHARLES (ABOUT LAURA FIGHTING WITH NELLIE): Now, Half-Pint, you heard what I said. You won't do it again?**
>
> **LAURA: Oh no, Pa, I promise. I won't have to. Nellie's scared of me now!**

On December 28, 2002, I got an e-mail asking me to be on the advisory board of a new organization, the National Association to Protect Children (PROTECT), whose goal was political action to change laws that directly affect abused children. But the group wasn't just planning to do this. The e-mail was announcing its victory in North Carolina; PROTECT had already gone into the state house and successfully changed the North Carolina "incest exception" law. And here was the most extraordinary part: PROTECT didn't even have an office yet. Some guy down in North Carolina had basically done all this out of his car with a cell phone. They had no T-shirts, no brochures—they didn't even have stationery yet. They had made a huge difference in child abuse laws with apparently nothing but fifty cents, a screwdriver, and a roll of duct tape. They were the MacGyvers of the children's rights movement.

Hell yes, I wanted to hang out with these people! But there was one little catch. I knew that when I did press about my work with the organization, one question was bound to come up: "So, Ms. Arngrim, is this a personal issue for you?" I knew that if I said yes to the e-mail, yes to the board, eventually there would be an interview or a Senate hearing, and someone would ask this question, and I would have to put up or shut up. I was no liar; I would have to go public with my own abuse story. I took some time to think about it. I talked to Bob and my shrink, and then I said yes.

I began getting calls and letters from the executive director, Grier Weeks. He did not directly ask me if I had been abused in our first conversation, but he posed several vaguely leading questions, which I answered with uncomfortable pauses. I decided to move things along.

"Okay, let's just clear something up right now," I started. "How can I put this? Like they say in the commercials, 'I'm not just president of the Hair Club for Men, I'm also a member.' Get it?" He got it.

At first, PROTECT seemed like it was going to be a low-effort type of charity gig, until we decided to "do California." It turned out that California was one of the thirty-odd states with the dreaded incest exception, a legal loophole that allows far lesser penalties than those normally given to perpetrators convicted of sexually assaulting children, sometimes not so much as one day in jail, as long as they are the "victim's natural parent, adoptive parent, stepparent, relative, or a member of the victim's household who has lived in the victim's household." It's a fact that the majority of child molesters are someone related to or known to the child. It's almost always a father, or a stepfather, or a brother, or the teacher, or the baseball coach who is molesting the child. This exception even included house guests. Why on earth would they call something an exception that allows the majority of child rapists to go free? Strangers make up the smallest percentage, which means this wasn't the exception, it was the rule.

This was the law that Grier and a skeleton crew of volunteers had overturned in North Carolina. They had managed Arkansas and were almost done with Illinois. PROTECT was on a winning streak, but Grier said California might be more difficult. Little did I know how right he was.

When I went to see my elected officials at the state capitol in Sacramento, I thought I would just go up there and explain this terrible mistake in the law books, and the nice elected officials would immediately rip this junk out of the book. Unfortunately, the scene did not play out as my fantasy script dictated it would. At my first meeting, I went with Paul Petersen from Minor Consideration and some friends of his, including other abuse survivors. They shared their stories. Afterward, a very nice Democratic female aide to a nice Democratic senator turned to me and said, "No one in Sacramento gives a shit that you were molested." Ladies and gentlemen, may I present your tax dollars at work! To be fair, she was trying to be helpful. She was in no uncertain terms (or censored words) giving me Lesson 1 in Politics 101: politicians only respond to political pressure, and one person's suffering is not considered political pressure.

The high point of my trip to Sacramento was meeting Republican senator James Battin, who told me that he thought this incest exception was one of the sneakiest things he'd ever heard of and was more than happy to take a shot at getting rid of it. He introduced a bill to remove it from California law but warned me that this was going to be a long process. We would have to go before the dreaded California Senate Public Safety Committee. He said that he had seen people "pour their hearts out, spill their guts in front of these people" only to be ignored and dismissed. "It could be a humiliating, soul-crushing experience," he said.

"Oh, so it's like going to an audition, then?" I replied. Senator Battin might be tough, but he'd never met a casting director before.

When I went before this committee, I was armed with a prepared statement, and I had both Grier Weeks and Dr. Bruce Perry from PROTECT by my side. I spoke from the heart about being raped by one's own flesh and blood and pleaded for the civil rights of victims. Dr. Perry spoke about the terrible effects of incest, the damage done to victims who see their attackers protected instead of punished, and the total lack of difference in psychology between incest and nonincest offenders. He was brilliant.

To say that our comments fell on deaf ears, however, would be an understatement. Senator Battin had been right. Talk about a tough room! The panel of senators staring down at me from their dais exhibited a cross section of emotions ranging from dismissive contempt to smoldering rage. Unbeknownst to me, I was testifying not just before some of the most powerful senators in

California, but some of the very politicians who had helped sign the incest exception into law in the first place.

When we were finished, the senators seemed to take almost gleeful pleasure in voting no on our bill. The incest exception would stand.

I didn't cry like those politicians expected me to. I was from Hollywood; I knew what to do. I called my publicist! Not just any publicist. Harlan Boll is the world's only gay Quaker publicist. He had a long-standing relationship with the producers at Larry King's show, having booked many celebrities for interviews, and called them immediately. "Now, I'm not saying I have this, but I'm saying *if* I were to tell you I had a celebrity, a woman who had starred as a child on a greatly beloved family television show—which shall remain nameless—who is now willing to come forward about having been sexually abused, would you be interested?"

"Which television show?" they asked.

"Little House on the Prairie," he volunteered.

They were extremely interested. He explained that the interview wouldn't just be about my own molestation, it would also be about the law, the shocking legal travesty that was the incest exception. He said this victim was now speaking out for millions of others. Then he told them the "theoretical" guest was me.

The producers had just one question. Not about the victim, *about the perp.*

"Was it Michael Landon?" they asked.

"Acckkk! God, no! Are you crazy? It was a relative!" replied Harlan in horror.

"Oh. We'll get back to you. . . ."

To their credit, they did. But they wanted to know *everything.* I was told that I needed to have breakfast with one of the producers before they booked me, so they could see that I could explain myself—and the law—in a clear, meaningful way.

And so I did. I met one of the producers the next day at a restaurant near my home in Los Angeles and told her everything. She quickly lost interest in her food. By the time I was done explaining the incest exception and the workings of Sacramento, she stopped me. She got out her cell phone and explained that she would be calling the office, and I would definitely be doing the show.

I told her this wasn't just about me, and, frankly, I didn't really want to be by myself for this one. "I have other people who can come on the show, like lawyers and psychologists. Senator Battin himself has agreed to appear," I offered.

She smiled at me. "Uh-huh. And what show were they on?" She explained that my intentions were all well and good, but that "people don't know them. They know you."

There was no escaping my *Little House* legend, and I had long ago decided I would not let it be a curse. But now Nellie was something else. She was a weapon I could fight this battle with, a sharp-tongued sword.

The producers still had many issues to work out, and I endured one conference call that was a bit surreal. Harlan and I were both on the line with another producer, and the issue of what "details" I would or would not be sharing came up. The conversation turned, well, graphic. Harlan was, as always, protective of me, and I finally had to stop for a moment and ask for clarification. "Excuse me," I politely asked. "I just want to be clear about this. Are we 'bartering' for the details of my rape?"

Following a brief, uncomfortable silence, the producer gave me an honest answer: "Yes. Yes, that is technically what we're doing here."

"Thank you. I just wanted to be clear," I replied. Oddly, this exchange made me feel better, not worse. If I was going to make a deal, I needed to know what the actual terms were. I now understood what they wanted. And so I explained what I wanted. I wanted to talk about the law, specifically the hideous reality of the incest exception and Sacramento's vehement defense of it. I wanted to talk about PROTECT and the fact that this was the only organization fighting this. My wishes were all granted. The producer even agreed to show footage from my testimony at the hearing in Sacramento (along with the required *Little House* clips, of course).

Now came the fun part: telling my father. I technically had to, because before the show could tape, the legal department required that I have a person who could "corroborate" my story. I said that my father would. I almost wanted to tell them to call my brother. He'd certainly acknowledged what he'd done to enough people, and I wouldn't be surprised if he'd have corroborated it himself.

I called my father, explained my involvement with PROTECT, and what had happened in Sacramento. He thought this all sounded great and was surprisingly quite enthusiastic about it

And then I broke the news: "I'm going on *Larry King Live.*"

He was silent for a moment. "Larry King? Did you just say Larry King?"

"Yup," I confirmed.

He went crazy. He sounded like he'd just won the lottery. "Larry King!" he cried with joy. "Larry King!"

"Um, I'm going on to talk about my abuse," I tried to remind him.

"Yes, yes, of course. This is fantastic! Larry fucking King! How long are you on for?" he asked breathlessly.

"Um, for the hour."

"FOR THE HOUR?" he shrieked. "Oh my God! Who are the other guests?"

"Well, nobody. It's just me."

He completely lost it at that point. "Just you? You're on LARRY FUCKING KING FOR THE ENTIRE HOUR, AND IT'S JUST YOU?"

He was ecstatic. He began to babble, "Oh my God, this is fantastic. I have to call everyone and tell them to watch it—"

I interrupted. "Look, Dad, I'm glad you're so happy about this, but you do understand that I'm going on the show to talk about being repeatedly raped as a child under your roof, okay?" This announcement did not seem to rain on his parade in the slightest.

"Oh, yes, of course, that's very serious." He pretended to calm down. "And, yes, of course, you have to do that. I always figured you would someday. It's for the best."

He was being far more supportive than I ever could have anticipated. But then he couldn't contain himself any longer

"But," he began again, "it's LARRY FUCKING KING! Oh my God! I'll invite everyone over." He began to think out loud. "Oh, God . . . do I have time to cook? No, wait, I'll call a caterer."

Yeah, sure, it was very bad that I got raped, and yes, of course, the legal injustice being visited on millions in the form of the incest exception needed to be stopped at once, but the important thing to remember was: I was going to be on TV! And in my family's universe, that was what really mattered. So he had no problem at all speaking to the producers at *Larry King* or corroborating my story or anything else.

I wasn't sure how to take this. On the one hand, it felt good to hear him be so supportive of what I was doing. Did he now truly understand what I'd been through? Is this what it took to get through to him? CNN? I sighed. No, this was not going to be an emotional breakthrough. This was just his favorite thing in the world. Publicity. He hadn't changed a bit.

After all these years, I understood how my father's brain worked, but it was a little hard to explain to Harlan and the gang at PROTECT, let alone other abuse survivors. "What sort of response did you get from your father?"

"Well, I think he's still somewhat torn."

"Oh?"

"Between the crab puffs and the spinach dip."

So I appeared on *Larry King Live* on April 27, 2004. Before the taping, Larry came into the green room and explained to me, "Look, I know we have questions we already agreed I wouldn't ask you. But I'm going to ask a couple of them. Do *not* answer them. I don't *want* you to answer them. You can say, 'I don't want to talk about that' " or 'None of your business' " or whatever you want. I'm not asking them to make you answer or upset you. It's just here, basically, I'm the audience. They're all thinking these questions. If I don't ask, they'll wonder why. But that doesn't mean you're supposed to answer me, okay?"

I was definitely going to be okay. Before I knew it, there I was sitting in front of the famous CNN "Light Brite" set with all the blue dots. And there was Larry King, sitting right across from me. On TV, the desk looks bigger than it really is. When you do the show, he is right there in your face. And like many celebrities, he has a really big head. Huge, out of proportion to the rest of him. It's one thing on TV, but in person it has the startling effect of making one feel that one is being interviewed by a giant praying mantis. I couldn't stop staring at his head.

There I was, trying to deal with talking for the first time in public about having been sexually abused at age six, trying to remember all the important things about the law and the bill and all I could think was, *Wow, he's* really *got a big head.* Perhaps it took my mind off the scary stuff and made me calmer. At any rate, I managed to spit it all out.

> LARRY KING: Why talk about this now?
>
> ME: I have avoided talking about this for years. I've seen a lot of celebrities go on television shows and come out about this kind of thing, and I've always sort of cringed and said "Oh, I just don't ever want to do that." But I've always said if I had to, if there was some compelling reason—in this case, I'm now on the advisory board of an organization called PROTECT, and we have a bill that we introduced in Sacramento. . . .

Then, after the first segment, Larry King turned to the camera and said "That's www dot PROTECT dot ORG!" I almost swooned. He kept it up, too, stopping at nearly every break to shout, "PROTECT dot org!"

When we finished taping, Larry asked someone (apparently in the ceiling) when this was going to air. A mysterious disembodied voice said it was "evergreen," that they could show it whenever they wanted. I started to panic. This had to get out now so it could help us with Sacramento. If they held it, we would be screwed. I felt a lump in my throat.

Then Larry turned to the voice in the ceiling and said, "Run it Thursday!" I could have kissed him.

People logged on to the PROTECT Web site from all over the world. And what did they see when they got there? All the senators from the Public Safety Committee who had said no to our bill to overturn the incest exception. Not just their names, but photos, with banners across them reading "BETRAYED." And below that were their phone numbers, fax numbers, and e-mail addresses.

The politicians were quickly inundated with faxes, e-mails, and phone calls from voters yelling at them, "What the hell is wrong with you! Are you sick?" The popular onslaught had the desired effect. Senator Battin reintroduced the bill in California. If nobody in Sacramento gave a shit that I was molested before, thanks to Larry King, they certainly did now. The bill began to pass, one committee, then another, first the Senate, then the Assembly, and finally to the floor. And when it went to a floor vote, the politicians did what they always do. *They passed it unanimously.* On October 4, 2005, the Terminator himself, Arnold Schwarzenegger, signed it into law. I was happy. Really, really happy.

And then I cried. I only really cry when I'm happy; I'm kind of nuts that way. I had fought city hall—no, the entire California state legislature—and won. I had helped to change an unjust law that had been on the books for decades and had hurt thousands of children. I had succeeded, not because I was a politician or a lawyer or a psychiatrist, not even because I had been a victim and spoken out. I didn't have the education or experience some of the others who fought alongside me did. But I succeeded because I had something going for me that the others simply didn't. I was someone people knew, someone who had been in their living rooms. Even better: I succeeded because I was Nellie—and that bitch sure could open up doors.

CHAPTER TWENTY

HAPPY EVER AFTER

> THE REAL THINGS HAVEN'T CHANGED. IT IS STILL BEST TO BE HONEST AND TRUTHFUL; TO MAKE THE MOST OF WHAT WE HAVE; TO BE HAPPY WITH SIMPLE PLEASURES; AND TO HAVE COURAGE WHEN THINGS GO WRONG.
>
> —LAURA INGALLS WILDER

On New Year's Day, 2010, I went to see Melissa Gilbert say "I do" again. Not to a new guy—thank God! She and longtime hubby, Bruce Boxleitner, were renewing their vows on their fifteenth wedding anniversary. For the record, Bruce is the only guy Melissa's ever dated that I could stand, and I think I can safely say she's given up dating idiots for life.

It was a small ceremony, at the Little Brown Church in the Valley, followed by a reception at Dupar's coffee shop, where we all got eggs and hash browns. Melissa table-hopped around the pie counter, in her high heels and lovely multicolored, tulle wedding gown, a strapless number that showed off the enormous heart-shaped "Bruce and Melissa" tattoo on her shoulder. For a girl who was so hoity-toity as a child, she's so down to earth now, I swear she's practically gone trailer. And I love her as much today as I did back then.

Yes, I still love my *Little House* family. Of course, we lost Kevin Hagen (Doc Baker) and Dabbs Greer (Reverend Alden) in the last couple of years, and Victor French (Mr. Edwards) some years back. They've all gone off to join Michael and Steve. But the rest of our gang is still going strong and, amazingly, still speaking to each other. Well, most of us. I admit, Melissa Sue Anderson and I haven't exactly been hanging out together at the beauty parlor getting our nails done, but sometimes I think maybe we should. Now that I'm older, I have a sneaking suspicion we probably have a whole lot more in common than either of us used to think. I've always said, if she wants to be friends, I'll buy the first pitcher of margaritas.

And where are the Olesons? Nobody ever really knows exactly where Willie is. Jonathan Gilbert took off and started roaming the world a couple years back, and he's been just about impossible to keep track of since. It's like a bizarre game of Where's Waldo? But I heard from him a while back, and he's still smart as a whip and enjoying driving us all crazy.

My "dad," Richard Bull (Mr. Oleson), lives in Chicago and still acts. And Mrs. Oleson? Come on, you know women like that never die. Indeed, Katherine MacGregor will be celebrating her eighty-fifth birthday this year. My guess is she'll outlive us all. She hasn't changed a bit, I mean, not at all. She will always be my mother, and I am convinced she will continue to try to boss me around to her very last breath. But how can you not love someone like that?

The Baby Carrie twins are now old enough that I can finally tell them apart. (They talk just fine now, too!) Rachel lives not far from me in Los Angeles, and I see her often. Karen Grassle

(Ma) and Charlotte Stewart (Miss Beadle) moved up north near Napa, so I have to be satisfied with e-mail most of the time, but we all try to get together at least once a year for cast reunions.

I think I'm going to need my *Little House* family more than ever as the years go by, particularly given that I've now lost all of my real family. It wasn't until almost a year after my mother died, in June 2002, that my father and I were able to spread her ashes in the Strait of Juan de Fuca like she wanted. But she's there now, with the killer whales and dolphins leaping around all day. In the spring of 2008, good old Jess Petersen, the caustic, chain-smoking other half of my dad's company, Arngrim and Petersen, the man who had somehow become my "third parent," finally succumbed to those damn Salem cigarettes he wouldn't give up and died. He had taken care of me when my parents weren't available and often did a better job of it. As my manager, he was involved in setting up my trust fund, a precarious position of great responsibility. He watched that money like a hawk and complained to the bank when the account failed to produce sufficient interest. Who ever heard of a guy breaking into a child actor's bank account to put more money in it? Jess loved to travel and used to tell me that one day he would take me to his favorite place on earth, Venice. Ultimately, it was I who wound up taking him. It was hard getting his ashes into the country at first, but I finally got him a nice spot at the cemetery on the Island of San Michele. It's got a beautiful view of the Grand Canal.

But this last loss was the toughest. On December 16, 2009, the world's craziest, most shamelessly publicity-loving stage father, the guy who clawed his way up from the Salvation Army orphanage all the way to Broadway and, eventually, Hollywood, took his final bow. My dad was eighty-one when he died. He had bravely battled Parkinson's disease and a severe heart condition for many years, firing up the electric wheelchair to go for oysters and martinis at five o'clock on weekdays and brunch on Sunday. After my mother died, he lived alone but entertained regularly. He attended all possible theater openings and political and charity events. Some people who met him were unaware that he was even ill. But eventually the disease did what it always does and began to attack his ability to speak, to swallow, and, ultimately, to breathe.

What made it hard for me wasn't just losing my last parent. It was that he's also the person I most resemble—in all too many ways. They say all girls turn into their mothers. No such luck in my case. Friends of his used to laugh and call me "Thor in Drag." The physical similarity was alarming. When my husband, Bob, asked me if there were personal items of my father's that I wanted to keep to remind me of him, I said, "It's okay, I have a mirror."

Dad and I were alike in more than looks. Having been in the orphanage during the Great Depression, and having suffered not just abandonment, but also malnutrition and neglect, my father had developed a survivor's mentality. He used to say that the thing about being an orphan is, "even if you get adopted, even if you have a family, you always know in the back of your brain: you're on your own." Whenever he said this, I always knew exactly what he meant.

I don't believe he or my mother intended to make me feel the way he felt, as an orphan. But when you're left all alone to fight for your life and sanity, it doesn't matter if it's on purpose or an accident. A child's soul doesn't know the difference. My father was left alone at the mercy of strangers in the orphanage. I was left alone at the mercy of my brother in my own living room. But we both learned the same thing. Sometimes it doesn't matter how loud you scream—nobody's coming. The only one who can save you is you. This sort of trauma affects people in different ways as they grow up. Sometimes it makes the scrapper, the fighter, the artist. Sometimes it makes the psychopath. And sometimes it makes the bitch.

My father had years ago made me the enforcer of his medical directives. He had always been adamant that he did not want to be put on life support. "If you ever come to the hospital and find me on a goddamn machine, pull the fucking plug! Trip over the damn cord if you have to!" he'd say. All of his instructions were quite detailed, sometimes bizarrely so, like the form I needed to sign and have notarized giving me permission to authorize the use of physical restraints if he should become mentally incapacitated and violent. I asked him what on earth he needed this for. But I should have known: he had thought it all out and done his research.

"Well, if I become incapacitated and have to go to a full-care type of facility, there are two kinds—the really good expensive ones and the cheap ones. The expensive ones know better. They won't take you if you're violent and crazy, unless they know they're allowed to legally restrain you. The only places that will take you in that condition without the restraint order are the horrible cheap places in the bad neighborhood." As always, with my father it was all about avoiding a bad address.

Well, what could I say? "Fine then. Will that be leather or latex?"

One time, I did ask, "Why, oh why, in the name of God, did you select me to be the one to make all these horrible decisions?"

He snorted with laughter. "Because you're the only person I know who's got the balls to kill me if you have to."

I suppose he was right. It didn't actually come to that, thank God. But I did have to sit with the doctors and go over the horrendous details of every possible artificially life-extending procedure and every possible outcome, and make the final call. His medical directive was quite explicit. When they finished offering to perform every single item that he had listed under "Do Not Do Any of These Things to Me EVER," my decision became pretty clear.

I told him that I wouldn't let them hurt him. I assured him there would be no more tubes, and that there would be lots and lots of morphine. At the end, I left him alone in his dressing room to prepare privately for his final performance. His last words to a family friend were simple, poignant, and, like my dad, a little weird: "I'm happy." And then after a thoughtful pause, "I don't know why."

Like I said, I'm my father's daughter. So in the midst of mourning, when my editor called to ask, "Alison, I'm so sorry for your loss. Do you think you'll be able to finish writing your book?" I cheerfully replied, "Are you kidding me? Not finish the book because my father died? Ha! If I don't finish it, the crazy bastard will come back and haunt me!" Stunned silence on the other end. Then we both laughed.

That's just me. I always manage to find ways to be happy, even when things are awful. It's more than just a "well, the show must go on" attitude. I just always see the humor in situations, no matter how dark. My husband says I'm the only person he knows who can figure out how to have fun doing absolutely anything. He says I can turn going to the supermarket for cat litter into an adventure.

True, but now when I'm happy, I'm *just* that. There's no static on the line now. It's not "I'm happy, but . . ." or "I'll be really happy when. . . ." I am just ridiculously, stupidly happy. I am often cheerful to the point of being annoying as hell. I don't know if this is a sign of good mental health or recovery, or if it means I've finally snapped and just gone the rest of the way to completely batshit crazy.

How? Why? If I knew, I would bottle it and sell it. But I have an idea. I read a study a long time ago about the effects of volunteering and activism on people with HIV and AIDS. It found that those involved in AIDS-related political activism and other activities that helped people with AIDS had higher numbers of disease-fighting T-cells, lower amounts of the virus, and lived longer than those who did not. Fighting back and helping others actually helps. I had figured it would certainly help psychologically, but it was nice to see it did something physically as well.

I wondered, *Could the same kind of activism work for survivors of severe physical and sexual abuse?* Apparently, the answer is yes. Back at the hotline, Bob told me that depression is defined as "learned helplessness and anger turned inward." I had learned I wasn't helpless. I learned it was okay to get mad as hell and scream my head off—especially if the cameras were rolling and an Ingalls was on the receiving end or some politicians who needed straightening out.

I don't have anything to do with my brother, Stefan, now. I don't go in for this faux forgiveness pop-psych nonsense that keeps getting foisted on incest victims. I just don't think it's fair. Nobody asks a robbery victim, "So, how are you and the burglars getting along now?"

When my father was ill, I did get stuck in the emergency room with my brother for several hours. I was focused on my father and in no mood to have a heart-to-heart with Stefan, so I just let him babble. It was like having an out-of-body experience. I decided it would be best if I just pretended I didn't know this person. I told myself I was a scientist doing a field study of crazy people, or perhaps more fittingly, Jane Goodall among the chimps.

I didn't see him after that; the night in the emergency room was enough. I can't do anything about the "outcome" of my situation. Time has passed, the damage has been done, the statute of limitations has come and gone. But I don't sit around pondering the injustice of what happened to me. I have been given the opportunity to affect the outcome of millions of other cases, many far worse than my own. This is a gift that has given me such healing, words cannot describe.

I owe it all to the bitch on the prairie. When I played Nellie Oleson, she allowed me to scream, to howl, to throw things, to pour out all my pain and rage over and over again in a safe place. All of us who have lived through abuse are terrified of our anger. Nellie taught me that I could be angry, and the world would not open up and swallow me. She also gave me a family for life that I made on the show, and she gave me friends all over the world (especially in France). When my friends began dying of AIDS, Nellie gave me the means to help them—to raise money for their care, to advocate for their rights, to educate their friends and loved ones about their illness. And when it was time to go to war for abused children, she gave me the means to do that as well. When Nellie talks, even Larry King listens.

So I'm happy, just like my dad. But unlike him, I *do* know why. I'm happy because I've finally realized this incredible gift I've been given and what I can do with it. I'm just getting started.

And now, I don't even have to put the wig on. . . .

ACKNOWLEDGMENTS

Main thanks: Kent D. Wolf, Didier Imbot, and everyone at Global Literary Management; Sheryl Berk and her invaluable seven-year-old research assistant, the appropriately named Carrie; Kate Hamill and HarperCollins; and Harlan Boll.

People without whom this book could not have been published: Jimmy Dykes, for his oh-so-comfortable pull-out sofa and for teaching me how to use the New York Subway system; Chip Duckett and everybody at The Cutting Room, where Kent found me; the inventors of Facebook, where Kent tracked me down, not having my phone number; Gerald Paras, for the use of his apartment and for all the totally "fan-boy" questions he kept asking me, giving me endless inspiration for new chapters; Melissa Gilbert, for going first into the line of fire with her book, even though she's supposed to be the "nice" one; Sue Hamilton, for making the "Confessions" show into what it is today; Howie Green, who actually came up with the title years and years ago; my sixth grade teacher, Mrs. Gerson, who figured out that none of us in her class could write a paragraph and made us all study the *Language Arts* basic grammar book until we could; and the late Lew Sherril, for sending me on that audition in 1974.

Thanks also to Michael Landon, Katherine MacGregor, Richard Bull, Jonathan Gilbert, Steve Tracy, and the entire cast and crew of *Little House on the Prairie.*

Special thanks to the real Laura Ingalls Wilder, the real Ms. Nellie Owens, and both of their entire families for making all of our careers possible!

The French: Patrick Loubatiere, Sandra Loubatiere, Sophie Epasto, Eric Caron, Christophe Renaud, Olivier Rigalot, Jamel Debouzze, everyone at *Les Enfants de la Télé,* and the people of France.

The Americans: Larry King, the producers and staff at *Larry King,* Nancy Grace and staff, Bob Schoonover, the entire Schoonover family, Angela Spataro, Sharon Phalon-Smith, Stan Smith, Pat Healy, Lindsay Ralphs, Sheri Freid, Pamela Fenton, Corinne Spicer, Pamela Clay Magathan, ANT, Thom Delorenzo, Will Denson, John McCormick, Daniel Cartwright, Rich Sebastian, Barry Horton and everybody at Tuesday's Child, Steve Pieters, Nadia Sutton (okay, also French), Albert Ogle (okay, and the Irish), Wendy Arnold, Thom Mosely, and everybody at APLA.

PROTECT: Grier Weeks, David Keith, Camille Cooper, Jennifer Allen, Dr. Bruce Perry, and everyone on the board. All those who helped carry the sword of justice to California: Betsy Salkind, Robin Tyler, Senator James Battin and staff, Ken Devore, Paul Petersen, Bikers Against Child Abuse (BACA), Ruby Andrew, Gloria Allred, and all those who do their best work by not being famous: "J.," "R.," "West Coast K.," "East Coast K.," "L.," and all the others.

And, of course, inestimable gratitude to the inscrutable Mr. Vachss.

APPENDIX

To find out how you too can help to change the laws to better protect children, visit:

National Association to PROTECT Children at www.protect.org

Promise to PROTECT at www.promisetoprotect.org

For more information on child abuse issues in general, visit:

The Zero's resources page at www.vachss.com

If you are in crisis right now, visit:

Rape, Abuse & Incest National Network (RAINN) at www.rainn.org, or call 1-800-656-HOPE (4673)

ChildHelp USA Hotline at www.childhelp.org/hotline

If you want more information on what law enforcement is doing about child abuse and child pornography, visit:

Internet Crimes Against Children Task Force at www.icactraining.org

the FBI's Innocent Images National Initiative at www.fbi.gov/innocent.htm

For issues concerning the treatment of child actors, visit:
A Minor Consideration at www.minorcon.org

To learn more about HIV and AIDS and link to resources, visit:
TheBody.com at www.thebody.com
National AIDS/HIV Hotline at www.ashastd.org/nah, or call 1-800-342-AIDS (2437)

For information on gay and lesbian issues, visit:
Parents, Families, and Friends of Lesbians and Gays (PFLAG) at www.pflag.org

To find out more about *Little House on the Prairie*:
The ultimate Little House fan Web site at www.prairiefans.com
Melissa Gilbert/Bruce Boxleitner Web site at www.gilbertboxleitner.com
Alison Arngrim Web site at www.hgd.com/alison
Alison Arngrim Web site (French) at www.alison-arngrim.com
Greenbush Twins (Baby Carrie) Web site at www.greenbushtwins.com
Laura Ingalls Wilder Web site at www.lauraingallswilder.com
Laura Ingalls Wilder Home and Museum Web site at www.lauraingallswilderhome.com